THE

Bay

OF

Pigs

THE LEADERS' STORY
OF BRIGADE 2506

by Haynes Johnson
with Manuel Artime,
José Peréz San Román,
Erneido Oliva, and
Enrique Ruiz-Williams

W · W · NORTON & COMPANY · INC · NEW YORK

Library of Congress Catalog Card No. 64-11143

ISBN-13: 978-0-393-33120-2

PRINTED IN THE UNITED STATES OF AMERICA
FOR THE PUBLISHERS BY THE VAIL-BALLOU PRESS, INC.

1 2 3 4 5 6 7 8 9

FOR *The Brigade*

CONTENTS

PUBLISHER'S NOTE

When the survivors of Brigade 2506 were freed from Cuban prisons they emerged into a world which knew only the outlines of the story of the Bay of Pigs, and those outlines were blurred by rumors, politics, and masses of misinformation.

The four commanders of the Brigade wished the story of the Brigade told in full. Their aim was to tell the American people the truth.

Because they were the leaders of the Brigade, they were able to persuade countless others of the survivors to contribute from their memories and documents. Beyond that Haynes Johnson had a totally free hand in interpreting the events, in judgments on individual behavior, whether or not criticism of the Brigade or anyone else resulted. He had a further free hand to add material gained from Washington, Guatemala, Miami and numbers of other sources which would set the story of the Brigade in a setting larger than any of the survivors themselves could know. This, Mr. Johnson has done.

His book is the history of a dramatic episode of our time. It is the full, true story, reconstructed by a man who now knows more about the entire episode than any man alive, including those who went ashore at the Bay of Pigs, and those who sent them ashore.

The four leaders of Brigade 2506 are dividing their share of the proceeds from the book with a fund for the children of the men who fell at the beach head.

AUTHOR'S NOTE

Despite all that has been written about the Bay of Pigs, most of the material in this book has not been printed before. The principal source is the men of Brigade 2506. With the leaders of the Brigade alone, the transcripts from the recorded interviews totaled more than three hundred fifty thousand words. The interviews were conducted individually—in Miami; at Fort Benning, Georgia, where more than two hundred men of the Brigade were undergoing U.S. Army officer training; at Fort Jackson, South Carolina, where another two hundred were serving as enlisted men; and in Washington and New York where other Cubans who participated in the invasion are now living.

In addition, a number of other sources have provided invaluable material. The Cuban Families Committee opened its entire files, including all cablegrams, telephonic and confidential memoranda, and personal letters between New York, Washington, Havana, and Miami. From Fidel Castro's side, the book draws on four works about the invasion and the Brigade published by the Cuban government and which, as far as the author knows, have not been made available in the United States. These and other specific citations are detailed in the Bibliographical Notes at the end of the book. The author also has gained information and other documentary material from sources which cannot be divulged, but which are irrefutable. The research for the book began three weeks after Brigade 2506 was liberated from prison on Christmas Eve, 1962, and it included a personal inspection of the areas where the Brigade was formed and trained in Guatemala.

The purpose of the book is to tell faithfully and with complete candor the history of the Bay of Pigs. It is not written as a polemic, a white paper, or to elevate or deflate political or military careers. In this respect, it should be noted that the manuscript was completed before the assassination of President Kennedy. The opinions and descriptions of the President's actions have not been changed, except in the final section where an attempt is made to assess what the President's death means to the cause of Cuban freedom.

HAYNES JOHNSON

December 15, 1963

PREFACE

This is the truth about the Bay of Pigs. We and many
men of our Brigade have told our story for the first
time to Haynes Johnson. We believe that the American people
must know what happened before the Cuban problem can be
solved.

The facts that Mr. Johnson relates in this book are the facts
as we know them. No member of our Brigade could know everything that happened. But Mr. Johnson, through his many interviews and other sources, has been able to write the Brigade's
complete history. We, too, have learned much about the Bay of
Pigs from reading this book, and we have found answers to
questions that we ourselves had asked.

We know that those who read this history will better understand why we fought, why we lost, and why we must continue
our battle.

THE

BAY

OF

PIGS

PROLOGUE

New Year's Day, 1959:

They were heralding the future. As the news spread
that Batista had fled and the dawn came, the city and
nation exploded. Horns sounded. Shots rang out. Men, women
and children ran into the streets of Havana singing, dancing,
cheering. Black-and-red pennants began appearing on buildings
and cars. Soon young women wearing black skirts and red blouses
joined the crowds. Students shouted their *vivas* to the balconies
above, and the old people opened the windows and shouted
back.

While the bells tolled in Havana, the bearer of the future was
preparing to come down from the Sierra Maestra Mountains
to begin a triumphal six-hundred-mile march to the capital.
Fidel Castro, a legend at thirty-one, had made his way into
those mountains three years before with only twelve men. Now
an almost unanimous Cuban public hailed him as something
close to a Messiah, or at least an apostle of a new order of
justice.

For seven days he traveled down the Central Highway of
Cuba as thousands blocked his path to shower him with flowers
and wave the black-and-red flag of his 26th of July Movement.
A large black helicopter lumbered overhead, marking the pro-
cession for the towns ahead. On January 8 he moved into Havana,
past the crowds along the Malecón sea drive, past decorated
Morro Castle, past warships firing a welcoming salute, and into
Camp Columbia. There, one week before, Batista had given his
own farewell party and, amid the popping of champagne corks,
departed by plane at two o'clock on the morning of New Year's
Day.

At Camp Columbia, in his green fatigue uniform casually open at the collar, Fidel faced the masses. As he began to speak, someone released three white doves. They flew directly to him and one perched on his shoulder as he said:

"There is no longer an enemy."

Summer, 1960:

The invasion was coming, and in Cuba everyone knew it. From Fidel Castro to the humblest *guajiro* toiling in the fields, everyone talked about it, prepared for it and waited for it.

It was almost inevitable. It was signaled by events, large and small: by the canceling of the Cuban sugar quota by the Eisenhower administration; by the visit of Anastas Mikoyan to Havana and of Fidel's brother Raúl to Moscow; by talk of a revolution-for-export throughout the hemisphere; by the humiliating aftermath of the U-2 flight over Russia and the resulting wreckage of the Paris summit conference. It was political and emotional and it involved not only Cuba and the United States, but Russia and the free world. And it involved personalities: Castro, with his repeated insults and threats and his massive campaign of government nationalization by which Cuba had seized $700,000,000 in United States property by July; Ernesto "Che" Guevara, the bellwether of Castro's revolution, who announced publicly that the revolution had found on its own the road set by Marx; Nikita Khrushchev, who threatened the United States with missiles if it intervened in Cuba and who pledged to help Cuba oust the U.S. from its Guantánamo Naval Base and stated that the Monroe Doctrine was dead; Eisenhower, the old general, replying with a clear, unequivocal and—for him—unprecedented counter-warning that the United States would never permit international communism to establish a regime in the western hemisphere; Allen Dulles, of the Central Intelligence Agency, saying in a speech that communism had perverted Castro's revolution; the young politicians, John Fitzgerald Kennedy and Richard Milhous Nixon, fresh from their respective national party conventions, vying for the Presidency and opening their debates by turning at once to the Cuban problem.

And it was also common knowledge within Cuba that a liberation army was being formed and that a civilian political structure in exile had been created to lead it.

As the word spread throughout Cuba, the flight from the country increased in size and fervor. It was the time to leave and join the liberators and strike the blow. And they left that summer, more of them than ever—doctors and lawyers and teachers; cattlemen and rice growers; writers, artists, bank clerks; skilled and unskilled workers—and with them came such disillusioned former top-echelon members of the Castro regime as Miró Cardona, the first premier.

They were new types of refugees. Instead of a home, they were seeking temporary asylum. They found it along the sandy beaches and curving coast line of Florida. They arrived by the thousands, in small fishing boats, in planes, chartered or stolen, and crowded into Miami. Along the boulevards, under the palms, and in hotel lobbies, they gathered and plotted their counter-revolution. Miami began to take on the air of a Cuban city. Even its voice was changing. Stores and cafés began advertising in Spanish and English. New signs went up on the toll roads slicing through the city, giving instructions in both languages. Everyone talked of home only one hundred miles away. And everyone talked about the great liberation army being formed in the secret camps somewhere far away.

From New Year's Day of 1959 to the summer of 1960
the events were set in motion that led, inexorably,
to the tragic denouement. What follows is the story
of that beginning, and that end.

BOOK ONE

Counter-revolution

CHAPTER 1

ARTIME'S STORY

The counter-revolution had not begun suddenly or dramatically. No martyrs vainly charged fortress walls or
declared to their judges, as Fidel himself had done, that "History will absolve me!" No heroic symbols, figures or dates provided a public rallying point. The future was foreshadowed in
Fidel's first year, of 1959, after he entered Havana in triumph.

Through all the events that year, the broken pledges of free
elections and a free press, the mass trials and executions, the
arrogant assumption of unlimited power and the bellicose
threats against the United States, Fidel remained the unchal-
lenged leader. It was his revolution. To the masses, as well as
to many in the professions, he was still *El Caballo* (The Horse),
the romantic, quixotic, legendary liberator from the hills. And
yet as the Cuban revolution—the genuine political, economic
and social revolution that Fidel had promised and the people
had prayed for—turned into another form of dictatorship, a
sense of betrayal began to grow.

Probably the first clear sign occurred on October 19, 1959,
when Major Huber Matos, one of the highest-ranking officers in
Fidel's rebel forces, resigned from the army in protest against
the increasing favoritism shown to known Communists. The next
day Matos was arrested at his home, charged with treason, and
subsequently tried and sentenced to twenty years in prison. A
few days after his arrest, a secret meeting of the National Agrarian Reform Institute (INRA) managers of Cuba was held in
Havana. There, the suspicions of Dr. Manuel Francisco Artime,
the young manager in Oriente Province, were confirmed. He
heard Fidel personally outline a plan to communize Cuba

within three years.

"I realized," Artime said, "that I was a democratic infiltrator in a Communist government."

Artime returned to Oriente, took a leave of absence, and with a group of college students began preparing the peasants to fight against Castro and communism. Many still had arms left over from the battle against Batista, and once more they stored them in the Sierra Maestra Mountains. By early November the basis for an underground movement in each province had been formed. It was named the *Movimiento de Recuperación Revolucionaria* (MRR) and it was the first action group originating from within Fidel's own ranks. When Fidel's G-2 began searching for the leaders, Artime took asylum with the Jesuits in Havana.

On November 7 Artime's letter of resignation from the rebel army and from the INRA was published on the front page of *Avance* in Havana. Addressed personally to Castro, the letter explained why Artime was resigning "my position in this Red army," referred to the "Red masquerade," and told how he "had heard from your [Castro's] lips the complete plans to communize Cuba." The letter was the sensation of the day. After it appeared a Jesuit priest said he would put Artime in touch with an American who could get him out of the country. Dressed as a priest and carrying a pistol hidden inside a missal, Artime walked up the steps to the American Embassy and met an American, a man he knew as "Williams."

While the American hid Artime in his own apartment, he asked many questions about Castro and Communist infiltrators. The information, Williams said, was being passed on to the United States; he thought the government would be interested in talking to Artime. On the night of December 14, 1959, Williams and two other Americans took Artime to a bar on the Havana waterfront where they met the captain of a Honduran freighter. The captain escorted Artime to his cabin aboard ship, moved a steel cabinet to one side, opened a trap door, and told him to get in. At midnight—an hour Artime will never forget —the ship began to move. It was raining heavily, the seas were high and lightning was flashing outside.

It is not clear whether or not the United States Central Intelligence Agency had decided that Castro was a Communist and must be forcibly overthrown by the time CIA agents spirited

Artime out of Cuba. As late as November 5, 1959, General Charles P. Cabell, the deputy director of the CIA, testifying behind the closed doors of the Senate Internal Security Subcommittee, said that "we believe that Castro is not a member of the Communist Party, and does not consider himself to be a Communist." General Cabell did say, however, that Castro already had delegated power to persons believed to be Communist sympathizers.

Months before Cabell's testimony, when Fidel had made his April trip to the United States, Vice President Richard M. Nixon had spoken privately with Castro for three hours in Washington. After that meeting Nixon wrote a twelve-page confidential memorandum for distribution to the CIA, State Department and White House in which he said he was convinced Castro was "either incredibly naïve about Communism or under Communist discipline" and that Castro would have to be dealt with accordingly. From that time Nixon urged, as he himself later described it, "stronger policy within Administration councils." In fact, Nixon favored a military solution, if necessary. His view eventually was shared by the CIA, but at that time the State Department and President Dwight D. Eisenhower opposed it.

The problem of fashioning a policy to deal with Castro's Cuba was determined partially by the past, for the history of Cuban-American relations reflected the history of United States relations with all of Latin America—neglect, economic exploitation and, by and large, inept diplomacy. The United States did not understand Cuba, or weigh the Cuban problem too heavily in the Cold War struggle. The performance of Fidel Castro and the enigma he presented—was he a Communist, or wasn't he? was his revolution merely another Latin insurrection, or was it something else?—made it even more difficult to comprehend. Whether the United States could have done anything, short of force, to alter the course of Castro's revolution is an unanswerable question. What is important is that a void in policy did exist. In time that vacuum was filled principally by the CIA, which for its own sources and purposes turned first to Manuel Artime.

As a man destined to play so important a role in the counter-revolution, Artime was in many respects an unlikely candidate for history. He was then only twenty-eight years old and he spoke no English. His career itself was one of contradictions. The son of a Communist, he was a devout Catholic, a product of the Jesuits. Although he had a degree as a medical doctor and was trained as a psychiatrist, he had been working with the peasants to improve agricultural production. Since his student days he had exhibited political ambitions and while he was a revolutionary, he was neither lean nor hungry. He was short, stocky, and black-haired, and possessed a rasping voice. "Manolo" Artime also was fairly naïve and trusting. He liked to express himself in sentimental verse and had a strong sense of the dramatic.

This was the man the CIA picked to help organize and carry out a plan to overthrow Castro—the plan that led to the Bay of Pigs.

Artime's escape from Cuba followed what came to be the standard CIA procedure. When the freighter carrying him from Cuba docked in the bright morning sunshine at Tampa, Florida, Artime was met on the pier by a tall, white-haired American with glasses who introduced himself as "Mr. Burnett, a friend of Williams." There on the dock Artime heard for the first time the story that would be repeated again and again: Burnett did not work for the United States government, but he was employed by a large group of wealthy capitalists who were fighting communism and who had influential friends in the government and in Washington.

Artime and Burnett left for Miami, and from that time on the young Cuban doctor was in the hands of the CIA. More "friends" of Williams and Burnett appeared in Miami. They, too, said they were interested in helping Artime get weapons for the Cuban underground, but first they had to be certain of Artime's motives. They questioned him extensively about his life and his thoughts for the future. After hours of interrogation in an obscure motel while another American "friend" took stenographic notes, formal testing began: first the Rorschach ink blot test, and then, they explained, they were going to give him a lie detector test. When Artime strongly objected that such a test was only for criminals, the Americans assured him that they all had taken it; all the top men in the Pentagon had taken it; in the United States it was a common test. Besides, they said, they were risking jail themselves in considering giving him weapons, so they had to be certain.

Grudgingly Artime agreed, and the questions were asked. How many times had he seen Castro? Was he serving another country or power at that moment? Had he told the truth about the INRA meeting and Castro? Did he have any intention of harming the United States? Was he certain his father had broken with the Communists? Had his father suggested he try to come to the United States? Was Artime himself a Communist?

After the test was over, the Americans withdrew to another room. It was late at night when they returned. He remembers their words: "O.K., Artime, you are our friend and we are going to be very close friends of yours."

From the beginning, the Cuban counter-revolutionists viewed their new American friends with blind trust. Artime was no exception. He, and later virtually all of the Cubans involved, believed so much in the Americans—or wanted so desperately to believe—that they never questioned what was happening or expressed doubts about the plans. Looking back on it, they agree now that their naïveté was partly genuine and partly reluctance to turn down any offer of help in liberating their country. In fact, they had little choice; there was no other place to turn. Some, of course, were driven by other motives: political power and personal ambition were involved. Even more important was the traditional Cuban attitude toward America and Americans. To Cubans the United States was more than the colossus of the North, for the two countries were bound closely by attitudes, by history, by geography and by economics. The United States was great and powerful, the master not only of the hemisphere but perhaps of the world, and it was Cuba's friend. One really didn't question such a belief. It was a fact; everyone knew it. And the mysterious, anonymous, ubiquitous American agents who dealt with the Cubans managed to strengthen that belief. As Artime himself said later:

"I don't know why, but in the bottom of my heart I believed those people would help me. I was impressed by the way they got me out of Cuba and took me through immigration with no problem at all. And I thought about that lie detector—you couldn't buy that in a ten-cent store. And besides that, it came to my mind that they were obviously more than a group of rich men. The kind of questions they asked me, and what they said, indicated a big organization. And there was always their preoccupation with my trustworthiness. Even though I didn't have anything concrete, everything indicated that these were people who could help me a lot."

He felt even more assured when the Americans arranged for him to leave the country and go into hiding until their plans had been completed. Artime was flown from Miami to New Orleans, accompanied by still another American known only by his first name, given a passport, and again cleared through immigration without question. On Christmas Eve, 1959, Artime flew to Mexico City. In Havana, Castro was warning of a Yankee invasion, and Cubans were receiving television lessons on fighting the imperialists. The year that Fidel had proclaimed as "The Year of the Revolution" was coming to an end.

On March 17, 1960, President Eisenhower authorized the CIA to organize, train and equip Cuban refugees as a guerrilla force to overthrow Castro. Six years before, the President had made a similar decision involving the CIA, "guerrillas," and a Latin country—Guatemala. That time it had worked, and the pro-Communist government of Jacobo Arbenz was overthrown by Castillo Armas, a man hand-picked by the CIA. The CIA and the administration clearly hoped for the same success in Cuba.

President Eisenhower had not acted precipitously; indeed, he had shown marked restraint in an increasingly difficult situation. Cuban-American relations had deteriorated steadily those first three months of 1960, with Fidel adding to the situation by inflammatory and insulting personal attacks on Eisenhower, Nixon, John Foster Dulles, and other leaders and institutions. When the President finally did agree to act, he probably could have counted on the support of a large percentage of the American public.

The ironic and tragic aspect of his decision was that Eisenhower, the moderate, the man of peace, was reflecting traditional American attitudes and principles: opposition to dictatorships and tyrannies, whether of the right or of the left; and the typically American desire to do good works and to safeguard freedom, not only in our own hemisphere, but around the world: and yet Eisenhower chose a method of accomplishing his goal that was alien to the American past. Instead of taking his decision to the people, enlisting their support, and then acting on it, or acting openly out of historical precedents, he relied on a secret agency to achieve good ends by dubious means. His decision was implemented, not in the public arena, but in the shadows of the CIA. And "Manolo" Artime became a central figure.

Artime, through the help of the CIA, had been on a speaking tour of Central and Latin America attempting to rally support for action against Castro. As he traveled through Costa Rica, Panama, Venezuela, Peru and Chile, he received calls from a "Jaime Castillo." In each country "Jaime" had a different voice, but always asked if there were anything he could do to help Artime. In Rio de Janeiro, at the end of March, "Jaime" called again. This time he wanted to see Artime urgently; he was in the hotel lobby and asked to come up immediately. "Jaime" turned out to be an American who spoke Spanish fluently. He insisted that Artime fly immediately to New York to meet some "friends" who wanted to talk to him. It was, he said, vital to the future of Cuba.

"He told me that as soon as I arrived in New York, I should go to the Statler Hilton and say I was George L. Ringo and that I have a room at the hotel," Artime said.

And so Artime flew to New York and checked in at the hotel. He had been in his room only a few minutes when the phone rang.

"Mr. Ringo?"

"Yes, I am Mr. Ringo."

But the caller was speaking in English and Artime could not understand him well. The caller hung up, and the phone rang again.

"Mr. Ringo."

This was a voice Artime understood and recognized. It was Oscar Echevarría, a friend from Cuba who had studied with Artime in college. Echevarría and another Cuban whom Artime knew and trusted, Angel Fernández Varela, came to the room. They explained that some prominent Cubans who had opposed Batista wanted to contact Artime to see if he would join them in a common cause against Castro. One of the men, Justo Carrillo, already had fled to the United States. The others, Manuel Antonio de Varona, a former Prime Minister of Cuba and president of the Senate; José Ignacio Rasco, a university professor and leader of the new Christian Democratic Party; and Aureliano Sánchez Arango, who had been Minister of Education and Minister of Foreign Relations, were still in Cuba. (Within two months these men and Artime formed their *Frente*, or united exile front, to overthrow Fidel.)

Artime said he opened his arms to them; then he asked what the Americans had to do with this. His friends told him an important American wanted to meet him now and explain that himself. They parted with an *abrazo*, or embrace, and Artime waited. There was a knock on the door and when Artime opened it he saw a tall man, expensively dressed, accompanied by one of his Cuban friends. The American introduced himself.

"It was the first time I heard his name," Artime said later. "I was going to hear that name until the Bay of Pigs. Frank Bender. The Great Frank Bender. 'All right, Manolo,' Bender said, 'we've got lots to talk about. I am the man in charge of the Cuban case.'"

Bender repeated the explanation that Artime had heard so often: the great company of wealthy people he represented had directed a large part of its money and effort toward the solution of the Cuban problem, and the defeat of communism everywhere. They had nothing to do with the American government, Bender told him, but they did have influence. Then he asked for Artime's thoughts on the future of Cuba.

"I told him that Cuba could not return to the old corrupt government," Artime said, "that a return to a military dictatorship would lead once more down the road to communism. I told him I believed we needed a genuinely democratic government. We needed social justice. We had to fight unemployment and raise the standard of living of the workers; we had to establish cooperatives to protect the small farmer and the small land owner; and we had to enact social laws to protect old people; we needed a progressive income tax, as in the United States. I told him that if we didn't do these things, we would go back to a corrupt democracy and then again we would have a military dictator who would destroy democracy. And, in the end, a reaction that would lead again to communism. I also told him that I thought the propaganda being used against Castro was wrong. When I went to South America, the people were being warned against Castro because he had taken the land of the rich people. The poor Indians said 'good' and applauded."

Bender apparently was impressed. He listened quietly as Artime discussed his ideas for a guerrilla uprising in Oriente Province, and then Bender asked, "Why not an uprising all over the island?" Artime said he didn't have enough men or weapons for that.

"Well, Artime, what if I told you that we have men who will help you to prepare for guerrilla warfare and others who will prepare men to fight in a conventional war with army training?"

"And you will give us the weapons?"

"All the weapons you need," Bender replied. "And also we will train radio operators so you can be in contact directly with Cuba."

Bender wanted to know if Artime could get men out of Cuba to be trained for such an operation. Artime replied that he could.

"Fine," Bender said, as he got up and handed Artime a piece of paper. "Call this number whenever you need me. Just say 'To Frank Bender from Manolo' and I will come to the phone." He instructed Artime to go to Miami where more friends would be in touch with him, and said he had reserved a plane ticket for him; Artime could pick it up at the hotel. "When you leave," the American said, "don't bother about paying the hotel bill. Just throw the key on the desk in the lobby."

As he left the room, Bender shook hands and said, "Remember, Manolo, I am not a member of the United States government. I have nothing to do with the United States government. I am only working for a powerful company that wants to fight communism."

PEPE'S STORY

On a Sunday afternoon in May, 1960, Manuel Blanco found his friend José Pérez San Román with his wife and children in the back yard of his small, rented house in Miami. San Román greeted him and led him to the rear of the yard. There he first heard of Artime, the mysterious Americans, a united political movement to overthrow Castro and the prospect of secret training camps to train a liberation army.

Then twenty-nine years old, San Román was a regular army officer who had served his country under a democratic regime, a dictatorship, and most recently and briefly under Fidel Castro. Tall, slender, dark-haired, quiet and reserved, he was among those freed from a Batista prison when Castro came down from the hills on New Year's Day, 1959. Before that year was out he had broken with Fidel, was again imprisoned, and finally succeeded in escaping to the United States. In Miami he was one of a group of ten former officers planning a campaign against Fidel.

As a group the officers had much in common: nearly all in their twenties, they were graduates of Cuba's military academy, the Cadet School, and all loved the army. While they had worn the yellow uniform of Batista and some had fought in the mountains against Fidel, they were not *Batistianos;* in fact they had organized their own insurrection within the army and planned to hold free elections after Batista was overthrown.

Because "Pepe" San Román was slightly older and was one of the few Cubans who had undergone United States army officer training—at Fort Belvoir, Virginia, and Fort Benning, Georgia—he had become one of the leaders of that rebellion. It had failed and now, in the spring of 1960, they were about to embark on another, more dangerous mission. One of their men was already in México trying to organize a military camp when Manuel Blanco brought the word that Artime wanted to see the officers.

San Román and Blanco left immediately, picked up several more in their group, and drove to meet Artime in an old house on Brickell Avenue overlooking Biscayne Bay.

Although Artime had requested the meeting, he was late. When he arrived, he was in a rush and obviously excited. He paced up and down and told them what he knew: they had an opportunity given to few men, they had a chance to liberate their country. He told of his meetings with the Americans and the promise of large-scale assistance. Even though the Americans he had talked to claimed they had no official connection with the government, Artime said he was convinced they did. Already, he said, the Americans were helping him to bring men out of Cuba and to transmit messages back to the underground. At length, he outlined the help the United States was going to give: arms, tanks, airplanes, everything they needed.

Only a few days before, he went on, a group of his students had left for a secret camp where they were beginning their training. The Americans had said they needed professional Cuban officers to train and lead the liberation forces. Artime urged them to volunteer. Within six months, he told them, they would have five thousand men trained and ready to move. When that time came, they would be so strong that Fidel would be overthrown in a week.

Although Artime's men and the officers in San Román's group had been enemies in Cuba and still distrusted each other, the officers believed that such a military force as Artime had outlined would certainly defeat Fidel. Despite their personal differences, Pepe remembers that they were unanimously confident. For them it was more than a matter of faith; they knew their country's history. Small groups of men always had triumphed over larger forces in Cuba. Batista proved that, and Fidel himself—he had started with only twelve men!

They talked enthusiastically for two hours. All of them seemed to feel as Pepe San Román did. "I knew the United States had to do something," he said, "and we were waiting for it. If a man waits, sometimes the home run ball comes by and he will hit it. We hoped this was the time."

They met with Artime several times more; on each occasion, they became more confident. In their own ways, they reacted as Artime had when he first learned of the liberation plans. They, too, were young, and they had been taken into a major, secret adventure which could help shape history. And, they were genuinely patriotic.

They agreed to send one man to the secret camp. If he reported back favorably, they would all go. Manuel Blanco was chosen, principally because he was single. When Artime called the next meeting, he handed over a letter from Blanco. Each man read it carefully and quietly. As San Román remembers it, "We all said, 'We will go!'"

The married men went home to tell their wives. They knew from what Artime had said that their families would not starve, for the United States was going to pay each man $175 a month plus $50 for his wife and $25 for other dependents. Nevertheless Pepe San Román found it difficult to explain to his wife. He waited until his three children were in bed and then began to talk as he and his wife sat down at the kitchen table.

"I told her that for her and my kids I had to fight Castro. And I told her I had found a way to fight him now, and it was a very sure way, and I was going to leave her for the camp, but she could be sure that in six months it would be over and we would be back in Cuba, happy with the family. I told her I wanted to go because it was my duty as a Cuban. I didn't want my kids to ask me after Cuba was free what I had done and be unable to give them a good answer. I promised it was going to be successful and that we would have a home in Cuba near her family that she loves very much."

On June 2, the day of their departure for the camp, the original group of officers met at an apartment in the northwest section of Miami. Including the absent Manuel Blanco and Alejandro del Valle, there were ten men—Pepe San Román and his younger brother, Roberto; Miguel Orozco, Hugo Sueiro, Ramón J. Ferrer, "Chiqui" García Martínez, Osvaldo Piedra and Alfonso Carol. (Within the year, three of them were dead.)

"We each brought a pistol and ammunition," Pepe said, "because regardless of Blanco's assurances we wanted to be sure of each other. That's the way this thing started. We distrusted each other, but we had confidence in the Americans."

As that day was ending, Artime met the officers at the house on Brickell Avenue and led them through the back yard, down an alley, and across a street to a vacant lot. There in the shadows, beside two parked cars, for the first time Pepe San Roman met one of the Americans involved in the affair. He was a man in his thirties, obviously strong, dressed in sports shirt and slacks, but with the bearing of a professional soldier. Pepe remembers noticing that he had green eyes and walked with a limp. Artime introduced him as "Carl" and said that he would take them to their first destination.

Speaking in English, Carl asked any of them carrying weapons to turn them over to him. They replied that they had none.

A three-hour ride through the night brought them to the west coast of Florida, somewhere near Fort Myers. There, they were taken to a waterfront area where they saw a power cruiser tied up at a pier with the motor running and two Americans aboard. Again the Cubans were told they must turn over their weapons; again they said they didn't have any.

As soon as they were aboard, the cruiser headed for the open sea. The Cubans talked quietly among themselves in Spanish. "We were afraid maybe they were taking us to a Fidelista boat," Pepe said. "We said if we are going to Fidel we will shoot the four Americans even if Fidel gets us. Well, we had a compass. So we saw that we were going west, always west. So we said, 'West, we cannot go to Cuba.'"

After a tense hour the Cubans saw a long shadow ahead in the moonlight. As they drew closer they made out a wide, beautiful beach. It was very white under the full moon and they could distinguish what appeared to be a number of small cabins. The cruiser pulled alongside a wooden dock, where they saw three more Americans carrying carbines and pistols. It was one o'clock in the morning.

Carl led them from the pier to a small truck. The driver also was an American, blond, young and smiling. He said he was glad they had come. He drove them across the sand and up a small hill, and there through the orange and grapefruit trees they saw the lights from a large building shining on smaller structures scattered across what seemed to be a golf course. They had arrived at the headquarters of the Americans.

When they were all inside, the Cuban officers asked to see Blanco. In a few moments he came in, still half asleep. "So we all embraced Blanco," Pepe said.

Carl said, "Now you have Blanco. Now give us your guns." They gave him their guns.

Before they went to bed, Carl gave them their first briefing. He began by telling them that everything was top secret. While they were on the island they must stay away from the shore to avoid being seen by boats and planes; they must not swim, for the waters around the island were alive with sharks. They would be permitted to write one letter saying they were well and happy, but they could say neither where they were nor what they were doing. They were told that they would be given various tests and that those chosen for the cadre would go to another secret base to learn to train others in the liberation army; the rest would stay on the island for a radio communications course.

When Carl finished, it was nearly two o'clock in the morning. For a moment there was silence, and then Pepe San Román asked the question in every man's mind: "What help is the United States going to give?"

"We are here to help Cuba, and if you are here for that reason we will get along well," Carl replied. Evasive as it was, Carl's answer satisfied the eager Cubans.

For the next three weeks the Cubans lived in comfort in the rustic golf club. They were on the resort island of Useppa, an island a Cuban named Freddie Goudie had leased on behalf of Frank Bender and the CIA. The papers were made out in Goudie's name and there was nothing to indicate the American involvement—except for the presence of the Americans themselves.

Aside from the Cuban recruits, everyone on the island was American. After Carl, the key people seemed to be "Jimmy," a towering, black-haired man who spoke Spanish; "Walter," who had an artificial eye; and "Gordon," quiet and diplomatic. There was a psychologist with blond hair who said he was from Nashville, Tennessee, and there were others whose names have been forgotten. "Max," the psychiatrist, has not been forgotten. He was genial, short, bespectacled and German. Max was in charge of testing.

Each man received a physical examination, and intelligence, psychological and general aptitude tests. As Artime had discovered months before, the lie detector was regarded as one of the most important testing devices. While the testing continued, each soldier received a serial designation numbering from 2,500. That, the Americans said, would confuse the enemy; it would make Castro think there were many men instead of only a handful present. By the next spring the serial numbers were high in the 4,000s.

The Americans always tried to give the impression that a Cuban millionaire was paying the bills, and that the United States government had nothing to do with the operation. The Cubans figuratively winked at the claim, and privately joked about the "Cuban millionaire" and referred to him as "Uncle Sam." "At that time we were so stupid," one of the men said later. "We thought Uncle Sam was behind us. He wanted to do this secretly. That was all right because he was Uncle Sam, and he is strong."

On June 22 Carl assembled the Cubans and introduced "Dick," a tall man in his fifties, quiet and pleasant. Dick told them that the twenty-eight men who had been chosen as the cadre would leave immediately for the next base. The others would stay until their radio course was finished and then they all would be reunited with the liberation army.

Pepe San Román was among the twenty-eight. With the others, he was taken back to the mainland on two cruisers. When they reached the pier near Fort Myers, they were told to run to a large truck backed up to the dock with its rear doors open. The doors slammed shut and they drove off, unable to see outside. Several hours later they got out in the middle of a deserted farm where they waited until the sun set; then they continued their trip in the closed truck. When it stopped again they saw a C-54 transport plane directly in front of them. Again they were ordered to run. They were able to catch only a glimpse of a few scraggly pines and untended fields before they got on the plane, the windows of which were masked from the outside. The engines started immediately and they took off. Eventually, nearly 1,500 more would follow them.

Some six or seven hours later their plane landed in darkness, and they were herded to a waiting truck. Again the doors slammed shut and they traveled for another hour in darkness. They were deep in a tropical jungle. From far away they heard a sharp, shrill whistle. It could have been a factory—or perhaps a ship.

An American of medium height and weight, with a scar on his face, who called himself "Peter," greeted them and introduced John, Dave, Wally and the rest of their American instructors. All of the Americans were in civilian clothing. Because they had arrived so late, Peter said, they would not have to get up early that morning, but after that each day would begin at five o'clock. They went to bed in nearby wooden barracks, tired and excited, hopeful and fearful.

Later in the morning Peter gave them a more formal briefing. Just as on Useppa Island, everything was top secret. Then he defined the camp boundaries.

"He said that we could not go to the top of the hill that was in back of the mess hall," Pepe said. "It was off limits. And we could not go around the road. And he said that if we see anybody we shouldn't say anything. Also, he said that sometimes there were hunters in that zone, so possibly we might hear some guns fired from time to time."

Peter explained that they would be trained at the base for eight weeks, and after that they would leave to instruct the Cuban liberation army. The training would be rugged, but when they finished they would be experts in guerrilla warfare.

Despite precautions including cigarettes bearing labels from a variety of American countries, the removal of labels from the uniforms they were issued, the obvious scratching out of "USA" on their weapons, the Cubans soon discovered where they were, and in whose hands. On Sunday, their first day off from training, Ramón F. Ferrer, later the Cuban chief of staff, explored the off-limits territory. When he got to the top of a hill he clearly saw the Panama Canal. Not long after his discovery, the men noticed one of their instructors carrying a Panama City newspaper. In fact, they were in the U.S. army jungle warfare training camp area of Fort Gulick in the Canal Zone.

The training was rugged.

"We were taught how to fight as guerrillas," Pepe said. "Sometimes they would make us walk a long way through the jungle to get the feel of it—to be wet, without food and to experience danger. There was the danger of getting lost, and there were snakes. It was a very deep jungle. The equipment and living conditions were poor, but we did not really mind. At that point we believed that we were going to train a large number of Cubans for guerrilla war, that we were going to Cuba, and that we would always have what we had then—organization and control, good control. We knew we might die in Cuba, but we were doing something organized by people who really cared. Those instructors did a good job with us. We never thought things were going to be handled the way they eventually were."

In the middle of August, in their seventh week of training, the men began a long, tactical field problem, with Pepe heading a guerrilla force that was supposed to attack the "army" back at the base. The mission went smoothly and everyone was pleased—especially the Americans.

As a reward for their arduous training, the Cubans were given a farewell party with beer and a big cake. In the convivial atmosphere, the Americans and Cubans drank and talked while a record player played Latin songs. As the party progressed, a short, stocky American brought out a Spanish guitar and began to play flamenco. The Cubans were delighted, and rather amazed, to see an American playing their music so well. As they sang together, one of the Americans said: "Well, we'll meet in a free Cuba." Another American told Pepe they were going to a new base the next day, "where there were five thousand men and everything was ready." The next evening, August 22, 1960, they again boarded a C-54 and flew off into the night.

CHAPTER 3
OLIVA'S STORY

Erneido Oliva had just celebrated his twenty-eighth birthday when he first heard of the invasion plan. Two Cuban underground workers had contacted him in Havana early in the summer of 1960. "They said there was going to be an invasion," Oliva recalls. "They were organizing troops in a camp in Latin America, with a recruiting office in the United States, and they wanted me to join."

Oliva, who already had decided to work against Castro, agreed to do anything he could. It had not been an easy decision, for Oliva was a loyal and dedicated officer, a graduate of the Cadet School, who at that time was serving the Castro government as a general inspector of agrarian reform throughout the island. And for Oliva, a Negro, to turn against the revolution was a contradiction of everything Fidel represented.

The question of race was important to Fidel; he capitalized on it and profited by it. As Oliva himself says, "When Fidel came in, it is true there were some districts in Cuba where the colored man was not permitted. Actually Batista, who had Negro blood, had helped to open up a lot of Cuba to the colored man. He broke the wall that existed in Cuba. But I really believed at the beginning that Fidel was working for the real solution of the race problem—and not as a Communist. As a colored man I was sympathetic.

"I discovered, however, that it was just another of Fidel's moves to divide and weaken. He was bringing division between the classes, races, and even between father and son—based on ideological differences—and in that division Fidel would find his power. By the time the underground came to me, I believed that Fidel was using the colored people as a symbol to divide the country. By the end of 1959 a lot of colored people were against Fidel Castro—not all; the people of the streets were hearing and listening to the propaganda.

"Beyond all that, however, was the fact that as a lifelong Catholic I could not support communism."

Oliva had begun working with the underground early in 1960, and after he learned about the invasion he made his final break. It came when Castro received a number of new 105-mm. howitzers from Italy and Oliva, as an expert artillery instructor, was ordered to train the troops. He refused. "I was sure," he said later, "that some day I would fight Fidel, and those weapons would be used against me."

On August 15 Oliva resigned from the army to avoid being a deserter, but his resignation was not accepted. It wasn't the proper moment, he was told; Castro might think he was against the regime. With the assistance of the underground, he obtained a seat on a plane and on the morning of August 18 flew from Havana to Miami, leaving behind his wife and one-month-old daughter.

After he left there were recriminations. Fidel's brother Raúl, in an unusual move, publicly attacked the G-2, the government intelligence force, for permitting an officer to leave without a permit. Fidel had erected what the United States called the "Cane Curtain" to isolate his people from the West. Oliva was only one of thousands who pierced it that summer, but in time his defection caused Castro more harm than did the flight of many men of greater reputation.

In Miami, Oliva went through the recruiting process set up by the *Frente*, the Cuban civilian exile structure that had been created by Artime and others with the assistance of the CIA. Oliva was questioned and tested in various offices throughout the city.

"They asked me if I thought a guerrilla force could overthrow Fidel," Oliva recalls, "and I said no, because I knew the regular army. Fidel had been too long in power and was too strong. They told me I was going to a secret place and from there I was going to fight Fidel. They said eight hundred men were there and that I would find all types of weapons, including artillery.

I asked what backing we had and I was answered, 'We have all the backing necessary.' I asked what the United States was going to do and they didn't answer, but I believed they had official government backing because they had to have the green light of authority to operate as they did. Everybody was convinced that the United States was behind us."

While he waited for orders, Oliva talked to many former regular Cuban army officers in Miami. Nearly all of them advised him not to go; they thought the soldiers in the camps were recruited almost entirely from Fidel's army. Oliva paid no attention, and soon he was ordered to report to a recruiting office. From the office he and twelve other recruits were transported in trucks in the conventional CIA manner—with the doors closed and locked—to some place called the "little farm." There, near a grove of orange trees, they pitched tents, were issued khaki uniforms, and waited until night when a second group of recruits arrived. They turned out to be Cuban pilots and aviation mechanics.

A Cuban colonel named Martín Elena addressed them.

"You are already in a military organization," he said, "and you will go as soldiers to the training camps and then to the fighting. You will find Cuban instructors."

He took their passports and other personal papers and ushered them through a door, single file. As each man went through the door, two Cubans searched him. Outside, Oliva saw his first CIA man—an American who appeared to be in charge.

After the usual mysterious ride in closed trucks, they arrived at the abandoned U.S. military airport of Opa-Locka in North Miami and boarded a plane. It bore no markings and the windows were taped but, unlike the plane on which Pepe San Román had flown, the tape was on the inside. Within minutes after they took off the men had stripped away the tape.

Hours later, at dawn, they saw the waters of the Pacific and then an airport. After they landed a jeep approached the plane. It was driven by a colonel Oliva knew. "He was from the Guatemalan army so I knew I was in Guatemala. It was drizzling and then after we got in two buses they had waiting for us there, it began raining like hell."

The buses left San José Airport and began driving inland along a narrow paved road past rolling fields of sugar cane.

They bounced through the cobblestone streets of small villages where Indians lived in thatched huts or dirty adobe buildings and walked barefoot through the mud. They saw women with baskets on their heads, men and boys leading donkeys with bundles of cane or fruit. The scene was unmistakably Central American; and unmistakably showed Yankee influence. DRINK PEPSI COLA and COCA COLA GRANDE signs adorned the highway. In the towns the sole gasoline station was either Esso, Texaco, American or Shell.

They drove on, climbing higher and higher, through the tropical foliage of the Guatemalan mountains. The road finally leveled off, and ahead they saw a cluster of red and yellow buildings set on the side of the mountain overlooking a deep valley. Minutes later the buses stopped in the midst of a large coffee plantation.

An American who limped approached them and introduced himself as Carl. He took them to a large wooden warehouse where they found another group of their countrymen. This would be their quarters for the time being, Carl said, as he gestured toward the hammocks strung about the building. A lot of work would have to be done before their training could begin.

When the American left, the Cubans met another group of their countrymen who had come from Useppa Island in July and questioned them eagerly: Where were the rest of the Cubans? Where was the liberation army of eight hundred to five thousand men? Where were the weapons and artillery? Where was the training camp?

"They told me that higher in the mountains there was another group of men, but there were only about one hundred men in all," Oliva says. "They didn't have weapons, they didn't have uniforms, they didn't have good food, they didn't have water, and there were no barracks to live in. We felt very sad."

Later that day Oliva discovered some old friends. One was Alfonso Carol, who had been the head of the Cadet School when Oliva first studied there; another was young Manuel Blanco, who had been a student of Oliva's later in that same school. The two men said they had arrived only four days before from Panama. They were going to be the Cuban instructors. Others in their group were already higher in the mountains preparing the camp.

That first night, August 27, Oliva said the rosary with many others. He asked God to help them in their mission.

Months before the Cubans arrived, Carlos Alejos, the Guatemalan Ambassador to the United States, had been approached in Washington about the massing of arms and training of Cuban anti-Castro forces on Guatemalan soil. The details of the final oral agreement between the CIA and Miguel Ydígoras, then president of Guatemala, never have been made public. Ydígoras has stated that the United States pledged to mediate Guatemala's claim to British Honduras territory, but the United States has denied it. Whatever the terms, a bargain was made. It was completed when Carlos Alejo's brother, Roberto, agreed to let the Americans use part of his vast coffee plantation in the Sierra Madre Mountains for a training area.

And so it was to Roberto Alejos' plantation, Helvetia, that Oliva and the Cuban pilots had come. The plantation was a self-contained city carved out of the mountains at an altitude of five thousand feet, with a hydroelectric power plant and a factory where the coffee was packed. Some two thousand Indian workers lived there. The Americans stayed in the headquarters of the plantation, and above them was the imposing home of Roberto Alejos, with a swimming pool, television, two or three cars and many servants.

Within four days a second group of forty recruits arrived at Helvetia. They showed the same surprise and disappointment at the size of the training unit. The next morning, September 1, under a driving rain, all the recruits prepared to leave for the new base. The forty-seven pilots and mechanics who were to remain temporarily at Helvetia, while an airstrip was being built next to the town of Retalhuleu on the plains below, were in high spirits. They had been told there were going to be many planes, and they waved cheerful farewells as the foot soldiers began the dangerous one-and-a-half-hour trip to the camp two thousand feet above. As the army trucks moved higher into the mountains, they got stuck in the mud and the Cubans frequently had to use chains to pull them forward.

"When we got to the highest place we had been able to see from the first camp," Oliva said, "we were at the base. We were still surrounded by hills. When we finally arrived at the camp we found it worse than we had guessed. We had three barracks. In half of one was the health office and the other half the quartermaster. And in a very long one were the one hundred and something men that were there before us."

With Oliva and the new arrivals, the liberation army numbered 160 men.

Alfonso Carol told the recruits he had been appointed base commander by the Americans. He introduced the other staff officers: Manuel Blanco was in charge of training and tactics; José (Pepe) San Román was in charge of weapons and demolition; and José Andreu was in charge of personnel. Carol explained that the new men would be formed into a construction platoon to help prepare the camp. When the next group arrived from Miami, they would be relieved to begin training.

Oliva took charge of the platoon. In the morning, after a cold wet night, their work began.

Base Trax, as the camp was called, was on volcanic soil that became spongy and swamplike in the rains. In the distance was the towering volcano Santiaguito; it was still active. In some areas of the camp the soil was covered by six feet of volcanic ash. In that terrain and handicapped by the heaviest rainy season in years, the Cubans worked to build their camp.

Oliva himself, who thought he had come to train an army, began working as a carpenter. By day the men built barracks and drainage fields, and attempted to pour cement foundations in the rain. At night they began receiving military instruction from the Cuban cadre. In their first class they met Colonel Vallejo, who was in over-all charge of the camp and the training.

Vallejo, a Filipino, told them he was an expert in guerrilla warfare and he claimed to have been famous in the Philippines against the Japanese during World War II. Briefly he outlined their training program: they would be divided into twelve small teams and trained to infiltrate into specific sections of each province of Cuba. Since they were going to be guerrillas, they would have to become accustomed to difficult conditions, but before they could begin training full-time Base Trax had to be completed. September 19 was the date set.

As the work progressed, Oliva was discouraged to find division among the Cubans.

"I had a place on a rock near a cliff, where I used to sit down and think a lot," he said. "Many times I wondered if I was right or wrong to be there. I was very sad to see the way the members of the rebel [Castro] army looked at the members of the constitutional army that had been betrayed by Batista. They looked at them with real hate."

Each time a new group arrived from Miami, the men would

divide among the three main factions in the camp—the ex-Castro rebels, the constitutional army, and the students who resented both sides. A fourth, much smaller group developed. These men had worn no uniforms; they had been civilians established in their own careers in Cuba. They worked to unify all. But only once in those early days in the camp were the men completely united—and then only by grief.

At midday of September 7 Roberto San Román, Pepe's younger brother, and Alejandro del Valle brought the news back to the camp. A group had left that morning on a platoon reconnaissance mission and as platoon leader Roberto had decided they would search for a trail from the camp to the *Rio Nil* below. He was followed by Del Valle, a man named Rafo and Carlos (Carlyle) Rafael Santana, an idealistic young student who was probably the most popular man in the camp.

"So we went into a very thick woods and started cutting our way with the machete, going down and down for about an hour and a half," Roberto said. "Then the slope became so nearly vertical that we had to hold on to roots to keep our footing. But we thought because we heard the river—we could not see it— we thought the river was something we could reach easily like any other river in normal terrain. And then we got to a place where we couldn't see more than a few feet ahead through the vegetation. We had to jump to a ledge anyway because a waterfall was in our path. When we jumped, Carlyle hurt his left knee. We decided to climb to the other side.

"In half an hour I think we climbed no more than fifty meters. It was all rocks and wet and the man ahead had to pass the word back, 'Put your hand here. Do exactly as I do.' I was leading and everybody had to follow, and after twenty-five minutes I grabbed the first tree, the first good solid tree, and in that moment I think Carlyle fainted or grabbed something that was loose. Anyway, he started going down, falling down, trying to grab hold of something, but he couldn't, and then he hit a little ledge. He was falling so fast that his body jumped about two hundred meters.

"We stayed there about ten minutes praying for him. Rafo had been studying to be a priest for two or three years, and he led the prayers. And then we started calling out very loud to see if Carlyle was alive, but nothing happened."

The Cubans immediately formed groups to search for Carlyle. It began raining—one of the hardest rains since their arrival. Until one o'clock in the morning they clambered up and down the mountains, in groups of five, tied together at the waist by ropes, searching and calling in the faint hope Carlyle might still be alive. Finally they had to stop. Early the next morning some Indians spotted the body. They started working at seven that morning to lift it with ropes, and by evening it was brought back to camp.

"That day we did not work," Oliva said. "Everybody was very sad. He was the first man to die. It was the day of *La Caridad del Cobre*, the patron saint of Cuba."

The food was bad, the rain was incessant, the living conditions were crowded, tempers were short and morale was low— but the camp was beginning to take form.

On September 19 Vallejo called together the Cuban command —Carol, Blanco, and Pepe San Román—to give them good news. The weapons were arriving, he said. Until that moment the Cubans had had none. An assembly was called, the officers addressed the men and the liberation army stood in the rain and mud and cheered at the news. "I wish you had seen these men," Pepe San Román said, "how happy they were. They were so happy that they made a party."

A truck arrived with the weapons, which were placed under lock and key. They had received thirteen Springfield rifles, vintage World War I, and a few pistols.

Days later about twenty men arrived in Base Trax. Europeans, Chinese, Mexicans and a few Americans, they had been brought together in some fashion by the CIA as guerrilla instructors. The Cubans called them the "Halcones" or "Hawks," after a comic strip depicting adventurers from many lands. A number of the instructors were from countries behind the Iron Curtain— Czechoslovakia, Latvia and Poland, and there was even a Russian called "Nick." They often talked of what it was like to live inside a Communist country, but they never referred to the CIA; it was always the "group" or "organization," and sometimes the "company." Their arrival signaled the beginning of training, but it was far from the kind of training the Cubans had expected.

"The training was so bad," Oliva said. "For example, a man came to talk about Cuba to us, giving us Cuban geography, and he said Trinidad was the second largest city in Cuba. Everybody laughed out loud at him."

By the closing days of the presidential campaign, Cuba had become the dominant international issue. Early in September Castro had announced that Cuba would recognize Red China; then he tore up a 1952 military pact with the United States and openly welcomed the military support of Russia and China. In the United States, pressure for action became greater. The rhetoric and the charges, the attacks and the rebuttals, grew sharper and more personal. Castro, perfectly gauging the American temper and characteristically acting in spite of it, called the United States a "vulture . . . feeding on humanity." Then he dared the U.S. to attack and be destroyed. Once again he repeated his charge that the Yankee imperialists were training mercenaries for an invasion.

To verify him, on October 30, *La Hora*, a newspaper published in Guatemala City, printed a story about the training camp and described the preparations for an invasion as well under way. Inside Cuba the invasion jitters increased, and became even more intense when a large force of United States Marines staged maneuvers off Puerto Rico.

The candidates kept up the attack. John F. Kennedy, who did not know about the training camp,* said: "We must attempt to strengthen the non-Batista democratic forces in exile, and in Cuba itself, who offer eventual hope of overthrowing Castro. Thus far these fighters for freedom have had virtually no support from our government."

And Richard Nixon, who did know about the camp, replied: "I think that Senator Kennedy's policies and recommendations for handling the Castro regime are probably the most dangerously irresponsible recommendations that he has made during the course of the campaign." Kennedy's call for United States support of a revolution in Cuba was "the most shockingly

* This point is disputed by Mr. Nixon. In his book *Six Crises*, Nixon states flatly that "Kennedy had been briefed on this [secret] operation" on July 23, 1960. After the book appeared, the White House, on March 20, 1962, denied that Kennedy had been told about the secret plans. Allen Dulles immediately backed up Kennedy and said it was an "honest misunderstanding" by Nixon.

reckless proposal ever made . . . by a presidential candidate," Nixon maintained. Such aid, he said, would be violation of five treaties with other American states.

The campaign entered November with Nixon accepting Kennedy's challenge to a fifth television debate—but with an important stipulation: the subject must be limited to Cuba. The debate was not held. At the same time the State Department solemnly warned United States citizens not to join military operations against Cuba.

Sixty-nine million Americans voted for a new President. When the ballots had been tabulated, John F. Kennedy was elected by slightly more than one hundred thousand votes. In Guatemala the Cubans, virtually one hundred per cent, were happy. Kennedy had promised more aggressive action against Castro and he, too, was a Catholic. Flushed from his victory, confident about the future, the President-elect went to Palm Beach, Florida, to rest after the rigorous campaign. There, on November 18, Allen Dulles, the director of the CIA, and Richard Bissell, the chief CIA architect of the Cuban training plans, told Kennedy of the existence of the camp in Guatemala.

Immediately, he was faced with making the first of many decisions involving Cuba that would mark his brief administration.

BOOK TWO

La Brigada

While the public clamor over Castro and Cuba increased, both in volume and emotion, the Eisenhower administration was wrestling with the same problem, but from a different perspective and with the utmost secrecy. Months had passed since the President had approved the forming of a liberation army, but still no final decision on what to do, or how to do it, had been reached.

Although the CIA was entrusted with the day-to-day operation of the Cuban counter-revolutionary force, the over-all planning was debated in Washington at the highest level by what was called "the special group"—a group of top officials of the State Department, Pentagon, CIA and White House who met periodically about Cuba. At first their plans were based on a guerrilla operation. In August, it was suggested for the first time that the guerrilla campaign be scrapped for an invasion of two or three hundred men with tactical air support by planes piloted by Cubans. This proposal won increasing support through September and October when confidence in the success of a guerrilla action declined for three chief reasons: *first*, it became apparent that supplying the guerrillas by air drops, as was planned, would be extremely difficult; *second*, as Castro became more openly allied with the Communist bloc, heavy shipments of arms and ammunition began arriving in Cuba; *third*, Castro's control over the civilians and militia was tighter than had been anticipated, making it difficult for even a long guerrilla campaign to succeed.

Finally, a decision was reached: the guerrilla operation was discarded and in its place was a plan to overthrow Castro by invasion and direct action.

On November 4, four days *before* the presidential election, the CIA sent a long cable to Guatemala informing its men there of the decision. The CIA ordered a reduction of the guerrilla force to a strength of sixty; "use conventional arms and training for everyone else." The cable spelled out, from A to Z, how the change in training was to take place, employing World War II infantry assault landing tactics. It became the Bible of the training camp. From that date any talk in the camp of guerrilla warfare was regarded by the CIA as a sign of weakness.

The idea that a few hundred men could overthrow Castro in a frontal assault is all the more astonishing in view of the known facts of Castro's forces *then*. On November 18, for example, the State Department made public details of military aid to Cuba from the Soviet bloc. At that time, the department said, Castro's army was judged to be *ten times* the size that Batista's had been. And from January, 1959, to mid-November, 1960, some twenty-eight thousand tons of military supplies had been shipped into Cuba.

In attempting to reconstruct the process by which the "special group" made its decision, one impression comes through strongly: Dwight D. Eisenhower was not a major participant. Eisenhower himself has said publicly that there was no plan for an invasion while he was in office; that the only plan then was to train guerrillas. His contention varies so sharply with the facts that an explanation for the discrepancy must be sought, for Eisenhower's integrity cannot be questioned.

One explanation lies in the nature of the Presidency itself and also in Eisenhower's personality. In those early days of November several factors were at work. It was clear that the final decision on Cuba would have to be made by a new administration—either Nixon's or Kennedy's. Eisenhower's health, his age, his method of operating by delegation of authority, the imminent change in office, his status as the first "lame duck" President since the Twenty-second Amendment limiting the term of a President to eight years was passed, and the tendency of his closest advisors to shield him—all these created an atmosphere of not bothering the chief, of going ahead in an interim period, in effect of postponing the final collection in the certainty that payment would be made.

The effects of the change from guerrilla operation to assault landing were felt immediately in Guatemala. Early in November an American known as "Frank" * took charge of Base Trax, and Vallejo and his guerrilla instructors, "The Hawks," departed as silently as they had arrived. Frank (not to be confused with Frank Bender), a florid, sandy-haired, aggressive and commanding figure, went to work energetically.

First, he inspected the men and their quarters and saw how some shared knives and forks. The men were too crowded, he said briskly; they would build more barracks immediately. After observing the lack of weapons, he said that, too, would change: every man must have a rifle. Soon all types of weapons—all new —and ammunition began arriving at the base. With the weapons came new equipment: beds, mattresses, uniforms. A fully equipped kitchen was built. An electric plant was installed. Base Trax finally became a true military camp.

But the greatest change was in the concept of the liberation army itself. Frank had brought with him plans for creating an assault brigade. As he explained it, the brigade would be only a skeleton force, but once it went into combat it would expand rapidly because more Cubans would join it.

Of the 430 men in the camp, sixty were separated to receive further training as guerrillas. Their mission would be to infiltrate into Cuba and prepare the way for the brigade when it landed. Carl, the American who limped, took charge of those men and they left Base Trax to receive guerrilla training in Panama. Left behind was the Brigade, the force that would defeat Castro. From that time on it was the principal concern of the Americans.

Pepe San Román was appointed Brigade commander and four battalions were formed. Pepe named Alejandro del Valle to command the First Battalion of paratroopers, while Hugo Sueiro headed the Second Battalion of infantry, Oliva led the "bomblene," or Armored Battalion, and Roberto San Román, Pepe's brother, was in charge of the Heavy Gun Battalion. In keeping with Frank's "skeleton" outline, the Brigade at full strength would be only eight hundred to nine hundred men. Its battalions would be the size of companies and its companies actually small platoons.

* He was an Army Colonel.

To the men in the ranks the new formations were confusing. "They told us that we were going to become a conventional force," one soldier said. "I didn't know what a conventional force meant. I just wanted to fight in Cuba."

In order to create *esprit de corps*, Frank suggested that the men choose a name for their Brigade. Pepe San Román and his officers at first wanted to call themselves Carlyle Brigade in honor of Carlos Santana, the first of their men to die; then Pepe decided to use Carlyle's serial number, 2506. The men liked the name and Brigade 2506 was formed. Pepe next designed an emblem—the numerals 2506 superimposed on a cross—which the men wore on their uniforms, and he also designed a flag.

Skirmishing day and night up and down the mountains, the Brigade was being whipped into an army under the close supervision of Frank and his American instructors. Although the Cubans knew the Americans only by their first names, a sense of camaraderie quickly developed. "Gordon," "Seabee," "Pat," "Big John," "Sonny," "Bob," "Jim" and the rest of the Americans were enthusiastic and seemed genuinely to believe in the Cuban cause. Most important to the Cubans, the Americans, unlike the "Hawks," knew their business. They were excellent instructors.

"I could never make up my mind just what was behind us," said Ramón Ferrer, whom Pepe appointed Brigade chief of staff. "I knew it was the United States but I didn't know exactly what. But when Frank and the other Americans came I knew that we were under the supervision of the American military."

Morale in the camp was high and the men responded eagerly to the training. They were happy, and so was Frank. As he watched the Brigade become more proficient, he told Pepe San Román they were developing a unit that would "sweep Cuba."

"Frank always referred to our part in the combat, or our part in the armed forces," Pepe said. "This thing was much bigger and we were just a piece there—one of the most important pieces—but he said there were many, many groups being organized like ours, and they were all going to be under us. We were only one-tenth of the force. He also talked about having the Guatemalan army with us, to help us in the rear."

The Cubans did not question Frank closely; they trusted in him and in the Americans who so obviously were behind them.

The *Frente* in Miami would ask what questions had to be asked; that was the responsibility of the civilian leadership. The leaders of the Brigade need have only one serious worry: their force was too small. While they worked in Guatemala with a few hundred troops, in Miami where the camps were an open secret, guesses as to their numbers ran as high as twenty thousand. With rumors of such a force, there seemed to be no urgency about enlisting. Censored letters from Guatemala added to the confusion. Some men wrote back requesting shorts, others asked for heavy sweaters. That certainly seemed to prove there were many camps in Central America. In actual fact, at the air strip at Retalhuleu, at sea level, the weather was tropical; at Base Trax, seven thousand feet higher, it was not.

In the Cuban colony, a game developed in which everyone tried to guess the size of the army. One young couple worked out what seemed to be a foolproof method: the husband said he would write his wife, when he reached the base, that he had read a certain number of books—five or four or three. Each book would represent a thousand men in the Brigade. The wife never understood why he failed to mention the books. They simply had not imagined the army could be less than a thousand men.

Slowly, in the same small groups of forty or fifty, recruits were transported from Miami to Guatemala. "This is the Hilton," they were told when they landed at the new field the Americans had built at Retalhuleu. Then, with a sweep of the arm toward the mountains: "Your home is over there in the clouds."

To speed up the flow of men, Frank and the Cuban staff sent a five-man recruiting commission to Miami on Christmas Eve, 1960. They were dismayed to find that the Cubans on the *Frente*'s command staff in Miami appeared jealous of the leaders in the camp. "They treated us as though we were enemies sent by Castro," said Roberto San Román, Pepe's brother. The commission was further discouraged to see that the Americans, too, had their differences. Those in Miami didn't agree with those in Guatemala. At the first of the year the commission admitted failure and returned to Guatemala, frustrated and embittered. It seemed they could trust only Frank and the other American advisors at the base.

But Del Valle told his paratroopers after the commission returned, "This is the only card the Americans have to play in the Cuban game; they won't waste it."

Nineteen sixty-one, the "Year of Education" as Fidel called it, and as it was to be for so many, began with Castro speaking hysterically on New Year's Day in Havana about an imminent American invasion.

On January 3 President Eisenhower, stating that the limit of U.S. endurance had been reached, announced the severing of diplomatic ties with Cuba. On January 4 Manuel Artime, discouraged at the political bickering in Miami and anxious to begin his own military training, left for the camp in Panama after conferring with Frank Bender. On January 5 the Fair Play for Cuba Committee, a pro-Castro group, asked Congress to investigate reports that the CIA was establishing secret bases for an invasion. On January 6 the State Department said it doubted newspaper reports that Castro was planning to let the Soviet Union establish missile bases in Cuba. And a week later a *New York Times* story discussed the suspicion that the CIA was training rebel forces in Guatemala and was also backing the *Frente* (none of it was true, "Tony" Varona, the head of the *Frente*, commented in Miami).

Then it was January 20, the day the oldest President in United States history stepped aside for the youngest ever elected to that office. From the windswept steps of the Capitol, John Fitzgerald Kennedy warned friend and foe alike that the torch had passed to a new generation tempered by war. It was, as the new President said, a day signifying renewal as well as change, for in the transition from old to new, unfinished business remained. Fidel Castro immediately offered the new President advice: relations between the two countries could begin anew, he said, but the United States must take the responsibility for improvement.

From Key Largo to Key West, the Florida Keys curve one hundred miles southwest into the Gulf of Mexico—coral island after coral island, with inlets, harbors and beaches, all facing toward Cuba. For more than a year a Cuban captain named Enrique (Kikío) Llansó had been sailing from those Keys to supply the Cuban underground with arms and ammunition.

Then, on the morning of January 27, 1961, one week after President Kennedy's inauguration, Llansó left in a small boat powered by an outboard motor with a crew of four and carrying five members of Brigade 2506. His mission was to transport them to Matanzas Province, where they would be met and infiltrated into Cuba.

When they reached the coast and flashed their lights in the prescribed manner, there was no return signal. They waited the specified time and went back to the Keys. Six days later they tried again. Halfway to Cuba, a defective pipe discharged gas from the engine into the boat. One by one the men felt sick, then sleepy, then each blacked out. The boat circled aimlessly until a patrol vessel, after failing to receive a radio answer, sent a boarding party and the men were carried to the United States.

On February 11 they sailed again. As they neared the coast, heavy seas buffeted the ship until it capsized. The men swam ashore practically naked, without weapons, money, or radio equipment. They were the first of the Brigade infiltration teams to land in Cuba.

The Brigade infiltration teams had been trained by the CIA to operate in the Cuban provinces and cities. Composed primarily of young, intensely idealistic students, who had been among the first to sacrifice their careers to join the counterrevolution, these teams had been instructed by the CIA to prepare the way for the invasion by creating internal strife and fomenting popular uprisings. Their job, for which they were well trained in Guatemala, Panama and the United States,* was a key to the success of an invasion mounted by a small force.

Once inside Cuba they took their positions throughout the island and, at great risk, began to organize rendezvous positions to receive supplies by sea and air. Soon radio nets were in operation between Cuba and the United States, under the coordination of a remarkable man named Rogelio González Corzo, well known throughout Cuba by his underground name of "Francisco." But immediately the infiltration teams encountered problems: supplies failed to arrive on time, and when they did they often fell into the hands of the enemy. Day by day the militia lines tightened and it became increasingly difficult to

---

* They received training in Florida, Louisiana and even in Maryland, near Fort Meade, twenty miles north of Washington.

operate. They found, also, that the CIA did not seem to trust them, for many messages sent from Cuba to the agency in the United States never were acted upon.

More than anything else the reaction of the populace kept up their spirits. As Félix Rodríguez, nineteen years old, who was in one of the teams, said later: "There were a lot of farmers, small people of all classes there, that were helping us, and I don't know why they kept doing it. Some of them were really poor people. That is one thing we had not been told in our briefing. We were not expecting that kind of cooperation. It was amazing, incredible, you couldn't believe it. Those were the most ardent people against Castro and yet they were the ones that were supposed to be his greatest support. The real poor farmers, the real poor peasants. It was a crazy idea, but those people had faith in us. They gave us the strength to keep on fighting."

In January the Brigade paratroop battalion, followed by Oliva's men, left the Guatemalan mountain ranges for a farm on the plains near San José. Once more they labored with machetes to clear the fields for a new training area, and once more they encountered difficulties. In the tropical vegetation there were many poisonous snakes, some resembling cobras, and one which for want of a better name the men called "yellow whiskers." At night they had to shake out their sleeping bags. Cattle ticks also were a problem and the base soon got the name "Garrapatanango," or tick base.

Later in the month Oliva was ordered to report back to Base Trax. There, Pepe San Román congratulated him and said the Americans had appointed him second in command of the Brigade. Oliva had no sooner returned to his old battalion when he was again summoned to Trax. This time San Román greeted him glumly, told Oliva he must assume command of the Brigade, and announced that he himself had resigned.

Pepe's resignation was an outgrowth of the long-smoldering feud between Miami and the Brigade staff. It was touched off when Manuel Villafaña, chief of the Brigade air force base at Retalhuleu, wrote a letter accusing the Cuban military staff in Miami of conspiring against the Brigade commander. When the letter was read to the Brigade, there was talk of a *coup d'état.* The situation was heightened by new arrivals from Miami; San Román suspected that some had been sent deliberately to create problems. A general strike occurred and 230 out of the more than five hundred men in camp resigned, including the entire second and third battalions. In despair San Román also decided to resign and join the ranks as a soldier, hoping that the men would reunite under Oliva. In his written resignation, San Román told the men they must stand behind Oliva because: "This unit is not mine, nor even of the *Frente*, nor even of the United States. This unit, Assault Brigade 2506, belongs to Cuba, our beloved country."

Since Frank was away from the base when the crisis occurred, the other Americans sent for his superior in Guatemala, a man they called "Bernie," who had come from time to time to check on the training. To the Cubans he was known as "Sitting Bull" because of his short, stocky, swarthy appearance.

Bernie assembled the Brigade, mounted a wooden platform and said: "A lot of you people have never seen me, but I am the boss here and the commander of this Brigade is still Pepe San Román."

He called Pepe forward and told him to take charge.

"Those that are willing to go with me and fight and forget about political things, walk to the right," Pepe said. "And those who are more interested in politics, stay where you are."

One hundred men stayed in place. They demanded to see the representatives of the *Frente*. When Frank returned, he was violently angry and summoned those who refused to train. They were soldiers, he stormed, and had to obey orders whether they liked them or not. After the men were assured that leaders of the *Frente* would come to Guatemala to hear their grievances, all but forty agreed to resume training. Twelve men considered by the Americans to be the principal troublemakers were transported to the *Petén*, the northernmost part of Guatemala, by truck, plane and finally by canoe, where they were imprisoned in the midst of the jungle, accessible only by helicopter.*

Then one by one the Brigade battalions moved out of the mountains to Garrapatanango for more intensive training.

The camp mutiny almost stopped the training. In an effort to

---

* They remained in that prison until after the Bay of Pigs invasion, after which they were flown back to Miami.

repair the damage the CIA once more turned to Manuel Artime, who was then in Panama taking a guerrilla training course. On February 4, after receiving a cable, Artime left immediately for Washington, where Frank Bender and another American outlined the problems. The *Frente* was hopelessly divided politically. A conspiracy had been discovered among members of its Miami staff; and there was the crisis in Guatemala where the dissidents were clamoring for a meeting with the exile leaders.

Out of that conversation came the eventual dissolution of the *Frente* and the formation of a new political exile structure—the Cuban Revolutionary Council—which included such men as Manuel Ray, Castro's former Minister of Public Works, and Miró Cardona, Castro's first Premier, both of whom, and particularly Ray, were far to the left of the *Frente* politicians. But before that organization was created, the politicians attempted to resolve the problem in the camp.

Artime, Tony Varona and Antonio Maceo, another member of the *Frente,* arrived in Guatemala in the middle of February. It was the first—and only—time that any member of the *Frente* visited the men in their camps. (Their military chief of staff in Miami, Colonel Martin Elena, had been there twice— one day in August, when he left during a rainstorm, and another day in the fall when he answered complaints about lack of mail and packages with the comment that the men didn't need any.) Varona, the coordinator and principal official of the *Frente,* spoke to the Brigade, and, in a definite rebuke to San Román, said the Brigade headquarters could not make decisions without first consulting the civilian structure in Miami. Those who had resigned were pleased: Tony was on their side. After his speech, Tony and the Brigade staff conferred at Helvetia with Frank.

"I told Dr. Varona that if he was going to demonstrate to the men that I was not backed by him then I wanted somebody else put in my place," Pepe said. "It was very easy for him to leave the camp and go back to Miami, but I was the one who had to stay there. He had to give me complete backing or I would not stay where I was. Tony was against us all the way."

Then Frank and Tony talked in private. The next day Varona again addressed the entire Brigade. This time he said he was completely behind San Román; anything Pepe did was all right, and there would be no changes in command. From the ranks of those who had cheered him the day before came catcalls and shouts of derision. Tony and the others returned to Miami. Their visit had helped in one respect: soon three and four hundred recruits a week were arriving in Guatemala. Photographs taken by an American while Tony and Artime addressed the Brigade helped to stimulate enlistments after they were released to Spanish-language newspapers and were printed widely—even inside Cuba. A great rush began to join *La Brigada*, as the Cubans called it, before the ships sailed.

"LET 'ER RIP"

I have been present at several great conferences where twenty or more of the most important executive personages were gathered together. When the discussion flagged and all seemed baffled, it was on these occasions Harry Hopkins would rap out a deadly question: "Surely, Mr. President, here is the point we have got to settle. Are we going to face it or not?" Faced it always was and being faced, was conquered.

WINSTON S. CHURCHILL

Soon after his inauguration, John F. Kennedy began meeting with his advisors on the problem of Cuba. Allen Dulles and Richard Bissell of the CIA were urging action.* Time was running out, they warned: if Castro was to be overthrown, it had to be done shortly. Intelligence reports indicated that even the month of May would be too late. By then more and more weapons and planes—Soviet MIG jet fighter planes, and the pilots to fly them—would be arriving in Cuba from Czechoslovakia and other countries behind the Iron Curtain. The CIA was certain that an invasion would succeed if it was undertaken soon, but the longer the decision was postponed the smaller would be the margin of safety. Dulles and Bissell not only endorsed the plan for an invasion; they strongly advocated it.

* On a "Meet the Press" television interview on December 31, 1961, for instance, Allen Dulles said the growing miltary strength of Castro determined the time of the invasion. The five months preceding April were, he said, "most auspicious" for getting rid of Communism.

The President asked for the opinion of his professional military men. The outline tactical plan for the invasion was sent to the Pentagon, approved at a subordinate level and then reviewed by General Lyman Lemnitzer, chairman of the Joint Chiefs of Staff, the nation's supreme military authority, and Admiral Arleigh Burke, Chief of Naval Operations. On February 3 they, too, endorsed it and predicted success.

At this time the plan called for an invasion in March near Trinidad, a city of twenty thousand on the southeast coast of Cuba at the foot of the Escambray Mountains. There the Brigade would make its assault landing and link up with guerrillas in the mountains. "Operation Trinidad" had evolved in the fall of 1960, after the Eisenhower administration decided to form an invasion army and discarded its plans for major guerrilla action.

President Kennedy had been in Washington fourteen years, first as a Representative, then as a Senator, and now as the new President. In those years, like all legislators he had to rely on the judgment of such men as Dulles and Lemnitzer and Burke— they were the pros, the men whose expert opinions had been tested and accepted by other Presidents in times of crisis, men on whose abilities the security of the United States had rested. And he, the President, was facing his first major decision.

The President had a variety of choices. Politics, of course, was deeply involved. The camps and the Brigade were a fact. They represented a tacit commitment by the United States. If he vetoed the plan, the men of the Brigade, trained under difficult conditions for nearly a year in the expectation of liberating Cuba, would be thrown back into the vortex of more than one hundred thousand embittered exiles in Miami. The angry Cubans certainly would accuse him publicly of betraying them. Just as certainly, the Republicans would attack. By scrapping the plans begun under Eisenhower, he would lay his administration open to the charge that it was soft on Castro and communism—and that the young "amateurs" in the White House had disregarded the advice of the experts. During the campaign Kennedy himself, in the celebrated fourth television debate with Nixon, had pledged to aid Cuban freedom fighters.

Aside from the domestic implications, there was a more significant consideration: the rewards of success. If Dulles and the military were correct, the invasion would eliminate Castro and his Communist base in the Caribbean without jeopardizing or directly involving the United States. If intelligence reports were reliable, such an opportunity would not come again. It was also clear that no more Cuban exile support could be expected if the invasion were halted. The United States would have to do it alone. That meant the risk of conflict with Russia. Was Cuba worth that risk?

There was another factor: the camps in Guatemala were attracting public attention, threatening to expose the United States involvement. As a consequence, the Guatemalan government was becoming nervous and asking when the Cubans would be removed from its soil. There was only one direction for the men to move—to Cuba.

Kennedy told the CIA to continue preparing for the invasion, but made it clear that he still might call it off. The President's doubts stemmed not only from the danger of conflict with Russia, but also from the possibility of damage to the relations of the United States with the neutral countries, as well as with its allies. The Cuban undertaking easily could be labeled another Hungary, in reverse, with the United States branded as a ruthless imperialist aggressor. It was vital, then, for the American involvement to be kept both secret and at a minimum in the actual landing and fighting. The reasoning was logical—and yet, with hindsight, it contained major flaws. For, in fact, the operation had long since ceased to be secret, and the United States would have to bear the responsibility for whatever resulted. Also, a failure could be disastrous to world confidence in a new administration. Success, it would seem, was an absolute necessity, if the invasion were to take place at all.

The original target date came and went—and so did the target itself. The reason for the change was complex, a jumbled mixture of political and military considerations. When the training resumed in February after the crisis in the camp, the Pentagon dispatched a special team to inspect the Brigade. The inspection was made from the 24th to the 27th of February. A report, praising the combat readiness and morale of the Brigade, was formally approved by the Pentagon on March 10. On the next day the National Security Council met and considered the Cuban venture. Out of that meeting and other high-level administration conferences in the middle of March, emerged a new landing area, and a modified invasion plan.

As one man explained the changes, "The plan came up as Trinidad but it was too big, too open, too big a deal. There was a kind of schizophrenic approach to the invasion: we wanted it to work, but it had to be kept under wraps so we wouldn't be implicated."

Trinidad, with a relatively large civilian population, might lead to a further American commitment. Also, by that time, the guerrillas operating in the Escambray Mountains had been eliminated,* ending one key advantage of Operation Trinidad—the link-up in the hills with the invasion force. A more remote area was sought, an area where the Brigade planes could operate from Cuban soil instead of making the long bombing runs from Central America.

In keeping with the political-military reasoning, one more change was made: instead of landing at daybreak, as originally planned, the Brigade would storm ashore at night and present the world with a *fait accompli* by dawn.

Before the invasion could take place, however, the political division among the Cubans had to be resolved and a provisional government formed. It wasn't until March 22 that the Cuban politicians came to an agreement and formed their Revolutionary Council. By then the new invasion site had been selected and the plan had taken its final form. The Brigade would land one hundred miles west of Trinidad at the *Bahía de Cochinos*, the Bay of Pigs. The new target date was first set for April 5; then it was postponed to April 10; and then a final date was selected—Monday, April 17.

More than a dozen meetings, conferences and briefings on the Cuban invasion were held in Washington between November 29, 1960, and April 12, 1961. All the meetings with the President were attended by one or more members of the Joint Chiefs of Staff. Perhaps the most important of the meetings took place April 4, with the President presiding in the conference room of

---

* On March 23, 1961, Captain Enrique Llanso picked up the twelve last survivors of the Escambray and took them to the U.S. They had fought their way out of the mountains and were wounded, starved and defeated.

the new wing of the State Department. Seated around the long table were Secretary of State Dean Rusk, Secretary of Defense Robert McNamara, Secretary of the Treasury Douglas Dillon, Assistant Secretary of State for Latin American Affairs Thomas Mann, Assistant Secretary of Defense Paul Nitze, Senator William J. Fulbright of Arkansas, the chairman of the Senate Foreign Relations Committee, and three presidential advisors and specialists on Latin America: Adolph A. Berle, Jr., Richard Goodwin and Arthur M. Schlesinger, Jr. Dulles, Bissell and Lemnitzer also were present.

Richard Bissell, the man who had masterminded the U-2 flights over Russia, was the first to speak. It was his final review of the Cuban operation. The Brigade would land and hold its territory until the Cuban Revolutionary Council declared itself a "government in arms" and rallied internal support to it. The situation inside Cuba was ripe for rebellion. The Brigade air force would control the skies and operate from the captured field near the Bay of Pigs. Castro's planes would be wiped out by a Brigade air attack before the invasion. He referred to the quality of the Brigade as a fighting force and mentioned the arms it would have. The history of Latin America was a history of rebellions, insurrections and *coups d'état*. The history of Cuba was one of small forces triumphing over larger ones, of the populace rising and joining the liberators. But the clinching argument came when the question was asked: What would happen if the invasion failed to bring down the Castro government?

An alternative plan had been prepared for use in the event of a total disaster. The Cubans would be told that if, somehow, the invasion foundered they would move inland to the Escambray Mountains as a guerrilla force.* The Brigade leaders themselves would have the option of deciding when to use the alternative plan. And, it was argued, a guerrilla force of nearly 1,500 men—well armed, trained and equipped—would be more than a thorn in Castro's side, as well as a major rallying point for further action.

From the beginning, the alternative plan had been a major

---

* "We were never told about this," Pepe San Román told the author. "What we were told was, "If you fail *we* will go in.""

element in the planning process. After Trinidad was eliminated as the target, the President and other important officials were repeatedly assured that the Bay of Pigs area was good guerrilla country and that the entire force could operate there. The President had also been assured that the Brigade had been trained as guerrillas when, in fact, there is no evidence that the Brigade received any guerrilla training after November 4, 1960, the date of the change in concept from guerrilla to invasion. Until November 4, 1960, the Cuban force consisted of only three hundred men. The alternative plan, then, seemed to minimize a disaster on the beach. As the CIA put it, if the Brigade can't do it one way (invasion) they will do it the other (guerrilla).

One who was there says Bissell gave the plan his unqualified support.

Dulles, who already had told the President he thought the Cuban venture was going to be easier than Guatemala, spoke briefly, and also backed the plan.

The President pointed around the table, man by man, asking for approval or disapproval.

No one opposed the invasion.*

"Let 'er rip," one man said.

On one point President Kennedy was clear: under no conditions were American forces to be committed to the invasion. It was a firm decision, one which was impressed on everyone, whether civilian, military, CIA or Cuban politician.

The CIA, principal architect of the invasion, was not distressed by the President's decision: it was so confident of success it believed that American manpower—and airpower—would not be needed. Air cover was one of the key elements in the CIA's invasion plan—but Cuban, not American, air cover. The CIA assumed that the Brigade would have the total dominion of

---

* Senator Fulbright's position is ambiguous. Although the Senator had reservations, the author has been told authoritatively that he did not—as has been written—oppose the invasion at the April 4 meeting. Later, he asked for, and received, a more detailed briefing. While he remained unconvinced, he did say he had not been aware of certain aspects of the plan that gave it a greater chance of success. It should be said, too, that Secretary of State Rusk, who also later was represented as harboring doubts, did not express them at the meeting.

the sky and thus would be invincible. Its invasion plan was based on its intelligence estimate of Castro's air force. In the official operations order for the invasion that estimate read:

The Cuban Air Force is entirely disorganized and lacks experienced pilots and specialists trained in maintenance and communications. The Air Force does not have organized squadrons, flights, or conventional units, depending instead upon Headquarters in Havana. The planes are for the most part obsolete and inoperative, owing to inadequate maintenance and the lack of spare parts. The few planes that are operational are considered to be in flying condition but are not in combat condition.* *The combat efficiency of the Air Force is almost non-existent; it has limited capability of early warning to oppose naval and air units, and could make raids against lightly armed invaders,* but in general terms it is limited to the transport of troops and material, strafing attacks, and reconnaissance patrols. *

When the CIA spoke of air cover, as it did at the Washington briefings and in Guatemala, it meant sixteen World War II B-26 attack bombers. The agency was certain these lumbering, veteran planes were all that was needed to control the air, without the support of fighters, either propeller-driven or jet. To deal with Castro's air force, the CIA plan called for two bombing attacks on Cuba—one two days before the invasion, and the other the morning of the invasion. When its bombers had finished their attacks, Castro's "almost non-existent" air force would be totally destroyed.

Only one thing seemed to worry the CIA: the President had said he still might call off the entire operation. The point of no return for the invasion was noon of Sunday, April 16. Then it would be too late to stop—the Brigade would be committed.

Now it was time for the public—already well informed of the camps by the press and talkative Cubans—to be further prepared for a major development in Cuban-American relations. In the diplomatic language reserved for announcing momentous decisions, the State Department on April 3 issued a "White Paper," or official policy declaration, on Cuba. It was the considered judgment of the United States that "the Castro regime in Cuba offers a clear and present danger . . . to the whole

* Author's emphasis.

hope of spreading political liberty, economic development, and social progress through all the republics of the hemisphere." Drafted by Arthur Schlesinger, the historian and presidential advisor, the declaration brilliantly and forcefully dissected the events from January 1, 1959 to the spring of 1961. "The present situation in Cuba confronts the Western Hemisphere and the inter-American system with a grave and urgent challenge," it stated. That challenge resulted from a betrayal of the Cuban revolution by its leaders. "What began as a movement to enlarge Cuban democracy has been perverted, in short, into a mechanism for the destruction of free institutions in Cuba, for the seizure by international communism of a base and bridgehead to the Americas, and for the disruption of the inter-American system."

In recounting how the revolution had been betrayed, the declaration called the roll of Cuban patriots who had turned against Castro: Huber Matos, Miró Cardona, Manuel Urrutia, Manuel Ray, Manuel Artime, and on down the list. Acknowledging "past omissions and errors in our relationship" to Cuba, it pledged "full and positive support" to achieve freedom.

Five days later Miró Cardona issued his own emotional call. "To arms, Cubans!" he said. "We must conquer or we shall die choked by slavery. In the name of God we assure you all that after the victory we will have peace, human solidarity, general well being and absolute respect for the dignity of Cubans without exception. Duty calls us to the war against the executioners of our Cuban brethren. Cubans! To Victory! For Democracy! For the Constitution! For Liberty!"

Two days after his public summons to battle, Miró was more specific and less emotional. Sitting on a bed in his suite high up in the Hotel Lexington, overlooking New York's East Side and only blocks away from the United Nations, Miró told Dom Bonafede of *The Miami Herald* that "there will be less talk and more action against Castro." The site for the establishment of a provisional government already had been picked, Miró said, and he would head the government as president. He discounted all the talk of an invasion; that, he said, was what Castro wanted. Asked when the council would land in Cuba, Miró said he didn't know. Then he added slyly: "I'm like a cab driver. I don't know where I'll be in ten minutes."

While Miró was preparing for that sudden trip, Tad Szulc of the *New York Times* was astutely reporting from Miami that "deep differences and rivalries" divided the Cuban exile leaders and that already various factions were unfolding plans for future Cuban regimes. In an ironic footnote to the day, the *Times,* in a dispatch from Guatemala, reported that leading Communists from the old regime of Jacobo Arbenz, the regime the CIA had helped to overthrow, were returning to Guatemala.

In Havana, while the invasion hysteria mounted, Castro said Cuba was growing stronger daily to counter the CIA's "imbecile" plan of counter-revolution.

On Wednesday afternoon, April 12, President Kennedy walked briskly into the new State Department Auditorium for his weekly press conference. It was a time of major developments. The day before Adolph Eichmann, the Nazi chief of the Gestapo's "Jewish Affairs" section, had gone on trial for his life in Jerusalem. That morning Major Yuri Alekseyevich Gagarin of the Soviet Union was hurtled into space in his rocket "Vostok" to become the first man to orbit the earth. In Laos, the pro-Western royalist forces were retreating before the pro-Communist Pathet Lao guerrillas. Even so, the first question at the conference was about Cuba. The President, in his reply, ruled out "under any condition, an intervention in Cuba by the United States armed forces."

"The basic issue in Cuba," the President said, "is not one between the United States and Cuba. It is between the Cubans themselves. And I intend to see that we adhere to that principle, and as I understand it, this Administration's attitude is so understood and shared by the anti-Castro exiles from Cuba in this country."

Why the President felt compelled to insist so firmly and so publicly that the United States would not use its force to aid the Cubans is not clear. The result was clear to all, however: the United States had tied its hands in advance. In Latin America the public reaction was one of praise. As the *Jornal do Brasil* in Rio de Janeiro commented editorially: "The last doubts about the sincerity of the new government of the United States were dissipated with President Kennedy's statement that no branch of the armed forces of that country would take part in an invasion of Cuba. . . . All this is very good because it shows the United States is beginning to understand Latin American psychology. . . ."

Whether the Latins—particularly the Cubans—understood the President was another matter. Later, the Cuban politicians claimed they had not understood or shared the administration's position on the use of American force. There is no record that *any* Cuban raised any official objection, public or private, to the President's statement. Neither did the Pentagon or the CIA.

The day after the press conference a cable was sent to a special emissary of the President in Guatemala, informing him of the President's statement. The emissary, a personable, professional military man then working with the CIA, was asked to reply by "emergency precedence" if in any way he had changed his evaluation of the Brigade. He immediately replied:

"My observations have increased my confidence in the ability of this force to accomplish not only initial combat missions, but also the ultimate objective, the overthrow of Castro. The Brigade and battalion commanders now know all details of the plan and are enthusiastic. These officers are young, vigorous, intelligent and motivated by a fanatical urge to begin battle. Most of them have been preparing under rugged conditions of training for almost a year. They say they know their own people and believe that after they have inflicted one serious defeat upon the opposition forces, the latter will melt away from Castro, whom they have no wish to support. They say it is a Cuban tradition to join a winner and they have supreme confidence they will win against whatever Castro has to offer. I share their confidence." *

A person who is able to speak with unquestioned authority said that that glowing report overcame the last of the President's doubts. The emissary was a Marine colonel with a brilliant combat record.

---

* When the author showed Pepe San Román this passage, San Román commented: "This conversation never took place with me or any of my commanders. He says that we knew all the details of the plan. Actually, we knew nothing."

CHAPTER 3

TURN LEFT TO HAVANA

At the end of March, after the Brigade had moved back to Base Trax, and after a brief inspection by Miró Cardona and the Cuban Revolutionary Council, Frank called Pepe San Román and Oliva to his headquarters. He told them the invasion was imminent, that there would be two beachheads, and that, as he had told them earlier, the Brigade would not be the only unit involved. The entire invasion force would assemble at a base he called Trampoline—the springboard—which would have to remain unidentified until they reached it. From there, ships that the Americans were in the process of buying would take them to Cuba. He showed them pictures of landing craft and told them their air force would include fighter planes as well as B-26s. When they got to Trampoline, they would see how strong their forces were.

"Frank told Pepe and me," Oliva said, "that the Marines were not going with us to invade Cuba, but they would be close to us when we needed them."

Then, in a casual manner, Frank remarked that the U.S. government had almost halted the program at the end of January because of the crisis in the camp. Now, however, the Brigade was going to move forward.

That was the end of the first briefing. Pepe and Oliva supervised the training with increased ardor. Near their headquarters they had installed a mock cargo net on a wooden fence. Now each day all the men practiced climbing up and down the net with weapons, simulating debarkation from a ship. Invasion fever was in the air.

Even tragedy at the camp seemed only to intensify it. When

Dr. Gustavo Cuervo Rubio Fernández, thirty-one years old, died in a car accident at Base Trax on March 30, Pepe wrote to Gustavo's father. "There is so little that I can tell you to mitigate the great pain you have in this moment," Pepe wrote. "However, if my words could help you in something, let me tell you that Gustavito was a complete man, a soldier completely conscious of his duty, with the Brigade and with his destiny, in the moment his country demanded his presence. . . . A companion will take his place . . . in this glorious campaign. . . . So when we fight he will be with us, as he wished. The expression of condolences was in the whole base when we knew about the death of your son, and believe me, during his crisis our prayers were stronger than the sound of our guns."

No longer were they torn by divisive political quarrels; they were about to enter combat, and they were united as they never had been.

The secret briefings continued. The Brigade leaders learned that they were going to have to establish and hold a beachhead until the civil government arrived, set itself up, and asked for help from the United States and other Latin American countries. There would be no problem, Frank assured them, because everything already had been arranged by the Americans. Once the provisional government was formally recognized, the free world countries, including the United States, would supply the Cubans. But that might not be necessary, Frank said, for inside Cuba the underground was ready and a general offensive would be ordered soon. The invasion would be the final blow.

It was now early in April and Artime was in the camp as the civilian representative of the Revolutionary Council. Frank called Pepe and Oliva again. This time he had startling information. There were forces in the administration trying to block the invasion, and Frank might be ordered to stop it. If he received such an order, he said he would secretly inform Pepe and Oliva. Pepe remembers Frank's next words this way:

"If this happens you come here and make some kind of show, as if you were putting us, the advisors, in prison, and you go ahead with the program as we have talked about it, and we will give you the whole plan, even if we are your prisoners."

Frank was quite specific: they were to place an armed Brigade soldier at each American's door, cut communications with the outside, and continue the training until he told them when, and how, to leave for Trampoline base. Frank then laughed and said: "In the end we will win."

Pepe and Oliva were disturbed by this plan, but they had such faith in the Americans that they agreed to follow it if necessary. They knew that they would have difficulty with the Brigade, because as Pepe said: "Most of the Cubans were there because they knew the whole operation was going to be conducted by the Americans, not by me or anyone else. They did not trust me or anyone else. They just trusted the Americans. So they were going to fight because they knew the United States was backing them."

Frank then called in Artime and privately told him the same thing. Artime was as stunned as the others. Frank never said who opposed the invasion—it was just "forces in the administration," or "politicians," or "chiefs above." He did say that if he received the order to stop the invasion, "I have also orders from my bosses, my commanders, to continue anyway." It cannot be determined what bosses, if any, gave Frank such instructions. But Artime, San Román and Oliva never doubted that he was speaking for his superiors. It seemed obvious to them that the Brigade could not be transported to another unknown base, and then placed aboard ships to go to Cuba without the knowledge and assistance of a great organization.

Out of more than ten secret meetings with Frank at Base Trax came several dominant impressions. Oliva summed them up. *First,* the forces that would land in Cuba were much larger than the Brigade's 1,500 men. *Second,* the Cubans would have the complete support of the United States government, including United States military—and air—support. *Third,* the invasion was going to take place even if Washington tried to stop it. And *last,* most important to the Cubans, the invasion was going to succeed and they would liberate their country.

In the next busy days nothing more was said about putting the Americans under "arrest." Trucks loaded with weapons were arriving in large numbers. The weapons were checked and sorted and then packed for the trip to the ships. An advance unit left for Trampoline to help supervise the loading. And now there was a new American at the base, an expert on amphibious landings according to Frank, who was helping to organize the move from the mountains to the air base below and then to the ships. (Although the Brigade did not know it, he was acting as an emissary of President Kennedy.)

On April 9 the commanders at Base Trax received the mobilization order: the next day they would begin their three-day move to Trampoline. Artime, who was quietly playing chess in the headquarters while the military men went about their preparations, sent a message through the Americans to Miró Cardona informing him that the Brigade was leaving and the invasion was approaching. The reply was: GO AHEAD. GOOD LUCK. MIRO (Miró has since stated that he never received a message from Artime and therefore never sent such a reply.)

San Román assembled the Brigade on April 10 and spoke about the future, instructing the men as to how they should behave with the civilians in Cuba and in the fighting to come. At two o'clock that afternoon a general formation was called and the men fell into line with their equipment. Everyone was joking. Soon the trucks began arriving. By five o'clock the last of the trucks departed, carrying Frank and the Brigade headquarters staff. It was raining and the men were singing the Cuban national anthem.

"It was a great spectacle," Oliva said, "very touching. Playing music, the charanga, singing, people saying *vivas*."

On the way to Retalhuleu, Indian peasants came to the side of the road and cheered and waved as the caravan moved slowly out of the mountains to the air base. There once again the windows of the transport planes were covered with tape and once again each man began wondering where he was going next. At 11:30 that night the first of the planes took off.

The *Río Escondido* moved slowly down the Mississippi to the Gulf of Mexico. As it neared the mouth of the river, one of the propellers was struck by a log. In midsea the Brigade frogmen aboard * checked and found it completely bent. As the old ship entered the Caribbean and neared a Central American port, the frogmen noticed a lot of activity. Small boats were darting across

---

* They had been trained by Americans on Vieques Island in an area marked, "Off Limits. U.S. Navy."

the harbor and men were at work on the long wooden pier. "We knew it was something big," Andy Pruna said.

The Cuban pilots boarded their B-26s on April 2 with sealed envelopes. When they reached an altitude of one thousand feet, they tore open the envelopes and read their flight plans. They headed south, and then east.

Enrique Ruiz-Williams, second-in-command of the Heavy Gun Battalion, took twenty men on April 2 and left Trax for Retalhuleu. That night they began loading planes with weapons and ammunition. It took them four days, day and night. Then in the last flight, they themselves left for Trampoline, still without knowing their destination. Williams talked to the American pilot, who said he had come from Miami the day before and expected to be back in Florida with his family for the weekend. The plane was flying south along the Pacific Ocean, away from Guatemala, away from Cuba, away from the Atlantic ports. "Where in hell are we going?" Williams asked.

He soon got his answer. From the Pacific the plane flew straight across Nicaragua, over the capital of Managua, and on to the Atlantic Ocean. There along the northern coast the Cubans saw a typical Central American coastal city: small houses, a long pier with railroad tracks going out into a harbor, flat ground, red earth. They landed, got in a bus and were driven to the pier. It was Trampoline, and it turned out to be Puerto Cabezas, Nicaragua, sometimes called "Bragman's Bluff."

At the pier the Cubans found Roberto Maciá, one of their comrades, and three or four others who had preceded them. Then they saw the ships—hulking old cargo vessels, unpainted and in bad condition. For the first time, Williams had what he describes as a "cold feeling." He didn't feel better when he inspected the loading machines. They were rusting and in even worse condition than the ships.

Williams' idea, and that of most of the Cubans, had been that they were going in large, well-equipped ships—the kind of American ships they remembered from the newsreels of World War II. Whatever their doubts, the men began working—again around the clock—loading the ships with old, incredibly noisy winches and hoists.

The Brigade planes landed at Trampoline one by one. When Oliva got off, he saw Pepe and his staff waiting for him with many Americans he had never seen before. Obviously, they were men of high rank, for Frank deferred to them. For nearly an hour they waited as a plane carrying Roberto San Román and his Heavy Gun Battalion circled the field. When it landed safely, despite a faulty wheel, all of the Cuban officers entered three or four vehicles and drove until they reached a number of tents surrounded by pine trees at the foot of a hill.

Early in the morning of April 12, the day the President held his press conference, "Seabee," one of the American advisors, arrived in a pickup truck with their breakfast. He explained that the Cuban officers would have to be kept apart because soon they were going to receive the final briefing. While Nicaraguan soldiers stood guard outside their tents, they waited throughout the morning. At noon they were taken to the air base, and along the way the officers saw a stirring sight: B-26s lined up on the field with Cuban flags painted on their wings. Alongside were a number of P-51 fighter planes. At the base they met Villafaña, the commander of the Brigade air force, who said that the B-26s were being prepared for combat and that some of the P-51s would be used in the operation as part of their air cover.

For the rest of the day the officers lounged in their tents until Seabee returned at five o'clock with some maps. After dinner in the air force headquarters, Villafaña remarked that his pilots were getting ready to go into action. When they heard that, the officers left for the base chapel to celebrate mass. At eight o'clock Seabee asked Pepe and Oliva to come with him to inspect the ships within the hour. While they waited, they studied the maps and drank beer. The maps were of Las Villas and Matanzas Provinces, covering an area from the Zapata Peninsula to the Cienfuegos Bay, but the invasion area itself was not pinpointed.

A pickup truck again arrived and Pepe and Oliva were taken to the pier. There, amid the bustle and noise and bright lights, they were introduced to García, a young man who owned the ships bearing his name, "the García Line."

"I felt a great deception when we got over to the ships," Oliva said. "It was something we didn't expect. That was not what we were waiting for."

Two of the ships already had been loaded and were anchored

far offshore with Brigade soldiers aboard. The men were crowded together, with hardly room to sleep, but morale was extremely high. Everyone, as one soldier said, was ready to start shooting. Pepe and Oliva, however, were professional soldiers. They saw much that worried them.

What put the "icing on the cake," as Pepe said, were the landing craft. They were fourteen-foot open boats, powered by outboard motors. They had no protection. How were the Cubans to land in those? Nothing could be better for a landing, Seabee said. Pepe and Oliva also wondered about the defenses on the cargo ships: the .50 caliber machine guns did not seem to be placed properly. Again, they were told: Don't worry; you are going to be supported by air and sea at all times. After a chat with the ship's captain, and a toast with 1800 brandy, Pepe and Oliva went back to their tents at one o'clock in the morning.

The next morning, April 13, two wooden tables and a blackboard were set up near the pines. Soon Frank and a number of Americans arrived. Pepe recognized one of them from Panama and shook hands and said: "Hello, Dave." All the Americans laughed. The man had been called "Dave" in Panama, but now he was known as "Bill." Bill was in charge of intelligence information.

The Brigade staff, all the battalion commanders and their assistants, as well as the doctors, sat down at the tables and waited for the briefing. It was hot and sunny, and some men wore shorts while others took off their shirts.

Frank spoke in general terms that morning. The landing would take place in three places on the south coast of Cuba, he said: Red Beach, Blue Beach and Green Beach. He pointed to a large sketch of a coastline on the blackboard, placed upside down so that south appeared as north, and covered with acetate to conceal landing positions. Frank spoke about communications and explained how the ships would form at an assembly point near the coast. Two battalions of the Brigade would land under the command of Oliva; the others under San Román.

As Frank spoke he glanced from time to time at several of the Americans, as if for confirmation of what he was saying. The Cubans particularly noticed one man who appeared to outrank everyone else. He was tall and thin, with glasses and slightly graying hair. Once or twice before he had inspected the camps, and although he was never introduced the Cubans remembered that he was called "Dick." The description of the man and his current responsibilities suggest that he might have been Richard Bissell of CIA. Most of the time he stood silently observing; occasionally he corrected Frank on a detail.

Later Artime talked to Frank alone. "I asked him about the trouble in Washington he had discussed while we were still in Guatemala," Artime said, "and he said: 'There is no trouble at all. We have orders for the invasion.'"

After lunch the briefing resumed, still in general terms. San Román told Frank his impression of the ships.

"He assured us," Pepe said, "that we were going to have protection by sea, by air, and even from under the sea."

The Cubans understood that to mean the United States Navy.

Frank also was asked where the rest of the forces were. He answered that the Brigade was going to be sufficient for the invasion, but another force would attack in a different part of Cuba to divert attention from the main landing. Then he told them that on the next day they would receive the complete operations order.

The Cubans returned to their tents in high spirits, joking about the superiority of one battalion over another. Someone had a radio tuned to Radio Swan and they all listened as it broadcast music and propaganda to Cuba. They sat up late drinking beer, studying the maps and talking. It was difficult to sleep.

In Miami excitement also was building. People were talking about *La Brigada* and the story that day in the *Miami Herald*. Under an eight-column banner headline, labeled "exclusive rebel story," the paper had quoted at length from "invasion-minded counter-revolutionary officials here." The men, the paper said, "have moved out—moved south."

On April 14, at five o'clock, before the sun had risen, Oliva left his tent and walked out of the base, thinking about the mission that was about to begin. "I felt very optimistic and I felt that all the sacrifices we had made would be rewarded by the liberation of Cuba. Sincerely, I was feeling happy." He walked until the tents were small in the distance and the sun came out. Before long he saw a man coming toward him. It was Artime. They sat on some rocks and talked about the future. Artime was also happy and optimistic.

Oliva explained his ideas for reforming the future army of Cuba, and he was gratified to find that Artime's ideas coincided with his. Oliva said, "The word he used more than any other in that conversation was love. And he told me that the only way that we could control the Communists in Cuba was with love, and the only way to liberate our country. That conversation was a great balm to me." They gave each other an *abrazo* and walked back to the tents for the final briefing.

The acetate was removed, the map was turned right side up and copies of "Operation Pluto," as the invasion plan was called officially, were distributed at nine o'clock. The Cubans read:

Commencing at H-Hour of D-Day, the Brigade is to engage in amphibious and parachute landings, take, occupy and defend beachheads in the areas of Cochinos Bay and Playa Girón of the Zapata Swamps in order to establish a base from which ground and air operations against the Castro government of Cuba may be carried out.

So it was to be the Bay of Pigs, where years ago Cuban engineers had dreamed of cutting a canal seventy-five miles to Cárdenas Bay on the northern coast, shortening the route from the Pacific Coast ports and the Panama Canal to the Atlantic.

The Bay of Pigs has a width of ten to twelve miles at its mouth and tapers gradually inland for eighteen miles from the Caribbean. At its northernmost point, not far from a lake called "El Tesoro" (Treasure Lake) is Playa Larga, or Long Beach. To the west is the Zapata Peninsula. To the southeast the coastline runs smoothly for twenty miles until it reaches the town of Playa Girón. Along the shore there is hard, rocky soil, and then for about three miles inland the land is smooth and firm. Immediately after that begins the Ciénaga de Zapata, sometimes called the "Great Swamp of the Caribbean," extending sixty-five miles from east to west and twenty miles from north to south. The Zapata Swamps are covered with hardwood timber growing in a vast expanse of marshy terrain.

Enormous deposits of peat and black muck, as well as many reptiles, are found within the Zapata Swamp boundaries. Farther along the coast, between the Bay of Pigs and the city of Cienfuegos to the east, is a large forest of valuable timber. Its potential for lumber has never been realized because of the sharp limestone rock, known to the Cubans as "dog teeth rock," which juts out of the ground. The rock is so sharp that iron shoes are insufficient protection for draft animals hauling timber. Until Fidel Castro came to power, the Bay of Pigs–Zapata Swamps area was virtually impassable. The peasants who lived along the coast and in the woods lived in squalor, existing by selling charcoal to pay for the rent of their land. In those days, the only routes across the swamps were two narrow-gauge railroads—one from a sugar mill at the town of Central Australia, straight north from Playa Larga and the Bay of Pigs, and the other running from the town of Covadonga to Girón sixty miles south. Under Castro, however, three major highways were built across the swamps: from Playa Larga to Central Australia; from Covadonga to San Blas, twenty miles northeast of Girón; and from Yaguaramas, approximately thirty miles northeast of Girón, to San Blas. San Blas, therefore, was a key junction of two of the three roads. A good major highway connected Playa Larga to Girón and Girón to San Blas. Due east of Girón was the road stretching to Cienfuegos.

The Castro government was busily transforming the area into a public vacation resort. Tourist centers were being built at Treasure Lake, Playa Larga and Playa Girón. At Girón alone, 180 buildings, resembling American motels and able to accommodate one thousand persons, were nearing completion by that April. On the weekends, for months, hundreds of Cubans had visited the area to see the new resort. May 20 had already been set as the official opening day for Girón.

Operation Pluto called for landings at three points—Playa Larga, called "Red Beach"; Girón, "Blue Beach"; and "Green Beach" a point twenty miles to the east of Girón cutting the road to Cienfuegos. Girón was the center of the invasion. There, at Blue Beach, San Román would land and establish his command post. From Red Beach to Green Beach, the Brigade would control forty miles of Cuban coast line. The first battalion of paratroopers would be dropped in three places—along each road crossing the swamps: at La Horquita, in front of Yaguaramas; at Jocuma, in front of Covadonga; and along the road from

Central Australia to Playa Girón. Del Valle, their commander, would establish his headquarters at San Blas. Thus the Brigade's initial holdings would extend inland for more than twenty miles.

Oliva would land at Playa Larga with the Second and Fifth Battalions of infantry. Near Playa Larga a paratroop detachment would seize an airport and town called Soplillar. San Román would land at Girón with the Sixth Battalion of infantry, the Fourth, or Armored, Battalion, and the Heavy Gun Battalion. The Fourth Batallion would send a reinforced company, with two tanks, to support the paratroopers at San Blas; the rest of the battalion was to enter the Playa Girón Airfield, a major objective, and be held in reserve until needed. The Heavy Gun Battalion was to give general support to the paratroopers, and also to the Third Battalion of infantry, which was to land at Green Beach.

The invasion plan carefully allocated supplies from D-Day to D-Day plus 10; then from the tenth day after the invasion, to the twenty-first day, and on to the thirtieth day. On D-Day itself seventy-two tons of arms, ammunition and equipment, enough to support four thousand men, would be unloaded. In the next ten days, 415 tons more were to be unloaded, and then 530 more, and then 607 tons. Everything was worked out, ton by ton, day by day. The plan seemed superb.

"Then Bill, the intelligence expert, told us that Castro could not react for at least seventy-two hours," Pepe said, "and also that Fidel didn't have any big forces close to the place. The closest were in Santa Clara and that was far away. And from his information they were so disorganized it would take them time to get together and come and give us a fight.

"He also said that there were no communications between Castro's troops in the area and if they saw us landing they would have to take a car and go sixty kilometers to Covadonga to telephone. He said there were no civilians in the zone. They were constructing a resort for tourists there, but it was still a very isolated area."

Bill also gave them this intelligence: Castro would have few tanks and no air force. Finally, there were supposed to be more than five hundred guerrillas nearby waiting to help the Brigade. On the ships were weapons for four thousand men, and the intelligence estimate was that in the first two days five thousand men would join the Brigade in a voluntary uprising. In addition, Brigade planes would drop thousands of weapons to the Cuban people who wanted to join the rebellion.

Then it was Frank's turn to speak. They were to hold the beach for seventy-two hours, he said. And what were they supposed to do after that? "We will be there with you for the next step," Frank said. "But you will be so strong, you will be getting so many people to your side, that you won't want to wait for us. You will go straight ahead. You will put your hands out, turn left, and go straight into Havana."

Frank made a sweeping gesture with his arm that no man present that day will ever forget. There was a great shout from the Cubans. Some had tears in their eyes.

When it came to support, Frank was equally emphatic: there was no question they would have air superiority. Nothing was said about United States air support, or about jets. It *was* said that the enemy would not be able to get to the Brigade; that it would be destroyed from the air; that no trucks or troops would be able to get through the roads because all the roads would be bombed; that "every five minutes there will be a plane over all the major roads of Cuba." The Brigade cargo ships were loaded with thirty to forty thousand gallons of gasoline so its air force could begin immediate missions once the field at Girón was seized. The air missions were already planned for that moment: the operations order called for them to destroy the main railroad and highway bridges in "the zones of Havana, Matanzas, Jovellanos, Colón, Santa Clara and Cienfuegos in order to isolate said areas from enemy operations."

Operation Pluto also included plans for a diversionary landing in Oriente Province by a commando group of 168 men, led by Nino Díaz, and a simulated attack, or "feint," in the vicinity of Pinar del Rió. The "feint" would be accomplished with special sound equipment that would make it sound as if a great battle were being waged.

When Frank had finished, there was a brief moment of silence and then a stir as the Cubans realized it was over. The plan sounded so good, the Cubans were so confident, that no one asked any questions. As Pepe said, "We didn't want to ask these men we knew any embarrassing questions."

Frank had said earlier, in response to a question, that if anything went wrong the Cubans should communicate with the rear base and he would give them instructions. *Nothing* was said about an alternative plan and as this is written, only one of the four leading Cubans knows that such a plan existed; he learned of it two years after the invasion. Later, in a secret top-level administration investigation that followed in the wake of the invasion, it was learned that the CIA decided, on its own, not to give the Brigade the alternative plan. The explanation was given that it might weaken the Brigade's resolve to keep fighting, that they might choose the alternative plan when the going became rough, even though the invasion still had a chance of success. The most charitable explanation that can be placed on this reckless action is that the CIA assumed such terrible responsibility with the best of intentions: it was convinced the Cubans would win and therefore in the classic sense the end would justify the means.

It was five o'clock in the afternoon on Friday, April 14 when the officers left the briefing area for the pier. At the last moment Frank took Pepe aside. He told him that if he were ordered to halt the invasion while the ships were at sea he would send Pepe a radio message saying: COME BACK, DON'T GO AHEAD.

That meant the opposite: it was really clear; they were to go ahead.

"But if I send you a message in code that says the bird—the Guatemalan bird, the quetzal—'The quetzal is on the branches of the tree'—that means Fidel is waiting for you so you will have to come back."

One of Frank's assistants named Phillips handed Pepe a big briefcase, locked and without a key, and told him to sign a receipt for it. Inside, he said, was $35,000—$10,000 in American money and $25,000 in Cuban. It was for use as the need arose. Pepe rejoined his staff and they prepared to board the ships.

There was one last bizarre note to the leave-taking. Luis Somoza, dictator of Nicaragua, came to the dock to say goodbye. He was dressed like a musical comedy potentate, wore powder on his face and was surrounded by gunmen. He waved and said, "Bring me a couple of hairs from Castro's beard"; then he clenched his fist, turned and walked away, followed by his sycophants.

The officers said their farewells to their American advisors.

It was an emotional moment. Seebee had tears in his eyes. The Cubans had no doubt that these were their friends.

As they neared the cargo vessels in the small outboard-motor launches, the officers saw the men of the Brigade lining the railings, singing and cheering. Each battalion had been issued a different-colored scarf. Now they were waving them—blue, yellow, white, black, red—from each ship. The officers boarded and the ships steamed slowly out to sea as the day ended.

CHAPTER 4

"THE FISH IS RED"

At two o'clock on the morning of Saturday, April 15, 1961, all Brigade pilots reported to the briefing room at Puerto Cabezas and received their orders. Later that morning they were to attack Cuba. Two planes were going to attack Managua, two San Antonio de los Baños, two Santiago de Cuba, four Ciudad Libertad, adjoining Camp Columbia, the main base for Castro's air force, and one plane San Julián and Baracoa. The pilots and co-pilots studied the recently taken aerial photographs and discussed the missions with the Americans. At 3:30, the missions to Managua and San Julián were canceled. No reasons were given.

Off the coast of Cuba in the early hours of Saturday a reconnaissance platoon of Nino Díaz' diversionary force set out for the shore thirty miles east of Guantanamo in the darkness. For a long time there was silence, and they could not be reached by radio. When they finally returned, the men were excited. They told of seeing militia waiting for them, of cigarettes glowing in the dark and stationary lights set to shine on them. What the men really saw probably will never be known. "Curly," the American with Díaz, was disgusted and there were hot words, but in the end they did not land; instead, as dawn came up, they moved out to sea and waited. They would try again the next night.

Fidel Castro was awake in those hours of early Saturday.*
He had received news from Oriente that a great number of ships

* This account is taken from Castro's published works on the invasion, particularly the pamphlet *Playa Giron: Victory of the People*. See the bibliographical notes for other sources.

had been spotted in the vicinity of Baracoa. For weeks now Castro had been strengthening his forces across the island as he waited for the invasion. He knew that the time was approaching. Indeed, he was so certain that he had taken to sleeping in the afternoon and staying awake during the night.

As he himself said, "The constitution of the Council of Worms in exile, the infamous 'white paper' of Mr. Kennedy, plus the things that filtered through the United States press, plus some disagreement among themselves about the strategy to follow, demonstrated that the moment of the attack was drawing near. News had come to us that the last embarkment of men and arms from Guatemala had been made, that the enemy was in movement, and it made us increase the vigilance."

Castro did not know where, precisely when, and how the invasion would take place. Would it be a full-scale invasion, or smaller landings at several points? If they landed their forces at several points, the invaders would not be exposed to a crushing defeat. Even after small pockets of resistance had been eliminated, they could still achieve propaganda advantage by claiming that other bands were still fighting in the mountains and interior. They would be defeated—but the defeat would be diluted and softened by many small battles. If they decided to land at one place in a frontal assault with all of their men, it would be better for Castro: he could liquidate the enemy rapidly and decisively. But apparently he became convinced that the United States would not take such a risk for, while a frontal attack at one point offered more immediate and dramatic prospects, it offered also the possibility of an overwhelming and total defeat. As he put it, the invaders would not concentrate their forces because of "the discredit to which they would be exposed through a defeat of this nature, discredit for the United States, discredit for the counter-revolution. . . ." Castro's judgment may have been good but the Americans were bolder than he imagined.

Acting on his decision, he selected what he considered the most probable landing points throughout the island; then he established posts manned by troops numbering from one hundred to five hundred men. He particularly concentrated on the access zones to the mountains—especially near Trinidad where the Escambray guerrillas had been eliminated in March. He was confident the invaders would not land on another likely position, the Isle of Pines, because for months he had reinforced that offshore island, where he kept his political prisoners, until it was impregnable. One more position had to be strengthened: when the attack came, he was certain the first objective would be to destroy his small air force. Planes that were out of service were placed together in groups of threes; the ones in service were dispersed, camouflaged and surrounded by antiaircraft batteries. Castro was ready. Now he waited.

When the news came of strange ships off Oriente, he went to his military headquarters at Camp Columbia, near Havana, and placed all of his forces in a state of alert. One battalion was dispatched to Baracoa, another to a point between Baracoa and Moa, and mortar and antitank batteries were moved closer to the coast of Oriente. A jet plane was sent aloft to circle the zone around Baracoa. The plane developed trouble. Then it was reported in flames two or three miles off the coast; it soon disappeared. Castro was waiting to send helicopters to search for the missing jet when, at six o'clock, a B-26 with a Cuban flag painted on its wings flew low over his headquarters. Moments later he felt the blast of bombs and heard antiaircraft fire.

"This is the aggression," Castro said.

He immediately tried to get in touch with the San Antonio airfield to order the planes to take off; and he also put in a call to Santiago de Cuba. He was told they were both under attack.

The high schools in Key West had planned an Olympics Day at the Boca Chica Naval Air Station, with track events, marching bands and proud parents. It was scheduled for Saturday morning, April 15. At seven o'clock that morning a bullet-riddled B-26, bearing the markings of Castro's air force, made an emergency landing at the airport. Olympics Day was canceled.

Minutes later another B-26, also bearing the numbers and flag of Castro, landed at Miami International Airport. One of the engines was dead and the fuselage had been pierced by a dozen bullets. The Cuban pilot, wearing a baseball cap, dark glasses and T-shirt and casually smoking a cigarette, was hustled away by United States immigration officials.

The press descended on the airport, taking pictures of the plane and pilot and clamoring for a formal interview. Edward Ahrens, the director of the Immigration and Naturalization

Service in Miami, issued a statement, supposedly drafted by the pilot. It said the pilot and three of his comrades had defected from Castro's air force in stolen planes. They decided to strike a blow against Castro and the treachery of those who remained in his service by attacking the fields. Because two of their planes were hit by antiaircraft fire and were low on gas, they flew to the United States, one landing at Key West, the other in Miami.

When reporters asked for their names, Ahrens said they were being kept secret to protect the pilots' families in Cuba. When it was suggested that the Havana regime would know the identity of its own fliers, Ahrens replied that the pilots had asked that their identities be kept secret—and the officials were going to do so.

Miró Cardona issued a statement from New York. The bombing raids, he said, were carried on "by Cubans inside Cuba." "The Council had been in contact with and has encouraged these brave pilots," he said. Miró appeared tired as he talked to the reporters in his suite at the Lexington Hotel. At one point he removed his glasses and invited those present to "look into revolutionary eyes that have known little sleep of late." Asked if the raids were a prelude to an invasion, Miró said, "No invasion."

But another Cuban seated near him said quietly, "Spectacular things have begun to happen."

At the UN the Ambassador from Cuba, Dr. Raúl Roa, rose to speak. "At 6:30 this morning," he said, "North American aircraft——"

Frederick H. Boland of Ireland hammered his gavel and called Dr. Roa to order. The business then before the assembly was the Congo, not Cuba. Valerian A. Zorin of the Soviet Union then demanded that the debate on the Congo be shelved in favor of "the aggression" against Cuba. That would require a two-thirds vote, the Assembly president ruled. Zorin next proposed an emergency meeting of the United Nations Political Committee. The Committee was immediately called into session.

Outside the United Nations building a crowd of Castro sympathizers, members of the Fair Play for Cuba Committee, were noisily marching up and down, waving placards denouncing the United States as "Murder, Inc.," and shouting "Cuba, sí, Yankee, no." Mounted police and foot patrolmen forced the crowd behind the barricades. Inside, a historic debate began.

Dr. Roa, the Cuban Foreign Minister, a slight man with a thin mustache and glasses, was acting on direct orders from Castro to accuse the United States government directly of aggression. He presented his indictment point by point. The attacks, he said, were the prologue to the large-scale invasion being planned by the United States and some Latin American countries.

When he finished, the United States Ambassador to the United Nations began his reply. It was to be the most humiliating moment in Adlai E. Stevenson's distinguished career. Twice a candidate for the presidency, urbane and eloquent, a man whose reputation for statesmanship and integrity was unquestioned, Stevenson was trapped by a tangle of lies. He had been assured by the State Department that the story told by the Cuban pilots was true, and he believed it.

Stevenson, with the oratorical skill for which he was famous, began by repeating what President Kennedy had said three days before: there would be no United States intervention in Cuban affairs under any conditions and his government would do everything it could "to make sure that no American participates in any actions against Cuba." He then read from a statement by the pilot in Miami. "These pilots and certain other crew members have apparently defected from Castro's tyranny," he said, and added:

"No United States personnel participated. No United States aircraft of any kind participated. These two planes, to the best of our knowledge, were Castro's own air force planes and, according to the pilots, they took off from Castro's own air force fields."

Stevenson leaned forward to the microphone and held up a photograph of one of the planes for all to see.

"It has the marking of Castro's air force on the tail," he said, "which everyone can see for himself. The Cuban star and initials F.A.R., *Fuerza Aérea Revolucionaria*, are clearly visible."

Anyone could paint such markings, Roa replied. And then he made a fateful remark: "These mercenaries bought by the United States have announced that tonight at ten o'clock they will again bomb Cuban citizens."

Stevenson answered, "Steps have been taken to impound the Cuban planes and they will not be permitted to take off for Cuba."

In Washington Pierre Salinger, the presidential press secretary, was telling reporters that the United States was trying to get all of the information about the attacks on the Cuban air bases. The government is naturally interested in events in Cuba, which is only ninety miles from the Florida coast, Salinger said. But, he stated, the United States denied any knowledge of the bombings except for what had appeared in news reports. At the Pentagon and the State Department there was no official comment. Unofficially, officials were being quoted anonymously as referring to the President's pledge on Wednesday that United States armed forces would not intervene in Cuba "under any circumstances" as reflecting the American position.

As the day wore on, however, questions became increasingly embarrassing and difficult to wave aside. How could the president of the Cuban Revolutionary Council in New York have advance knowledge of the mission if the pilots were all members of the Cuban air force who made their decision suddenly, only Thursday, as the B-26 flier said in Miami? Why did the immigration authorities in Miami continue to withhold the name of the pilot who landed there even after newspaper photographs were published clearly showing his face and the serial number of his plane? What about the rocket fragments bearing the inscription "U.S.A." which Castro said he had recovered after the attack? What about the two auxiliary fuel tanks recovered twelve miles off the northern coast near Havana? Didn't that prove the planes came from a distant point, rather than inside Cuba? The Cuban Revolutionary Council announced that six planes took part in the bombings, but that directly conflicted with the statement of the pilot in Miami who said only four defected. Who was right?

To all questions the same "no comment" was given. No matter what was said, on or off the record, it was apparent, as Attorney General Robert F. Kennedy remarked later, that "things were beginning to surface."

If President Kennedy was concerned about that "surfacing," he did not show it. Late in the morning he left the White House and flew by helicopter to join his wife and children at Glen Ora, their rented estate in the rolling Virginia hills. Spring had come to the Virginia hunt country: the dogwood was in blossom and a bright sun was shining as the President and his wife, Jacqueline, drove to the Glenwood Park race course on the two-hundred-acre farm of Daniel C. Sands. From a rail fence near the first jump, he watched part of the first race of the Middleburg Hunt Race Association. "That was an interesting race," he said. "First time I've seen one of these steeplechases." After ten minutes he said, "I've got to go back and do a little work." He drove back three miles to Glen Ora, leaving his wife to watch the races.

Saturday morning's Radio Swan broadcast carried the reassuring news of the bombing to the convoy in the Caribbean. On board the five transports and two escort ships, living conditions were bad. Men slept where they could—on deck, in lifeboats, in hammocks strung in holds loaded with ammunition and gasoline —and ate C-rations, either cold or heated by sterno lamps, and bathed with salt water. Smoking was prohibited; a stray match or spark could touch off an explosion.

On the horizon was the comforting sight of the American navy—several destroyers and one or two larger ships. On the first night out the men aboard the *Houston* watched an American submarine circling the ship.

By Saturday afternoon the entire Brigade knew its mission. The officers had made their speeches outlining the battle plan. The troops were asked to respect prisoners as fellow Cubans. The men responded with cheers and singing.

Toward the end of the day, San Román received a message from Frank. It said the bombing mission had been accomplished successfully and nearly all the enemy aircraft had been destroyed. That message resulted in one of the great miscalculations of the invasion. The Brigade air force report stated that eight to ten planes had been put out of service at the San Antonio base; six to eight at Ciudad Libertad; and twelve planes at Santiago de Cuba—all of which would have left Castro with almost no air power. While the attack *did* inflict considerable damage, Castro actually still had four fighters, two "Sea Furies" and two jet T-33s, as well as two B-26 bombers.

Soon after the message from Frank, there was an accident on

board the *Atlántico*. Three men had been practicing firing the .50-caliber machine gun when its mountings came loose, and bullets sprayed wildly about the deck. One man was killed and two wounded. During the burial ceremony the men on the *Atlántico* stood at attention in full uniform on the deck at sunset and prayed for their comrade, for Cuba, and for their mission.

That night, for the second time, a reconnaissance team was dispatched from Nino Díaz' group of commandos off the coast of Oriente Province. Again there was a long wait; and again the men returned to their ship, *La Playa;* and again the 168 men did not land. The mission, in the words of the accompanying Americans, "aborted primarily because of bad leadership." Diaz and his men, now thoroughly dispirited, moved out to sea. They had failed to create the vitally needed diversionary movement.

The Miami Sunday papers told the story of the bombings in streamer headlines. In *The Miami Herald,* James Buchanan was reporting one of the "inside" stories under a headline: WHERE ARE CASTRO'S JETS? "Asked about Castro's reportedly well-equipped and well-trained jet air force, counter-revolutionary leaders here merely shrugged. 'He keeps telling the people his friends behind the Iron Curtain have given the country jets to protect itself. But where are they? Why don't they fly. . . . When the real bombs begin to fall, where are they?' "

In the competing *Miami News,* Hal Hendrix, whose interpretive reporting on Cuba later won him a Pulitzer Prize, began his Page One story with another inside view: "It has been clearly established now that there will be no mass invasion against Cuba by the anti-Castro forces gathered at bases in Central America and in this country. The *News* has stated this for several months."

In Cuba, the populace was girding for another war. Early in the afternoon radios in Miami picked up a broadcast from Havana. It was Castro delivering a funeral oration for those who died in the bombing attack the day before. A funeral cortege stretching thirty blocks moved slowly through the streets of the capital carrying the bodies from Havana University, where they lay in state, to the edge of Colón Cemetery where Castro was waiting. As a crowd of ten thousand, mostly militia, stood massed before him Castro, for the first time, publicly described his revolution as Socialist. Flailing his arms and speaking hoarsely, he said, "The United States sponsored the attack because it cannot forgive us for achieving a Socialist revolution under their very noses."

The crowd roared back, "Fidel, Khrushchev, we are with you both!"

Amid cries of "War! War!" Castro continued. "If the attack on Pearl Harbor is considered by the American people as a criminal, traitorous, cowardly act, then our people have a right to consider this act twice as criminal, twice as cunning, twice as traitorous, and a thousand times as cowardly."

He also said, "The United States delivered the planes, the bombs, and trained the mercenaries. The Yankees are trying to deceive the world but the whole world knows the attack was made with Yankee planes piloted by mercenaries paid by the United States Central Intelligence Agency." With heavy sarcasm, he read a translation of dispatches sent by American news services from Miami. They were sheer fantasy, Fidel said, and "even Hollywood would not try to film such a story."

Castro was correct on both points—the world was becoming aware that the United States was sponsoring the invasion and that its news reports were unreliable. In Moscow and in Peiping, the Communist empire broadcast warnings: the safeguarding of Cuba was the goal "not only of the Cuban people but also of all peace-loving nations who should not allow the United States to attack Cuba." Zorin of the Soviet Union had already warned, "Cuba is not alone today. Among her most sincere friends the Soviet Union is to be found." The Soviet Union was not satisfied with the official American explanation, Zorin said, for "with one single word from the United States, not one plane would have bombed Cuba. The fact was that this word was never spoken."

By twelve noon of Sunday the Brigade forces were committed; it was then too late to stop the invasion. Sometime after this hour had passed, President Kennedy made one of the most difficult decisions of his administration. While he had shown no outward concern over the "surfacing" Saturday, by Sunday the situation had become more complicated. Russia and China were threatening action—if not in Cuba, then perhaps in Berlin, or

Laos or Vietnam. The realities of the Cold War, the life-and-death stakes involved, the gamble Cuba represented, the apparent success of the Brigade air attack on Saturday, the President's pledge against direct American intervention in Cuba, and the assurance of his advisors that the invasion had a chance of success without such American support, led him eventually to a decision: the second air strike, scheduled for dawn Monday to coincide with the invasion, was canceled. Retrospect or hindsight does not alter the central fact about that decision: it was consistent with the President's policy, stated unequivocally both publicly and privately, that the Cuban affair must not be allowed to jeopardize larger United States interests.

When Bissell was informed he and an assistant, General Charles Cabell, an airman, urged Secretary of State Dean Rusk to reconsider the decision. Rusk, who was acting for the President, did not agree with them. He asked if they wished to appeal directly to the President. Neither did. The order went out to Puerto Cabezas to cancel the attack.

At 1:30 P.M. the Cuban Revolutionary Council began what was publicly announced as a long afternoon session at the Hotel Lexington in New York. The day before it had been easy for reporters to see Miró Cardona. Then the Council had announced its new "cabinet posts." Tony Varona was named Secretary of War; Antonio Maceo, Secretary of Health; Manuel Ray, Chief of Sabotage and Internal Affairs; Justo Carrillo, Economic Administrator; Manuel Artime, "Delegate in the Invading Army." But now, Sunday afternoon, five Americans in plain clothes barred the door to Miró's suite. About 3:30 P.M. the Council members left the hotel, avoiding the lobby exits. They would continue their meeting at a secret location, the press was told.

While the council was being taken to its confidential hideaway, Alejandro del Valle was briefing his paratroopers in Nicaragua. By 6:30 P.M. the briefing was finished and the 176 men were issued camouflage uniforms and ammunition. They inspected their weapons and were taken to the Puerto Cabezas air base. After a steak dinner they were given apples to carry for their breakfast; then they put on their parachutes and climbed into five C-46 transport planes. "Sonny" and "Big John," two of their American instructors, had asked the Cubans to conceal ex-

tra equipment on the planes for them, so they also could go.
Somehow, Frank learned of this and ordered that if any American instructors were missing no planes would take off. "So,"
as Néstor Pino said, "we said goodbye crying. I remember I told
them I wasn't going to my death or my funeral." As the paratroopers boarded, Big John handed a Negro paratrooper his
knife and told him to take care of it until he joined him in Cuba.

Del Valle shook hands with one of his assistants and said,
"I'll see you in Cuba." Standing nearby was the "paratroop
priest," Father Segundo de las Heras. The priest wondered if they
wouldn't need more air power and Del Valle replied, "Father,
don't worry. We'll just be mopping up what is left."

Sunday afternoon the men lounged on the ships, listening to
the radio, talking, trying not to appear nervous. They fussed
with their new camouflage uniforms, packs and cowboy hats
and joked about their return to Cuba. Some played poker; some
took sunbaths; still others talked quietly about their families.
For many it was, as one soldier said, "like a Caribbean picnic."
Yet the jokes and shouts could not hide the inward nervousness.
Everyone was afraid of acting afraid, and most adopted the philosophy that they were going to win or die. No one voiced doubt.

Later, Castro would speak disparagingly of the Brigade as
mercenaries, war criminals and sons of the jaded rich who were
coming to regain their vast holdings at the expense of the workers. In reality, Brigade 2506 was a cross-section of Cuba. The
men ranged in age from sixteen to sixty-one, with the average
age twenty-nine. There were peasants and fishermen as well as
doctors, lawyers and bankers. A large percentage of the men
were married and had children: and there were a number of
father-and-son pairs aboard the ships.

By profession, students, with 240, were the largest group, but
there were mechanics, teachers, artists, draftsmen, newspaper
reporters, engineers, musicians, three Catholic priests and one
Protestant minister, geologists, cattlemen and clerks. Some fifty
of the men were Negroes and many more had Negro blood. One
man, a naturalized Cuban, had been a Brooklyn truckdriver.
While the vast majority were Catholics, there were also Prot-
estants and even Jews in the Brigade. With the exception of the
135 former professional soldiers—who had served both under

Castro and Batista—most of the men had had no previous military training or experience. Indeed, some had never held a weapon until that weekend aboard ship because the Fifth and Sixth Infantry Battalions were not recruited until the end of March, and some arrived at Base Trax just as the Brigade left for the Trampoline base.

In so many ways these were men of differing backgrounds, and their differences—both political and intellectual—had divided them bitterly in the past. The Brigade had its cowards, its self-seeking men; it had its gamblers and privileged rich. Their motives varied: some were stirred by hate, some by greed, some by adventure, but most—especially the young—felt a sense of duty and ideals, and some bit of everything mixed together. Few tried to analyze their reasons. One who did admitted to being a wealthy playboy in Cuba. "What I was doing," he said, "was what a psychiatrist might call a wish to atone, or something like that. I was like Rhett Butler putting on the uniform of the South when the cause was hopelessly lost and he knew it. Or maybe I was like a kamikaze pilot." Whatever their reasons or differences the men were bound together by a common belief: they were going to be victorious.

One of the elements in their tragedy was a complicated attachment to the United States. Many had gone to school in the States and spoke English. They were proud of America, they knew its history and its record of victory in war, and they liked to compare themselves with Americans. In truth, they felt closer to the United States than to Latin America: "We even look more like Americans than other Latins," they would say proudly and in many cases it was true. They had a genuine fervor that many Americans found difficult to comprehend. They were, in fact, intoxicated by thoughts of heroism. It was old-fashioned; it was flags and patriotism and religion and country. They and their country had not experienced the disillusionment of warfare and its aftermath, the cynicism of the victor who has discovered that wars usually lead to other wars and that the lines of peace were more difficult to maintain than those of combat. Cuba had not experienced this: it had remained unscathed during the twentieth century while World War I led to World War II and then to the atomic and hydrogen age of the Cold War. And in back of everything was the conviction that the United States would not let them fail.

"It was so many hopes and so many important people and it was difficult not to feel that there wasn't something very big behind us," one man said. "There had to be. We couldn't, we just couldn't, be wasted."

At sunset, as the ships neared the southern coast of Cuba, Pepe San Román called the men on the *Blagar* to attention. They saluted as the Cuban flag was raised. Artime cried. "I thought it was the beginning of the liberation of Cuba."

With the night, radio stations in the United States—including NBC and CBS—began picking up a strange message broadcast repeatedly by Radio Swan. It crackled out over the air waves of the Caribbean—a fifty-six word message referring to a rainbow, the running of fish, the sky and "Chico." "Alert! Alert! Look well at the rainbow," the message said. "The first will rise very soon. Chico is in the house. Visit him. The sky is blue. Place notice in the tree. The tree is green and brown. The letters arrived well. The letters are white. The fish will not take much time to rise. The fish is red." Later, it was explained that this was the message for the Cuban underground to rise. No one in the Brigade, or in its infiltration teams, received that message —in fact, San Román, Artime and Oliva never heard it.

By 7:45 o'clock the five principal ships and their two escort vessels had reached the rendezvous point thirty miles south of Cienfuegos where they were joined by landing craft from Vieques Island carrying the tanks, heavy equipment and Cuban crews. Aboard Oliva's ship, the *Houston*, the men spontaneously began singing the Cuban national hymn. Then the convoy began moving up the coast toward the Bay of Pigs.

BOOK THREE

The Bay of Pigs

CHAPTER 1

MONDAY: TIGERS FROM THE SEA

Pepe San Román first began to doubt the intelligence information when his flagship arrived at Playa Girón. Instead of the deserted resort houses the CIA had said he would find, the shore was ablaze with lights.

His ship, the *Blagar,* anchored two thousand yards offshore while the *Houston,* carrying Oliva and the Second and Fifth Battalions, and accompanied by its escort ship the *Barbara J,* moved west along the coast, into the mouth of the Bay of Pigs and north toward Playa Larga.

At eleven o'clock, five Cuban frogmen prepared to leave the *Blagar* in two rubber rafts to place white and red lights on the beach to mark the landing zone at Girón. The frogmen embraced Pepe and Artime and, weighted down by their Browning automatic rifles and ammunition, their signal lights and black rubber suits, masks and flippers, entered their inflated rafts and silently moved toward shore. There was no moon to light the way. Gray, the American who had trained them, was with them and Gray, the American, was the first to land in the invasion— despite the insistence of President Kennedy that no Americans participate in the action.

Instead of the smooth approach and sandy beach they had expected to find, it was rocky terrain with razor-sharp coral reefs offshore, poorly suited to an amphibious operation. By the time they had succeeded in placing the first landing light, it was fifteen minutes before midnight. The light flashed on the beach, from beside a concrete pier, and as it did the men aboard the *Blagar* saw other lights: a small vehicle was moving rapidly toward the beach from Girón, a half mile to the east. It was a jeep. It stopped, backed up and turned its lights toward the sea. The frogmen, led by Gray, opened fire with their automatic rifles; but the alarm had been sounded and now a truck carrying Castro militiamen was heading toward them.

As the firing began, the lights of Girón went off. By radio the frogmen called for support from the *Blagar* and soon the shooting was intense. Farther out to sea the Third, Fourth, Sixth and Heavy Gun Battalions lined the rails of the troopships, straining to see through the darkness, tensely wondering if their men or Castro's were winning. And near the northernmost point of the Bay of Pigs, the soldiers on the *Houston* saw red and orange tracers lighting the sky over Girón. It was, as Oliva said, "a very emotional moment for us, because they were the first shots fired toward Cuba."

While the shooting continued, the first landing craft edged toward the coast line carrying men of the Fourth Battalion from the *Caribe*. Because of the unexpected opposition, San Román decided to go ashore in that boat to direct the fighting. Just before he left he handed the still-locked briefcase containing the $35,000 to the American task force commander on the *Blagar*, and asked the American to safeguard it until the beachhead was secured. Accompanied by Ramón Ferrer, his chief of staff, and two radio operators, San Román boarded the landing craft. In the darkness and confusion they headed in the wrong direction. When the pilot moved back on course, the boat was caught in a spotlight from the beach and the men came under direct fire. The pilot veered sharply, landed where he could, and San Roman and the men jumped into the water and waded ashore.

Pepe, the calm and quiet soldier, yielded to the emotion of the moment when he reached the beach: he knelt, under fire, took a piece of earth and kissed it; then he organized a small beachhead and began fighting the militia. Seventy-five milimeter cannons from the *Blagar* found the range. Twice the cannon boomed out. There was no answering fire; everything was quiet, everything seemed well.

Now the trouble began. It stemmed from an almost incredible miscalculation by Americans who, by record, by reputation and by experience were the unsurpassed experts at amphibious operations. During World War II, not one assault landing had been attempted at night. Yet, in the first such landing planned by Americans, the coral reefs inexplicably had been ignored or forgotten. Certainly the reefs were unknown to the invasion troops —until their boats struck. Some were sunk, some merely delayed. The invasion schedule was set back and surprise, the only advantage of attempting a risky landing at night, was lost. A way had to be found through the reefs—especially a channel wide enough for the large LCUs (Landing Craft, Utilities) carrying the tanks. José Alonso, commander of the frogmen, began working with his men to chart a path for the invaders.

While the frogmen were in the water, the Fourth Battalion began landing, cursing the darkness and the small boats. On the beach their commander, Valentín Bacallao, was ordered to Girón with part of his men and another group was dispatched to the Girón Airport. The airport was the principal objective, and at the briefing the Brigade leaders had been told they would have to do some work with heavy equipment before their planes could land. Bulldozers and graders and an electric saw to cut trees had been brought from Nicaragua especially for that job.

Soon the word came back to San Román. "The strip was ready. It was a perfect strip, very long, very nice and very clean, and there were no piles of sand, as we had been told." Another, more serious difference between intelligence forecast and actuality was all too apparent: the area was not deserted—civilians who were constructing the resort houses were living at Girón with their families.

Soon San Román himself was on his way to Girón to select his headquarters. Along the way an old peasant, one of the charcoal workers in the swamps, saw the Brigade passing. He shrank in terror beside the road and asked fearfully, "Who are you?" He was reassured to learn that they, too, were Cubans. With their faces painted black and their spotted camouflage uniforms, the old man thought they looked like tigers from the sea.

From their small fiberglass boat approaching Playa Larga the second team of Cuban frogmen could see, far away, flames in the sky over Girón. The waves were high and they moved rapidly toward the shore until they could distinguish shacks along the waterfront. Fifteen yards from the beach their boat struck coral; they jumped out and raced toward a grove of pine trees. Leading them ashore was "Rip," an American who had joined them in Nicaragua. Rip had said he was an ex-Marine with many combat missions behind enemy lines in Korea and also that he was a personal friend of Somoza, the dictator of Nicaragua. Because of his toughened skin, the Cubans called him "the alligator." Thus, at the second beachhead of the Bay of Pigs, an American was also the first to land.

Once ashore, the frogmen began placing the markers they had made on their voyage from Nicaragua. On the tops of one-hundred-gallon gasoline tanks they had painted in luminous yellow: WELCOME LIBERATORS—COURTESY OF THE BARBARA J. While one of the men put up the signs, another lighted the smudge pots and placed a flashlight so that it shone directly on the signs. They were finishing the job when they were suddenly attacked by Castro militia from one of the nearby shacks.

"We opened up almost automatically with our BARs and we really gave them hell," said Andy Pruna. "We knocked out perhaps as many as twenty in a few minutes and the rest ran away and left their weapons."

Then from their left flank they saw the lights of a truck heading toward them, and behind that the lights of more vehicles. They called the *Barbara J* to speed up the landing and heard on the radio the message to the *Houston*: "Is *Aguja* (code name for the *Houston*) putting the little boys ashore?" It was a quarter to one in the morning.

Aboard the *Houston*, Oliva was told that the invasion force had been seen and therefore his men must be ready to disembark at once. The first of eight fiberglass boats swung over the side and down to the sea. On the deck all other sounds were lost in the screeching of the ancient winches. It was obvious to Oliva that they could be heard for miles.

Oliva told Hugo Sueiro, the Second Battalion commander, to hurry. The plan called for the men to board boats at three stations, ranging aft from the bow. Problems developed immediately. The motors on the boats sputtered and choked out in the sea. By 1:10 A.M., as Sueiro was approaching the beach in the first boat, machine guns began firing from the coast toward the *Houston*. The *Houston*'s guns answered, and the frogmen were caught in the crossfire. The Castro machine guns were knocked out but when the firing ceased one of the invaders was dead—the first to die at the Bay of Pigs. The frogmen headed back to the *Barbara J*, carrying the body with them, and the invasion proceeded.

In the first group of small boats heading toward Playa Larga there were nervous jokes and an occasional cry to "shut up! shut up!" from an officer. The darkness and the knowledge that they had been detected lent their own peculiar terror. Each man has his own impression and memory: the boat pilot saying "here it is, jump," and the first man over the side sinking to the bottom over his head, to be dragged back aboard by his comrades and then an angry quarrel to force the pilot closer to shore. The image of the shoreline varied according to the imagination. To one soldier it "was a dream, a modern picture"; to another it was "something that looked like the entrance to a cemetery with buildings around it." Worst of all, the moment when the lights of Playa Larga went off and in the deathly silence they knew the enemy was waiting . . . the sense of relief when the machine guns began firing and things were happening too rapidly to dwell on anything else . . . Then, reaching the shore, in small groups of ten, and at a soft whistle and the whispered passwords, "Eagle," "Black," being reunited with Sueiro and assigned to positions along a road facing tall woods in front, surrounded by the shadowy buildings of the new tourist center. In their nervousness, some had forgotten their spades and they had to dig shallow foxholes with their hands.

One of the first prisoners the Brigade took was a young Negro militiaman. When a Brigade member said to him, "Things are really bad here," the Negro said, "Really bad, sir. Really bad."

There was little comfort for the commanders. Nothing was going according to plan. Consequently, as Pepe had done, Oliva, too, decided to go in with the early waves of troops.

"I changed the order of landing," he said, "and ordered my staff to get ready because I was going ashore. The people on my ship were a little nervous; it was their first time in battle. They hadn't expected the shooting to start so soon. I told them to be calm, that Sueiro was fighting the enemy and controlling them, and that I was going to the beach."

He climbed down the rope ladder, followed by a radio operator and several assistants. But in jumping from the ladder to the small boat below, one of the men struck the pilot and knocked him into the water. The boat drifted away. None of the seven men aboard knew how to operate the outboard motor and so they floated helplessly. At one point they were so close to the *Houston's* propeller they were certain they would be destroyed. Then for forty-five maddening minutes, while they heard the sound of battle on the shore, they drifted in the midst of the Bay of Pigs awaiting a launch from the *Houston*. Finally it came and at 2:30 A.M. Oliva ingloriously reached the shore. By then only sporadic firing was heard.

Oliva headed toward the front where Sueiro reported they had destroyed a truck of militia and had taken prisoners. As he walked toward a shack not far from the beach, Oliva made an alarming discovery: "I saw the antenna of a micro-wave station and we captured it at once. You could see that they had transmitted from there recently." It was another crucial failure in intelligence, for the plan was predicated on the inability of the enemy to communicate with larger forces.

Oliva instantly recognized the seriousness of the situation; but of more immediate concern was the landing itself. The outboard motors on the eight fiberglass landing boats were not working. Two of them went out of service immediately (on one the propeller fell off and into the sea as soon as the boat was launched). One after the other the other six failed in the middle of the Bay. Although there were only 185 men in the second battalion, by 5:30 in the morning the last of the men still had not come ashore. Also left to be unloaded were the entire Fifth Battalion and *all* of the supplies, including ammunition, for the area. Oliva is convinced that had they had only three LCUs, both battalions and the supplies would have reached the beach by three o'clock.

By 4 A.M. the invasion was foundering on both fronts. Pepe reported to the American task force commander that Girón had been taken with little resistance; and he requested that his tanks be sent in immediately. Hearing that message, Gray came to him.

"Pepe, you are the commander and you make the decisions, but I think it is better to wait until daylight to bring the tanks in because this beach is very difficult and at night you can't see what you're doing. You might lose one or two tanks. My advice is to wait for daylight."

Although he had doubts, Pepe agreed to wait two more hours —until six o'clock—before ordering the tanks sent in regardless of the difficulties. Shortly after that he received more bad news, which he promptly reported in his second message: two microwave stations had been found at Girón and it had to be assumed that the militia had been sending messages to Castro.

At 3:15 in the morning Fidel Castro was awakened in Havana. He was told the enemy was landing at Playa Larga and Playa Girón and that his platoons on guard duty in those areas were resisting. Castro first ordered this information confirmed because, as he himself later said, "In this kind of thing you must always be sure." The check was made and in Castro's words: "The news came for certain that an invading force was giving heavy fire with bazookas, with recoilless cannons, and with .50-caliber machine guns and ship cannons, that they were attacking strongly at Playa Girón and Playa Larga in the Zapata Swamps."

The micro-wave stations at Girón and Playa Larga continued relaying details of the attack "until the very moment when, as a result of the attack itself, the stations stopped functioning." Then there was complete silence from the invasion zone.

Castro alerted the forces he had in that section—a battalion of nine hundred men commanded by Osmani Cienfuegos, his young minister of Public Works, already stationed at the Central Australia sugar mill on the road to Playa Larga, and several platoons of armed militia, drawn from the peasants of the area, in position at the small towns of Cayo Romano, north of Girón; Soplillar, slightly to the south and west of Playa Larga, and Buenaventura, adjoining Playa Larga. But it was not until dawn that Cienfuegos' battalion went into action. A battalion of militia in Matanzas Province, containing three mortar batteries, was also mobilized and ordered toward Playa Larga. At Matanzas an infantry battalion was ordered into service. Three battalions from Las Villas Province were dispatched to Yaguaramas and Covadonga to protect the other two major highways through the swamps. Orders also went to Castro's air force to take off at dawn and attack the ships facing Playa Larga and Girón.

Castro's principal objective was to crush the invaders at Playa Larga which, being at the head of the Bay of Pigs, was nearly twenty miles inland. "The most important point was that we had to try to keep the beachhead on the other side of the Ciénaga [swamp], that is: a beachhead in the territory they were supposed to take possession of . . . our main proposal was to hold . . . at Playa Larga." Castro, astute as always, recognized that time was vital and that he had to prevent the landing of the provisional government at all costs. He therefore considered it necessary to mount wave after wave of attacks against the invaders.

With his orders given and his plans made, Castro left immediately for the Bay of Pigs. When he arrived, he received a message that it was only a feint and that another landing was being made simultaneously at Pinar del Rio Province where in fact Americans had sent rubber rafts ashore containing radio equipment simulating the sound of battle. He hurried there only to find it was a false report. Castro's reaction here and the initial disorganization of his troops in the field lead to the unanswerable question: What might have happened had Nino Díaz' men carried out their assignment to land in Oriente and created a genuine diversionary movement?

INVASION OF CUBA
REPORTED BEGUN
BY A REBEL FORCE

———

Miro Cardona Says Group
of Hundreds Has Landed
in Oriente Province

———

CONFIRMATION LACKING

———

Castro Challenges Kennedy
to Produce the Air Base
Raiders Before U.N.

The great presses of the greatest newspaper started to roll. The Late City Edition of *The New York Times* was on the streets before the sunrise.

The story, quoting an announcement by Miró Cardona, said a seaborne invasion had been launched Saturday night in Oriente (where Nino Díaz was supposed to have landed) and the invading Cuban troops had successfully carried out the first stage and encountered "no opposition." At the same time in Washington Joseph W. Reap, a spokesman for the State Department, was telling reporters that "the State Department is unaware of any invasion." At the Pentagon the reporters were told the Defense Department knew nothing but what it read in the news dispatches.

At 6 A.M. Juan Luis Cosculluela, a young Cuban navy captain, called the *Blagar* to report the completion of a mission. He and the frogmen had charted a path through the coral reefs. At 6:25 landing craft carrying tanks and the men of the Heavy Gun Battalion began arriving at the beaches. Cosculluela, after supervising the landing, was returning to the *Blagar* in a launch when a B-26, painted blue with a Cuban flag on its wings, flew over and dipped its wings in salute. Certain that it was one of theirs, Cosculluela and others waved back. Then the plane opened fire. Following it was another—and then another. Soon they were joined by Sea Fury fighters and T-33 jets. The remainder of the Heavy Gun Battalion and all of the Sixth and Third Battalions had to land under fire.

"I saw those planes pass over our heads three times going to the beach," said José Sosa, a fifty-one-year-old cattleman who had a son and two nephews in the Brigade. "I saw the red tongue of the flames and the machine guns shoot, shoot, shoot. Bupbup, bupbup, bupbup! The best thing was when I arrived on the coast and found my son."

Others were not so fortunate. The slow landing craft were easy targets at best but, to make it worse, the LCUs and four LCVPs (landing craft, vehicle-personnel) were stopped 150 yards short of the beach by impassable coral. Men waded through water chest-high, carrying their weapons—including even the 4.2 mortars, weighing 640 pounds each—and boxes of ammunition on their shoulders. When the planes passed over, they ducked under the water. Consequently, most of the small radios were wet and could not be used that first day of fighting. It was a nightmare. Immediately the doctors began receiving casualties and treating men on the beach, under fire.

The first attack ended with one of Castro's B-26s shot down. In the momentary lull C-46 transport planes carrying the Brigade paratroopers flew over Girón on their way inland. One of the planes dipped low to salute the invaders and as it did the men on the ground opened fire. Bullets passed through the fuselage. "What the hell's going on?" one paratrooper yelled. "They've gone crazy."

Rip and the frogmen had gone to the *Houston* in a launch to assist in the landing. By then only a few men of the Second Battalion were left aboard; but all the Fifth—the greenest in the Brigade, with only a few days of training—was still aboard. Rip began yelling for the men to get off but they were reluctant. In anger he shouted: "It's your war, you bastards. Get off!" Ten men got off and headed for the beach. From behind them they heard the motors of an airplane. It was a B-26 and they, too, thought it was one of theirs. The plane attacked them. As it turned toward the horizon and came back, Rip stood up and shouted: "Everybody fire at the God damn thing!" This time they hit it, and when it made a third pass it went down in flames.

More aircraft were on the way—first a Brigade B-26 to provide cover for the invaders and then three of Castro's planes, two T-33 jets and a Sea Fury. The slower Brigade plane didn't have a chance. (The Brigade B-26s flew without tail guns to permit them to carry more fuel for the fourteen-hour round trip flight from Nicaragua.)

"I remember," a Brigade survivor said, "looking toward the sea and seeing a small plane—a Sea Fury, a fighter—at a very high altitude. I could see it sparkling in the sun and shooting and I remember admiring the courage of that pilot. It looked pathetic, that plane. I couldn't help admiring him and even feeling sympathy. He looked so childish, like a fly. I watched it go up and down and then someone told me they were bombing the *Houston* and I didn't feel sympathetic any more."

With the *Barbara J* under attack and unable to give support, the *Houston* was defenseless. Two planes came low over the mangroves and one made a direct rocket hit. There was a hollow clang and the ship started taking in water. Miraculously, the rocket had passed through the deck and on through the bottom of the ship without exploding. Laden as it was with ammunition and gasoline, the *Houston* would almost certainly have blown to bits had the rocket detonated. And almost all her troops were still on board! A small fire broke out below decks but as Alberto Pico said, "God was with us." The water coming through the hole that the rocket had made extinguished the fire. Luis Morse, the captain, headed the stricken ship toward the coast and succeeded in grounding it three hundred yards from shore. There it stayed—a broken vessel, oil oozing from its holes, a sitting target for the planes. Without weapons, some stripped to their underwear, the men jumped into the oily water and were strafed by Castro's planes. Some drowned, some were attacked by sharks. At least twenty-eight men died in the sea. Those who got ashore were dispirited and defeated. They huddled under the trees and awaited orders from the commanders.

Minutes after the loss of the *Houston* a second, even greater, disaster overtook the Brigade. It was shortly after seven o'clock when Oliva, at Playa Larga, heard a tremendous explosion from the vicinity of Girón; even from that distance black smoke could be seen mushrooming into the sky. It looked as if an atomic bomb had been dropped over Girón. A Sea Fury, diving out of the sun, had made a direct rocket hit on the *Río Escondido*. Those who survived the enormous blast jumped into the sea where they, too, were strafed by the planes. It was an irreparable loss for the *Río Escondido* carried the supplies for the first ten days of fighting—ammunition, food, hospital equipment and gasoline. Also lost was the Brigade's communications trailer— the primary method of communications with the battalions in the combat zones, as well as with the flagship and the rear base in Nicaragua. Why such a vast majority of all the supplies needed for any success whatsoever was committed to one ship is a question still unanswered by the CIA.

By radio, the task force commander told Pepe he had been ordered to withdraw his ship, because he was unable to hold his position. The air attacks already had brought another change in the invasion plan: instead of landing at Green Beach, thirty kilometers to the east toward Cienfuegos, the Third Battalion was forced to come in at Girón, where Pepe immediately sent them on foot two miles to the east to protect his right flank. The departure of the ships was an even more critical change in plans, for the Brigade had unloaded less than 10 per cent of its ammunition, and the *Blagar* and *Barbara J* were supposed to patrol the coast from Playa Larga to Girón, supporting the Brigade with its guns.

"He could not do that, he [the task force commander] told me," Pepe said, "because he had to leave. But he said they were coming back that night to unload the supplies—the ammunition, the trailer, everything we needed. So the ships left and they did not give us a single case of anything. We fought with what we had. The doctors took care of the wounded with what they had, and that was very little."

Pepe saw his brother Roberto and explained the situation; then Roberto left, according to plan, with two tanks and other men and equipment to support Del Valle and his paratroopers at San Blas, the junction of two of the three roads through the swamps.

Over the western (Playa Larga) front at the drop zone on the road to Central Australia, Del Valle's heavy equipment was dropped first; his paratroopers followed. They never saw their equipment again—it was lost in the swamps. In addition, an advance group was lost in the swamps, another badly missed its drop zone, with some landing behind the enemy lines. They landed under heavy fire. When they reached the ground they found one of their men dead, dangling from a tree by his parachute. Another had been shot and killed before he hit the ground.

In the confusion one unit, commanded by Tomás Cruz, unable to make radio contact with headquarters, tried to take Palpite, was driven back and forced to retreat, leaving the road to Playa Larga open. The main road to Central Australia, where Rubén Vera's paratroopers were lost in the swamp, also was open.

On the eastern front the paratroopers fared better. The various units landed successfully, without strong opposition, and moved to assigned forward positions designed to block the roads from San Blas to Covadonga and San Blas to Yaguaramas.

Each of these assigned strong points was manned by nineteen men armed with one 57-mm. cannon, one .30-caliber machine gun, one bazooka, an automatic rifle squad and a forward observer to direct mortar fire. These strong points bore the brunt of the first attacks on the eastern front. Almost immediately after Del Valle landed at San Blas to establish his headquarters, he received word that Juan Quintana, the commander of the advance post before Covadonga, was under attack.

Del Valle discovered, on landing, that part of the advance intelligence proved to be correct. A number of citizens of San Blas joined his forces as volunteers, helping to carry supplies and working as nurses. Five were given camouflage uniforms and weapons and fought with the Brigade. Other civilians gave the soldiers food and water.

Del Valle dispatched men along the two roads to select a place for the 4.2 mortars. They walked forward until they lost radio contact and by that time, in midmorning, the mortars were arriving by truck. Roberto San Román and his reinforcements had made the link-up from Girón. As they were placing the mortars on the road to Yaguaramas, word came that a battalion of Castro soldiers was attacking the advance post.

At Brigade headquarters, when Pepe San Román made the first faint contact with Oliva at Playa Larga, the report was equally discouraging. It was ten o'clock in the morning. Oliva said his situation was difficult and that his men had been in continuous combat since landing. He had lost contact with the Fifth Battalion and had been unable to reach the paratroopers forward of his position. He asked about the support—a tank with a squad from the Fourth Battalion—he was supposed to receive from Girón.

"I told him," Pepe said, "that I had no communications with the rear base or with Del Valle or Roberto; that the ships had left; that they were supposed to get back that night; and that I had sent him the tank."

Even with their supply lines cut, their backs to the sea and no communications, San Román and his commanders were not in despair. It was not false heroism, or naïveté, but an unshakable conviction that they would not be let down; that victory therefore was inevitable. It was inconceivable that they would be stranded.

Once established in his headquarters, Pepe had inspected his positions and dispatched messengers to the various battalion commanders for first-hand reports from the front. From the beginning he had expected the main enemy attack to come through San Blas toward Girón. He knew that the body of Castro's army was stationed in Las Villas. But instead it was headed toward Playa Larga. Another concern was his right flank and the road to Cienfuegos. The Third Battalion, supported by a tank and 4.2 mortars from the Heavy Gun Battalion, was up the road but far from where it was supposed to be. While Pepe awaited reports he gathered what intelligence was available from 150 prisoners taken at Girón. The prisoners disclosed little of military value, but a great deal about the situation inside Cuba.

"They had been told that we were killers," Pepe said. "Most of them were scared of us in the beginning. When they saw that we were Cubans and that we were trying to treat them gently, that we were going to give them food and that we were not going to kill them, they changed. They did not want to fight with Castro but they were frightened of us."

More than fifty—including uniformed militia—joined the Brigade and worked as volunteers under the air attacks that continued all day at Girón.

The attitude of other prisoners, however, disturbed the Brigade staff—and most particularly Manuel Artime. Artime, who had landed after Pepe, had first started worrying about the invasion "when I saw that Fidel's air force was not completely destroyed." He spoke to a large gathering of prisoners and civilians inside Girón and felt gratified when nearly half said they wanted to help the invaders. Then he was told about a twelve-year-old boy who had been wounded wearing a militia uniform.

"I went to see this boy and he asked me why we had come to fight against them. And I told him we had come to liberate the country from Russian control, from the Communist regime.

"The boy replied: 'I am a Communist.'

"I started explaining to him what communism meant, what it meant to lose your liberty; that he was only a little part of the big machine; that it was a regime that would destroy anybody who opposed its policies; and when I finished the boy said to me: 'I think you believe what you say, but my teachers and my father tell me different. I believe them. You are mistaken.' "This incident made me very sad," Artime said.

To the mildest in manner among the high officials of the Kennedy administration fell the task of explaining the United States position. Dean Rusk called a press conference that Monday morning in Washington. Conservatively dressed as always in a dark suit, looking tired, he stood before a battery of microphones, and in his Georgia drawl pronounced the United States policy. "The American people are entitled to know whether we are intervening in Cuba or intend to do so in the future. The answer to that question is no. What happens in Cuba is for the Cuban people themselves to decide." The Secretary of State then opened the floor to questions.

1. *Q. Mr. Secretary, does your categorical statement that we are not going to intervene in Cuba, period, mean that this administration is abandoning the traditional reservation that we reserve the right to intervene to protect American lives?*

   A. That particular question is one for the future, and I would not wish to relate it particularly to Cuba because of the debate now going on in the United Nations at this very moment.

2. *Q. Mr. Secretary, in the past the Soviet Union, indeed Premier Khrushchev, has said that the Soviets would go to the aid of Cuba. I believe at one point Premier Khrushchev said "rockets will fly." What would our attitude be in the event of intervention by the Soviets to help the Castro regime?*

   A. I would not wish to answer a hypothetical question of that sort this morning.

3. *Q. Mr. Secretary, could you tell us what contact our government is maintaining, if any, with the so-called Revolutionary Council in New York, whose representatives came down and called on you a few days ago, and would you tell us when the last contact with the group was?*

   A. I am very sorry not to answer questions on Cuba, but I must stand on the statement I have just made.

4. Q. Mr. Secretary, can you answer questions about the United States Immigration Service?

A. Why don't you ask it and I will see. (Laughter.)

5. Q. Well, there is a very puzzling case of this pilot who landed in Miami after saying he had defected from the Cuban air force. The Immigration Service, although his picture was printed—Castro has challenged us to produce him to verify the story that he told. Why do we not allow the press to see this man? Is the Immigration Service making policy for the State Department?

A. I think this is a question which started as one on the Immigration Service and became one on Cuba, and I would not wish to answer it this morning.

6. Q. Mr. Secretary, there is another question that arises. If the rebels succeed in establishing a solid foothold in Cuba, would we be prepared to consider or to grant diplomatic recognition?

A. That is a question for the future, into which I can't go this morning.

7. Q. Mr. Secretary, I will get off Cuba.

A. Thank you. (Laughter.)

No one else could get away from it, however. In the United Nations, where Roa and Stevenson continued their debate; in Sochi, on the Black Sea, where Nikita Khrushchev conferred hastily with his Foreign Minister Andrei Gromyko; in Bogotá, where windows were broken and crowds threw rocks at the United States Information Agency; in Caracas, where tear gas was used to break up demonstrations; in Moscow, where *Izvestia* said "The news agencies report alarming news"; in Gettysburg, Pennsylvania, where Dwight D. Eisenhower, tanned and rested after a six-week vacation, returned home to begin his retirement; and in London, Paris, Bonn, Rome, the extraordinary tension of crisis was felt as the world anxiously turned its attention to what was happening in Cuba.

Until 7:20 that morning the Cuban government messages were monitored in Miami; then the radio network was shut down on the grounds that the messages were "alarming the public a little." Through the static came early indications of confusion, edged with panic, as one extract showed:

6:43 A.M.—*The aircraft are asking for reinforcements. They are firing in the boats.*

6:45—*(Havana Central to Laguna) Please report the message from the boat in the inlet that picked up the call from the planes asking for help.*

6:47—*(From Laguna) According to the boat, they are asking for help.*

6:50—*(From Havana) The chief of operations wants to know who is authorizing information bulletins.*

—*(Another voice) They are being authorized by Osmani Cienfuegos and by Sergio.*

—*Listen, Osmani, this is Captain Ruiz of the detachment at Jovellanos. The problem is this: you know that the army bulletins can't be transmitted by the micro-wave stations of the various departments. The adjutant says it must be done exclusively through official channels because all the departments are picking them up and they are alarming the public a little.*

—*(From Cienfuegos) Listen, this is the problem: we are here in direct communication with Fidel and we are using a part of this information to keep up to date on what is happening.*

—*(Havana) Osmani and Sergio are at the headquarters of the militia. They are still using the station at Jagüey. (Static interrupts) Ask if our people also are dropping parachutes.*

—*Tell him no.*

—*What are they dropping? Men or cases?*

—*They are dropping parachutes and bombs. In the Boca de la Zanja they are dropping bombs. The lieutenant says the enemy is among the works of Playa Larga. (Interruptions) The four planes are already passing over the beach. . . .*

At eleven o'clock the network was heard again briefly in an urgent call to the Red Cross in Havana to pick up "many wounded"; then the news blackout resumed. The lack of accurate information did not deter some reporters at news desks in the United States, particularly in Miami. In its first edition, *The Miami News* carried a banner story by its Cuban expert, Hal Hendrix, who reported the rumors that the Isle of Pines had been shelled by sea and bombed, and that Raúl Castro, Fidel's brother, had been captured. Before long Miami's Cuban exiles were reading in the second edition "unconfirmed reports" that the Isle of Pines had fallen "and the thousands of political prisoners freed," and the flat assertion that "the invaders seemed to be using their aircraft to increasing advantage. After covering the landings, the planes swept inland, shooting up and bombing Castro's defenders who were gathered in large numbers." Also duly reported was the rumor that Fidel himself had a four-engine jet prop plane ready at the San Julián Air Base to flee the country.

Rumors were not confined to the United States. Inside Cuba there was talk and hysteria and, for one particular group, heartbreak.

Shortly after twelve noon José Basulto, of one of the Brigade infiltration teams, received a message with the identifying code marks "QSP" meaning very, very urgent. Basulto and all the other members of the Brigade infiltration teams inside Cuba had been told to take immediate action if such a message ever came. Quickly Basulto decoded the message: A LARGE WELL-ARMED FORCE HAS LANDED IN SOUTHERN LAS VILLAS PROVINCE. INTERRUPT COMMUNICATIONS. BLOW BRIDGES. "I don't remember the last part," Basulto said, "but it was something like 'rise up,' and the way I felt at that time was here they were sending me propaganda, a propaganda speech. I already knew more by the Castro radio. I sent back this message: IMPOSSIBLE TO RISE. MOST PATRIOTS IN JAIL. THANKS FOR YOUR HELP. CLOSING TRANSMISSION, and then I went to the beach. There was nothing else to do. We were the last to be told."

All over Cuba that day similar CIA messages arrived. But it was too late. As Félix Rodríguez said: "The roads were closed, the houses were surrounded and they were arresting thousands of people. I cried."

While the Castro radio played soothing music, a reign of terror had begun. In Havana more than two hundred thousand were arrested. In theatres and ballparks, auditoriums and public halls, men, women and children were packed together indiscriminately. At the Blanquita Theatre, where more than five thousand citizens were confined, there were only two bathrooms.

Of all the failures that day, the failure to alert the Cuban underground in time was one of the most damaging and certainly the most baffling. From the beginning, from the days when Artime had been smuggled out of Cuba to set in motion the events leading to this April 17, the underground had been a vital part of the CIA's plan. In the original plan the underground was to aid a guerrilla force. Later it was to support and join the invasion. In any case its role called upon it to create confusion, sow discord and fashion an environment in which the populace would join the liberators. Later, Allen Dulles would say the CIA had never counted on a spontaneous uprising; but nevertheless, his agency *had* trained Cubans to perform the dangerous jobs that would lead to that end—in the strictest sense, it would not be spontaneous—and then in the crucial moment it had ignored them.

The diversionary landing at Oriente, the sabotage campaign through the island presaging the signal for revolt, the propaganda broadcasts of Radio Swan, all were a part of the overall plan to distract attention from the invading army. And now those 1,500 invaders stood alone. The implications were clear to every Cuban who had worked with the CIA as an infiltrator. It was apparent to Enrique (Kikío) Llansó when, at four o'clock in the morning, he was called by a friend, Carlos Arteaga in Miami, and told the invasion had begun without him. It was apparent hours later at Girón beach when an MRR man who had been working inside Cuba came to Artime and told him that the underground had no idea the invasion was coming and that thousands had been taken prisoner by Castro since the air raids on Saturday. It was even apparent to Miró Cardona and the leaders of the Revolutionary Council when they learned of the invasion by radio that morning in a house near Miami where they had been flown secretly to be kept in isolation by the CIA until they could return in glory and proclaim their provisional government.

One final act underscored the tragedy: on that Monday, April 17, Francisco, the underground leader, was executed.

Operation Pluto called for the Second Battalion to land, divide and advance in three directions: straight north toward Central Australia, northeast to the Soplillar airport and west to the town of Buenaventura. The Fifth Battalion was to have been held in reserve at Playa Larga, and then was to move up as the Second advanced.

With the *Houston* sunk and the Fifth Battalion out of action, Oliva deployed his men as best he could. To the front, as the vanguard of the battalion, he sent a company commanded by Máximo Leonardo Cruz. To the northwest, to take the entrance of the road to Buenaventura, went a company led by Oscar Luis Acevedo. The third and remaining company of the battalion, headed by Pedro Avila, was kept in reverse at Playa Larga.

Cruz had in action only three of his four squads: the fourth squad had drifted in the Bay of Pigs, stalled by a defective outboard motor, until they were picked up by the *Barbara J* and taken out of the combat zone. Cruz' total strength was three squads of twelve men each, plus a reinforced squad armed with 75-mm. and 57-mm. recoilless rifles and .50-caliber machine guns. They were desperately short of ammunition. Acevedo had four squads in position. Before the day was out Cruz and Acevedo and their small groups of men faced everything that Castro could throw at them—and held their positions. That they did so was due partly to the lack of leadership, morale and egregious errors of Castro's men. Partly it was due to the quality of the Brigade's training and superiority of arms. But principally it was due to their nerve.

On the surface, they were not particularly impressive men. Cruz, twenty-three years old, dark hair, dark eyes, 5 feet 5, weighing 120 pounds, quiet, not well educated, was distinguished among his comrades for his large nose. For months there had been jokes in the training camp that he would not be able to get his nose out of the way of the bullets. And Acevedo, thirty-one, also short and dark, was remembered best for his constant laughter and talk.

Cruz' first major encounter with the enemy was decisive for hours. It began when a number of militia appeared coming toward them out of the brush. "I let them take a certain time to get together and I took advantage of the *agrupación* (massing). They were very close and when they were together I fired at them with the 75-mm., with the .50-caliber machine gun, and with the 57 cannon. I destroyed them completely. The 57 made a direct hit on their truck with a grenade of *fósforo vivo* (white phosphorus). I was looking when the grenade hit the truck and the whole truck blew up and I saw the men jumping, dying and being burned by the *fósforo vivo*. The rest ran away and did not come back until 2 P.M." He took advantage of the time to camouflage and strengthen his position.

At Playa Larga, the lull in the fighting gave Oliva a chance to assess the situation. Some wounded and dead, including women—all Castro's militia—had been brought back from the front and more than forty prisoners had been taken.

"The dead men were from some family that lived there at the beach and we had problems with the family crying and all that," Oliva recalled. "The medical men tried to take care of the wounded as best they could (even a woman had a shot through her breast) they tried to do the best they could but they didn't have very much. In the meantime, I went to see the prisoners and I put the militiamen on one side and the civilian workers on the other. A few of the militiamen told me they were very happy that we had landed and wanted to join our troops. I could not accept them because I had no weapons to give them." He did accept two peasants who were mechanics; they were put to work immediately repairing captured trucks. By twelve noon Oliva heard Radio Swan saying the Brigade was winning. "The radio of Castro was better," he said.

About that time Oliva made contact with Luis Morse aboard the *Houston*. He ordered the Fifth Battalion commander to reorganize his men and within an hour Montero Duque, the commander, reported by radio that he had organized the landing of the remainder of his personnel in rubber boats and that a great number were together on the shore, about ten miles from Playa Larga. At twenty minutes to three, Oliva ordered an assistant to take two trucks and an infantry squad from Avila's company to pick up men of the Fifth and bring them to the front. Minutes later he canceled the truck mission after receiving a fateful message from Cruz at the front. That message signaled the beginning of what came to be known in Cuba as the "Battle of the Lost Battalion"—the 339th Battalion of Castro militia leaders from Matanzas. The name itself today carries the connotation of scandal, for when the battle was ended there had been unnecessary slaughter. The encounter began with a report by two of Cruz' scouts.

"I had two men about six hundred yards ahead to the front," Cruz said, "so they could observe the enemy. They came back about 2:30 P.M. and they told me that the enemy was advancing in a column. They were coming through the center of the highway, straight on it, in a close formation. These people were crazy coming that way down the hill in the middle of the road. We were in a very good position at both sides of the road, camouflaged. Between the enemy and me there was a swamp and trees on both sides of the road. We were able to shoot well from this position."

Cruz told Oliva what he could see through his binoculars. Instantly Oliva called Sueiro, the battalion commander, and prepared to leave for the front. Fortuitously, the tank from Girón, driven by Fernandez Torres Mena, arrived at that moment with the squad from the Fourth Battalion. "With a little reinforcements and feeling a little happier, we went to the front lines," Oliva said. They were in place by the time the first columns of the 339th Battalion reached Cruz' position.

"When they were about five hundred yards from us they stopped," Cruz said, "and they started putting up their mortars and getting their weapons prepared. They didn't send any forward observers to see where we were and they didn't know our positions. When I saw that they had all their weapons ready, I gave the order to open fire. I had to do it because they were getting organized there. When I gave the order to fire, you could see them flying up in the air. I threw everything at them with the three shells of the 75 I had left, with the 57, with the machine guns and all the weapons we had there. In ten or fifteen minutes there was a big mound of dead men all over the road."

Then at exactly 3:05 P.M., as Oliva said, "They were so unlucky that in our area appeared two B-26s." It was the first time that the Brigade had made contact with its air support that day. The first pilot radioed for instructions, and Oliva told him to make a pass and observe what was coming. When he reported back, he said there were approximately seven hundred men in sixty or seventy vehicles—jeeps, buses, trucks—heading straight toward them. "He asked me what he should do and I said, 'Give it to them,'" Oliva said.

The planes made two or three passes, dropping rockets and bombs.

"How beautiful it was from the ground!" a soldier murmured. "How beautiful from the ground and our airplanes in the air!"

But the carnage was horrible. The road was a solid wall of flames.

"*No quedó ni el gato* (not even the cat was alive)," Cruz said.

Out of nearly nine hundred men in that battalion only a handful survived. This, indeed, was air support.

The planes had been supporting the Brigade for twenty-five minutes, and no Castro fighters had appeared. On the ground Oliva heard, by radio, one of the pilots say to the other: "Let's go because I've finished my ammunition and don't have much gasoline."

"No," the reply came back, "there's a son of a bitch in there that shot at me and I'm going to get him."

The men watched as one plane circled over Playa Larga and the other headed toward Central Australia.

"I hit him, I hit him," came the cry of the pilot.

At that moment a T-33 jet and a Sea Fury appeared.

"I've got a T-33 on my tail. Shoot at him! Shoot at him!"

The second Brigade pilot answered: "I don't have any ammunition."

"They hit me. They hit me," were the last words. Both Brigade planes were shot down.

As the sound of the battle ceased, a soldier at Playa Larga squinted into the sun toward the front. "There were crowds of vultures flying to the battlefield and it made me think how quickly the human body can corrupt itself."

Oliva returned to his headquarters and personally questioned prisoners. He learned that a great concentration was being formed at Central Australia and that he could expect a major assault that night. He dispatched a messenger to Girón, requesting reinforcements, tanks and ammunition. As he was interrogating the prisoners, Cruz again called from the front. Two ambulances were coming down the road.

"If they come to pick up their wounded, let them do it," Oliva said.

The ambulances came closer. Behind them was a white truck painted with a Red Cross emblem, and behind that Cruz saw other trucks with troops. Again he called Oliva.

"I told him to start shooting," Oliva said. Cruz did. The enemy was routed. It was the last combat of the afternoon at Playa Larga. But out of it Castro eventually reaped a propaganda advantage: when the fighting was over, he displayed pictures of the Red Cross vehicle riddled with bullets to show the barbarity of the "mercenaries."

Some time after 4 p.m., Montero Duque of the Fifth Battalion reported to Oliva by radio that all his troops were on land and "had started walking toward my [Oliva's] position." "I told him that I expected them to arrive to my position about seven at night and I told him to hurry because I was awaiting an attack and I wanted them to be in position when it came. He told me, yes, he would be there early."

Oliva next turned to his defenses. Less than a mile north of Playa Larga there was an intersection where a number of roads met and merged into one that led toward the Bay of Pigs. When the reinforcements came, he decided to establish his lines there at the Rotunda, or traffic circle. In the meantime, his mortar batteries prepared their concentrations of fire along the roads so they would be ready when night came.

On the San Blas front, too, the Brigade was digging in for the night. Since midday the advance post in front of Covadonga had been under artillery fire and was requesting air support that did not come. At the other post, in front of Yaguaramas, there had been a brief, bloody fight in which a Brigade tank was decisive—after almost being disastrous to its own men.

When Roberto San Román arrived at San Blas, he left on the road to Yaguaramas in a tank, carrying a 3.5 rocket launcher, to support the paratroopers. As they moved forward the sound of battle increased. It was at that point that he learned that they were being attacked by a battalion. San Román sent the tank and bazooka along with eighteen infantry men.

One of the paratroopers at the front recalled what happened next. "The tank commander got confused and shot at one of our men. And the man in front whirled and fired his 57 recoilless cannon at the tank, but fortunately his aim was poor. That recoilless rifle had no sight and the tank gun—the 76—wasn't working right so I think that God was on our side. The shell landed in front. Everyone started to eat the ground. We started to fire back and then we saw the camouflaged uniforms and knew it was our own men. We got reorganized in less than a minute and counterattacked. We gave them all we had. And they [Castro's forces] retreated and we hit them and hit them and hit them, and all we saw were dead men at that point."

By 6 P.M., as the sun was setting, the two strong points on the San Blas front had held their positions with thirty-eight men. At that time the closing market edition of *The Miami News*, in a two-line banner, proclaimed:

CUBAN NAVY IN REVOLT;
INVASION FORCE MOVES IN

and stated that the navy revolt—actually there was none—"had been planned for several months under the code name 'bounty.' " As to the fighting itself, "according to various accounts the invaders hit the beaches in four of Cuba's six provinces, sparing only Havana Province and Camagüey in Eastern Cuba."

For the Brigade to hold on that first day against overwhelming odds and with such slight casualties—less than one hundred died that day—was a tribute to the men, also to the invasion area. In that important respect, the plan proved to be correct: Castro's troops had no choice but to come down the highways through the swamps. With tanks, heavy mortars, cannon and bazookas the positions were relatively easy to defend. Only two elements were missing—air cover and sufficient ammunition to keep going.

When it became clear that the Brigade could not win unless Castro's air force was eliminated, the restrictions imposed by Washington on bombing attacks were lifted. By midday the Brigade air force issued this report: "Our infantry forces shot down a Sea Fury and damaged a B-26, leaving the enemy with two jets (the T-33s) two Sea Furies, and one or two B-26 bombers. Our air force has the following missions for today: from 3:30 to 4 p.m., protection of objective zone; at night, 6 planes will try to destroy rest of the enemy air force."

The afternoon mission resulted in the disaster of Castro's "lost battalion." The night mission was scheduled to attack the San Antonio de los Baños field. That was where Castro's jets were.

While the six Brigade B-26s at Puerto Cabezas were being loaded for that three-hour-and-twenty-minute flight to Cuba, at Girón Pepe San Román ordered Bacallao to assemble his Fourth Battalion and march to Playa Larga to reinforce Oliva. The Fourth, less one of its companies fighting with Del Valle at San Blas, left at six o'clock with the two tanks Pepe had in reserve at Girón. At 6:45 the reinforcements and ammunition reached Oliva. The two mechanics who had joined Oliva at Playa Larga jumped up and embraced each other.

"Didn't I tell they were not crazy to come just alone in that little boat?" one said. "See, more are coming from Girón."

Militia prisoners asked for weapons to fight. Oliva had none to give them. Oliva assembled the Fourth or "Bomblene" Battalion. He was particularly proud of them for these were the men he had trained and led in Guatemala before he was appointed second in command of the Brigade.

"I am very happy to have you," he said, "because this is going to be a strong fight." Then he put his men in the line. To support Cruz and Acevedo at the Rotunda, he sent one company. Another company went to Avila's squad along the beach on the east. He placed the six mortars and all the mortar shells that had been brought from Girón to support his front and flanks. Two tanks were sent to the Rotunda with Cruz and the other to Acevedo nearby, where they commanded the Rotunda roads and had a wide range of fire. Oliva held nothing in reserve. He was waiting for what was to be the fiercest battle of the Bay of Pigs, "The Battle of the Rotunda."

Far away in New York City a press agent named Lem Jones, the president of Lem Jones Associates, Inc., a Madison Avenue public relations firm, was issuing "Bulletin No. 3" on behalf of the Cuban Revolutionary Council for "immediate release." In the past Jones had done public relations work for such clients as a lay committee of the Armenian Apostolic Church and corporation stockholders waging proxy fights; but his present client, he told a reporter, was "a very serious thing, too."

Bulletin No. 3, issued at 7:15 P.M., began: "The Cuban Revolutionary Council wishes to announce that the principal battle of the Cuban revolt against Castro will be fought in the next few hours. Action today was largely of a supply and support effort to forces which have been mobilized and trained inside Cuba over the past several months. The tremendous army of invincible soldier-patriots has now received its instructions to strike the vital blow for the liberation of their beloved country. Our partisans in every town and village in Cuba will receive, in a manner known only to them, the message which will spark a tremendous wave of internal conflict against the tyrant."

The Bulletin quoted a "spokesman" for the Council as saying: "I predict that before dawn the island of Cuba will rise up en masse in a coordinated wave of sabotage and rebellion which will sweep communism from our country." The Bulletin also referred to "the ever dwindling portion of the militia which has not already come over to our side" and said that "our information from Cuba indicates that much of the militia in the countryside has already defected."

"The night came and we were expecting the ships," Pepe said. "Everybody turned their faces to the sea waiting for the ships. We knew that without the ships we could not make it."

On the shore, Roberto Pertierra, the G-4 or supply officer of the Brigade, placed landing lights on the beach and waited with a large group of men to unload the vital supplies.

What Pepe did not know was that the ships had left the area pursued by planes that morning in a desperate, disordered flight for safety, each on its own. Attempts to round them up failed. The *Caribe* went *218 miles* south of the Bay of Pigs and was *never* again available for resupply operations. The other merchant vessel, the *Atlántico,* went *110 miles* south and it was not until 4:45 *Tuesday afternoon* that it returned to a rendezvous fifty miles off the coast. What happened aboard those ships helped to doom the Brigade. Even the flagship *Blagar* had trouble with its crew. Juan Cosculluela, who was on the *Blagar,* described that Monday night:

"We prepared to go north, but we had difficulty with the

crew. The crew was made up of Cubans. They were supposed to be there because they were patriotic, because they wanted to liberate our land. The officers were Americans; for them it meant another job. When we talked about going back the crew said, 'We do not go back. They are killing the people in the land. We are lost. This is a disaster. We have been betrayed and we are not going back unless the American destroyers come with us.' So I told them that they should be ashamed. They were Cubans, and they don't want to go back, while our brothers were fighting and dying and needed the ammunition. The Americans that we had accused before of doing mercenary work, wanted to go back. A minority of the crew wanted to go back, but the great majority was quiet."

Aboard the *Barbara J,* with Rip and the Playa Larga frogmen, there never was any talk of going back that night. All afternoon, on their race for the deep sea and international waters, they had seen American planes flying overhead and heard the radio messages, "Friendly, friendly."

By midnight Pepe San Román, "mad as hell," took a twenty-five-foot boat with his radio operator and Varela Canosa, a liaison officer between the Cuban navy and the Brigade, and left for the open sea to search for the ships. In one of the most bitter moments of the invasion, Pepe went nearly six miles offshore in the darkness calling in vain for the ships. There was no answer. From the boat he could see the red blasts of artillery at Playa Larga. At 1:15 Tuesday morning Pepe returned to Girón and sent another man to take his place in the boat. Young Luis Sosa spent hours calling on the radio, over and over again, the code names: DOLORES. THIS IS BEACH. DOLORES. THIS IS BEACH. I AM TRYING TO FIND YOU. WE NEED YOU. WE NEED YOU. There was no answer.

The first attacks that night came on the San Blas front. Amado Gayol, a short, muscular young student, asked his paratroop commander, Del Valle, if he could move forward to help his comrades at Covadonga. By early evening Gayol reported to the advance unit nine miles north of them on the road to Covadonga. No sooner had he arrived than the sound of tanks was heard. "We heard the noise of the tanks but we didn't hear what was in front of them." Armored cars with .50-caliber machine guns, followed by infantry, were only yards away when they opened fire. "Some of them were running among us and when I shot I was afraid I was shooting my friends. That was my baptism of fire." The first tank came into range and a Brigade bazooka made a direct hit. When the order to stop firing was given, "we heard the yelling of the wounded. There was a concert of the dying."

Along that front the plan was to resist and fall back, resist and fall back. But the enemy kept coming: they couldn't be stopped without more support. Gayol went back to San Blas and asked Del Valle for assistance. "I told him they were smashing our defenses and our men almost surely would die." By midnight a Brigade truck evacuated the small band in front of Covadonga. Strong Point 2 was crushed. Del Valle called for 4.2 mortars to halt the advancing columns. With three forward observers, Roberto San Román moved from San Blas to Covadonga. What they saw was terrible! Castro's men were walking down the road, illuminated by the lights of their own trucks, straight into the Brigade mortar fire. It was a massacre.

One of those forward observers was Juan Pou, twenty-four years old, tall, slender, quiet, who had been studying animal husbandry at the University of Florida until he enlisted in the Brigade. During the first part of the evening, Pou was supporting the paratroopers at the advance post of Yaguaramas with mortar fire; then at midnight he was told to report to Del Valle.

"O.K., *guajiro*," Del Valle said, "go out and get in touch with my lines."

"So I walked through the night until I found the enemy and directed mortar fire on him. Fidel's troops were very close to me. I could hear their screams and see bodies blown into the air." For the rest of the night the 4.2 mortars stopped the advance toward San Blas.

But in halting one advance, Del Valle had left himself open for another. When he moved Pou, he failed to replace him— or to notify his forward positions at Yaguaramas. At that front, Néstor Pino and his paratroopers had come under mortar fire themselves and moved to a new location where the highway crossed a small key in the middle of a lake. While the enemy kept firing on the old position, Pino placed his men, carefully camouflaged, alongside the road with bazookas and machine guns. At 4 A.M. the first scout car appeared. "In trying to reach Del Valle on the radio I got the enemy frequency," Pino said. "And I learned they were coming with four infantry battalions with 105-mm. howitzers and two companies of tanks. They were stupid; they didn't use any code; it was plain language over the air." Two companies came, massed and walking straight down the road in columns of four. "I let them come. I called the mortars back for support, but I found that there were no mortars behind us. I don't know why. So I grabbed the phone again and tried to get them. There was no answer.

"When the enemy was 150 yards away we opened fire. Everyone fired pretty good. It was amazing the quantity of people we could hit. They went into the water on either side of the road and it was easy to keep shooting them. I sent a runner a mile back to the 4.2s. He was Manuel Casaña. And he came back and said: 'No one is there.' I told him not to say it very loud and don't repeat it to anyone else. I told Casaña to try to reach San Blas and say we need support or we can't hold—we need mortars or air support. He left for San Blas. By then everyone was firing, including me. You know, in a war, I didn't think an officer could fire so much."

After Pepe returned to Girón after searching for the ships, Enrique Ruiz-Williams of the Heavy Gun Battalion came to him and volunteered to take men and mortars to reinforce Oliva. Although he did not say so, Williams was certain the failure of the ships to return meant their defeat. "I was completely convinced of three things," he said. "*First,* that we were going to die; that there wasn't a chance for us. *Second,* that because of my position I should be optimistic up to the end, to keep the boys fighting. And *third,* that I was sure that they were going to kill us if they captured us, because I had seen those big signs, the Communist propaganda all over, 'MUERTE AL INVASOR' (death to the invaders) and that what we had to do was kill as many as we could before they killed us."

Williams, called "Harry" by his friends, had already been talking with his men and the Brigade staff about making a quota. Manuel Penabaz, a lawyer for the Brigade, asked what he meant. "If we are 1,500 men," Williams replied, "and we kill fifteen guys each we are going to kill a hell of a lot of people in here and even if we die something is going to happen."

In that frame of mind, Williams, burly, black-haired, forty years old, a mining engineer by profession, asked to leave for Playa Larga. Pepe approved. With thirty volunteers and a truck loaded with mortars and ammunition, Williams headed toward Playa Larga. In the darkness the truck driver, Jorge Larrázabal, only nineteen, struck a bomb crater, swerved to go around it and ran off the road. The truck turned completely over and the men and weapons were thrown out. Ahead was the noise of the battle.

Before the battle began, an old soldier who had served under Batista said to a young one who was about to enter combat for the first time: "If they have artillery, we are out." He waved his right fist and thumb like an umpire. "Out!"

At a quarter to eight the first rumble of artillery was heard at Playa Larga.

Four batteries of Russian-made 122-mm. howitzers had opened fire.

Oliva passed the word to be quiet and stay in the trenches.

Slowly, almost yard by yard, the shelling moved closer. At 9:30 the first barrage hit the Brigade position. No matter what came after, for many men those hours under artillery were the worst. "You feel like running, desperately, but no one runs. They shoot three times, bam . . . bam . . . bam . . . and we count, one, two, three, and blam, blam, blam, they are hitting us." The concussion of the shells grabbed at their clothes. There was a shower of steel. "Ping, ping, ping."

During World War II, Rommel's crack Afrika Corps broke and ran under such an artillery bombardment. They had the desert; the Brigade had only the sea. "It was like being in a plane that is falling down and we had this horrible feeling, pounding, pounding, pounding." There were flashes all around them. Some posts were abandoned and men crept inside large open pipelines intended for the resort under construction at Playa Larga. In the shock of the bombardment, some acted as if they were asleep. Everyone was terribly tired. An officer tried to rouse his men with the words "Oliva wants to see you at the command headquarters" and walked away. When he came to Oliva he said, "Oliva, here are the men."

"What kind of joke is this!" Oliva answered sternly. The men had not followed.

Oliva was standing by a tree when Tarafita, one of his radio operators, shouted that he had got the enemy frequency on the radio. Oliva ran the twenty yards to Tarafita. Suddenly, there was a tremendous explosion. Oliva turned and saw that a shell had struck the tree where he had been standing seconds before. Still under that tree was Juan Figueras, a mortar man. "I went on fighting, I say I am hurt and I faint." Figueras lost his leg.

From the radio Oliva learned that El Gallego Fernández, the head of the Militia Training Center at Matanzas, was in charge of the enemy operations. Then Oliva heard a message that "had to make the Gallego happy": "forty toys" had arrived from Managua. Immediately, Oliva sent two bazookas to Cruz and Avila. At 11:55 the artillery barrage ended and the battlefield was silent. Castro had fired two thousand shells in slightly more than four hours, but because of the Brigade's long and narrow position and the small number in place it had been difficult to adjust fire directly on them. Many shells went over their backs into the Bay of Pigs.

Oliva passed the word to prepare for an attack. In the distance they could hear the sound of engines. To his mortars, placed only 150 yards from the final line of protection, Oliva said: "Don't fire until I give the word!"

In that final line, Cruz gave his own orders. "I told everybody including the tanks to take advantage of the enemy by surprise." The tanks had also been told by Oliva to fire alternately at a high angle to make the enemy think they were facing artillery.

The first firing came from the west when two machine guns opened up. Then, from one hundred yards in front of him, Cruz saw a Stalin tank at the head of a column of infantry entering the Rotunda. Twenty yards behind it was another tank, and behind that still another. Despite the difference in manpower, the Brigade position was ideal: the enemy could come only through one place and they had to come slowly. Oliva quickly ordered the tank with Acevedo to move to Cruz, and the battle was joined: tank against tank, twenty yards apart, firing point blank. Along the line the firing was intense and the smoke and smell of gunpowder enveloped the men. The first two Castro tanks were knocked out; the third moved around them. The climax came when the Brigade tank driven by Jorge Alvarez fought *cuerpo a cuerpo* (body to body) in the Rotunda.

"They were like two prehistoric monsters, firing point-blank at each other, and then actually physically hitting each other," said Felipe Rivero of Avila's company in the Second Battalion. "Then the Russian tank withdrew and ours did, too!" The Russian tank had been hit in the caterpillar tread and it went limping off.

Now the road was blocked and the enemy had an even more difficult time getting through. The firing was so fast and the fighting so confused that the enemy tanks even ran over their own wounded, Cruz remembered. By 12:20 the tank fighting was over. Infantry assaults came next.

"Oliva said, 'Everybody out of positions and shoot,'" a soldier recalled, "and we shot everything we had. We couldn't see the enemy but we heard his screams. We started shooting from our positions but Oliva stood up and said, 'Oh, no. This way.' And he stood up and began firing."

At one o'clock Oliva ordered the mortars to fire for the first time.

Two hours later, after continual battle, Oliva ordered the mortars to fire white phosphorus grenades.

"The shouting of the enemy at that moment was just like hell," he said. "Everything was on fire. They were completely demoralized because that *fósforo blanco* really burns the skin. It was like a curtain, completely covered with *fósforo blanco*. The tanks and the mortars saved us."

At 3:45 Oliva saw one of his tanks heading very fast from the Rotunda. It was Torres Mena. He said he was running out of ammunition and the tank needed repairing; the loading mechanism had broken and each shell had to be pried out by hand before another could be fired.

"I asked him if he could take the shells out with his hands every time he fired," Oliva said. The answer was yes. "Then I told him to go back to his position."

At that moment one of the incredible mischances of war occurred. A soldier from the Fourth Battalion ran toward them shouting that a tank was approaching only yards away. "Is it ours or theirs?" Oliva yelled. Then the tank appeared, stopped and the driver got out and began running toward Torres Mena, vigorously waving his arms. Suddenly, he stopped short, screamed, "It's the enemy," and dashed back to his own tank—a Russian T-34. "I was so surprised that I didn't shoot. None of us shot," Oliva said.

But Torres Mena reacted. He climbed in his tank and from twenty-five yards, firing his shells by hand, he shot his explosives. There was a VOOM as the shell hit the Russian tank in the middle. For a second the tank turned a bright lobster red; then it was black; then there was a booming explosion and the turret erupted like a volcano as the ammunition began exploding. Torres Mena went back to his position at the Rotunda.

It was a night when heroes were made. There was Felipe Rondón, only sixteen years old, baby-faced, called the mascot by older men, who stood in the Rotunda with a 57-mm. cannon and faced a tank. When the tank was ten yards away he fired. The shell pierced the armor, but in the explosion the boy was knocked to the ground and the tank crushed him. There was Gilberto Hernández, another young boy, who lost an eye at 3 A.M. and continued fighting with his recoilless rifle for another hour until a grenade killed him.

By that time the men were seeing visions. Some saw cars in front of them. One saw two men dancing before his eyes, another saw a large Mexican hat. The fighting continued, but more slowly. At 4:45 Alemán's tank headed back from the Rotunda. He had no more ammunition. Fifteen minutes later González Colmenares reported the same. Still the enemy tanks were coming, passing the wreckage and rumbling toward the Brigade. Two more entered the circle in single columns. The first was knocked out by a bazooka. The second advanced but the bazooka men failed to see it in the dark. Cruz stood up and, by firing tracer bullets, outlined the tank's position. Beside Cruz was Adalberto Sánchez, who had left his family and his job as a designer in New York City to join the Brigade. He had been with Cruz all that day and night as radio operator. Earlier, Sánchez had been wounded and burned slightly and only minutes before he had asked if he could go back to have his wounds treated. Cruz replied: "There is no retreat. We stay here and fight." It was after that exchange that Cruz stood up and fired at the tank. The next events occurred too swiftly for Sánchez to recall precisely. "A shell exploded and Cruz fell. I was knocked down and remember feeling blood spurt from my back. I remember also I feel all through my body, blood, and I am on my way to the ground bleeding, calling out to Cruz, 'Don't leave me,' but there was no reply."

Wounded severely in four places, Cruz was carried back to Playa Larga. Sánchez was left for dead. It was five o'clock, the sky was beginning to brighten, and shapes that in the darkness had assumed nightmare qualities turned out to be trees and construction material and houses.

"Many of our men were dead, the rest terribly tired," Acevedo said. "They had no water, no food, nothing. It was a desperate situation. I couldn't support another attack from the enemy so I sent a message to the head of the Battalion [Sueiro], explaining our situation. At that moment we could hear tanks coming. But suddenly, I cannot explain it, the enemy retired. I don't know what happened. So I had a chance to take my company out to Playa Larga."

Part of the explanation came an hour later when the shout went up at Playa Larga that a Stalin tank was approaching.

For the first time in that long day and night, after fighting valiantly and with extreme heroism, a group of the Second Battalion momentarily lost its nerve. They were desperately low on ammunition and dead tired. Some began running.

Oliva and Sueiro cursed and shouted for the men to return to their positions. Oliva grabbed a 57-mm. cannon with the only shell he could find and ran to the middle of the road and knelt down and faced the tank. When the men saw him, they resumed their positions. Luckily for Oliva, the tank stopped and the driver got out and approached.

"Are you the commander of these men?" he asked Oliva.

"Yes."

"I congratulate you because these men are heroes. I would like to fight with you."

He was the first prisoner taken there. From him Oliva learned what they had faced—and defeated—that night: 2,100 men—three hundred regular soldiers, 1,600 militia, and two hundred policemen—plus twenty tanks, including Sherman and Stalin tanks.

"I asked him what happened to those two thousand men," Oliva said, "and he said a lot of them were dead, a lot of them were wounded, and the rest were running back." Of the tanks, five or six were destroyed, several had developed mechanical trouble and the rest had left when they ran out of ammunition. The best available estimate of Castro's casualties that night, from a Castro doctor who later defected, places the dead at five hundred with over a thousand wounded.

Oliva's force, numbering less than 370 men, had sustained an almost unbelievably low number of casualties: forty to fifty wounded, ten to twenty dead. They were well trained, they massed their fire superbly and they were brilliantly led. After that battle, the men began calling Oliva "Maceo," after Antonio Maceo the great Cuban hero of the Wars of Independence against Spain. Maceo, like Oliva, was a Negro. At one time Oliva had wanted to become an architect; but those who saw him in the battles of Playa Larga never doubted where his true talent lay. He exhibited complete steadiness under fire and a quality of strength and decision that made men want to follow him.

At five o'clock Oliva had sent a messenger to Pepe reporting that his situation was desperate. At 6:15 a jeep arrived with Pepe's reply: "Resist until the last moment—the moment of death." Oliva summoned his staff and the two battalion commanders into conference. They were out of ammunition and they expected an even greater attack to follow in the daylight. Oliva decided that the time had come to withdraw to Girón. The decision was fortunate: Castro had massed a tank company, four howitzer batteries, eight antiaircraft batteries, a battery of 37-mm. cannons, a company of bazookas, a special combat column, a battery of mortars, a police battalion and the 111th Battalion to attack and take Playa Larga.

At 6:35 as the Brigade forces were racing to get on five trucks, some in their haste leaving their canteens behind, Oliva was called on the radio by Montero Duque, the commander of the Fifth Battalion.

"He told me that his battalion had had an attack, which was a lie, that it was disorganized, and that was the reason they could not arrive to help us in the fighting." Oliva reproached him sharply. In fact, the Fifth had not been attacked and had not marched to the front. It never fired a shot in combat.

Since Sunday night the Brigade had taken two hundred prisoners. Now Oliva went to them and said that since the enemy was defeated, the Brigade was moving to another place in its advance toward Havana; the invaders were so strong they didn't need to take prisoners and they were giving them their freedom. "The real reason," Oliva said, "is that we did not have any way to take them with us."

Battered and without ammunition, Oliva's troops began the retreat to Girón. As his small column moved down the road, he saw an overturned truck and a group of Brigade soldiers: Williams and his men. "He told me with tears in his eyes that it was impossible for him to come and help us when we needed him."

On the battlefield, Adalberto Sánchez opened his eyes to a sight of horror: vultures were circling slowly overhead, coming lower and lower. The ground was covered with the reminders of battle: weapons and equipment, the dead and the dying, and most horrible of all the sight of a woman and a little girl, dressed in cheap peasant clothes, lying together, dead. Soon the enemy arrived. Sánchez was lifted roughly and thrown in the back of an open truck and taken to a village, while militia shouted insults along the way. The truck stopped in the middle of the small town. While Sánchez lay there in a haze, the sun in his face, bleeding from shrapnel wounds throughout his body, a large crowd of civilians slowly gathered until the truck was surrounded.

Suddenly, he felt them spitting at him and shouting, "*Paredón, paredón, paredón*" (the wall, where prisoners are shot). He was probably the first Brigade prisoner.

CHAPTER 2

TUESDAY: "JETS ARE COMING"

As usual, President Kennedy's Tuesday morning break-fast for Congressional leaders began at 8:30 in the family dining room on the first floor of the White House. When it was over the guests walked out the front door of the Executive Mansion and faced a battery of reporters, photographers and TV cameramen. Instead of their customary show of optimism after conferring with the President, on this day everyone seemed glum. Old Sam Rayburn bluntly spoke for all: "I think it is a serious situation down there. I don't know whether it will work or not. I hope so."

At dawn the six B-26s, each carrying a full bomb load, were over the San Antonio de los Baños airfield. Fate, destiny, an act of God or simply bad luck intruded, for the target was covered by heavy haze and thick low-lying clouds. The mission, like Nino Díaz' landing, "aborted." Castro's small air force was still intact—and still able to range at will over the Brigade.

At 8:45 Oliva arrived at the one-story concrete house beneath the Royal palm trees at the intersection of the roads from the west, north and east that Pepe San Román had chosen as Brigade headquarters at Girón. Oliva reported the situation as Pepe, Artime and Ramón Ferrer, the Brigade's chief of staff, listened and studied the large maps on the wall. In Oliva's opinion, the forces approaching from Playa Larga were so great that the Brigade would be unable to resist. He therefore made a proposal: they should pull back the troops from the San Blas front, reunite the Brigade with its five tanks, form an arrow-

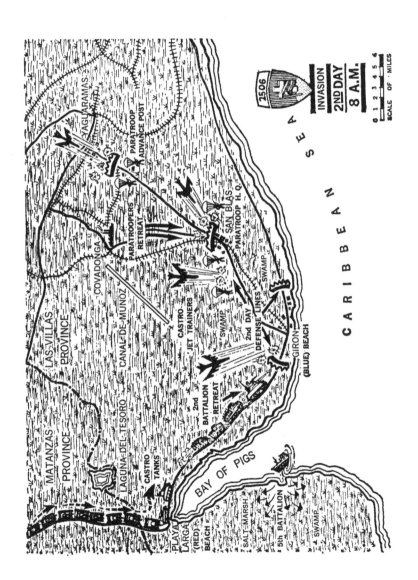

head, strike toward the east along the road to Cienfuegos and fight on into the Escambray Mountains. On his own, Oliva had come up with the alternative plan. A debate on the proposal began. Pepe made the final decision.

"I told Oliva that it was too far away; that I was expecting an enemy attack along that road because Cienfuegos is a very big and important city, and I thought that there must be some enemy concentration there that was going to hit us. I told him that we didn't have enough transportation to move the whole Brigade in a rapid movement from Girón to there and that we didn't have enough ammunition to fight the enemy for that long a distance. And we didn't have any communications at all, so that as soon as we left this position our support wouldn't know where we were. I was sure they were coming today with help. I was sure of that, so we were not going."

In the end, Pepe's decision was based on his confidence in the Americans—confidence, as he expressed it, that something was coming and "if we could hold this position for two or three days everything was going to be all right. We didn't feel demoralized. I knew that we were in a very rough situation, very dangerous, but I felt optimistic about everything."

Had Pepe and his officers been prepared from the beginning to take alternative action, had they known that the Americans had drafted such a plan for use at such a time, perhaps the Bay of Pigs would have had a different ending. No one will ever be able to say for certain. But one thing is certain: in the very moments that San Román was explaining his reasons for rejecting Oliva's proposal, an event occurred which ended forever any chance of using that alternative plan.

Sometime between 10 and 10:30 in the morning "a man came running like hell," saying radio contact had been made with a ship through a radio of the G-4 at the ammunition supply point. Pepe, Oliva, Artime and Ferrer raced to the supply communications post where Orlando Cuervo, a radio operator, excitedly said he had picked up the ship. Faintly, but getting stronger, they could hear a voice on the other end. It was the *Blagar.* The first words from the sea were congratulations to the fighting men of the Brigade for their victory at Playa Larga. The message of congratulations was given in the name of the Cuban Revolutionary Council. "I don't know how they knew about our fighting," Oliva said, "but that is what they said."

Pepe's reply to the voice on the *Blagar* was to call him a son of a whore and report that the troops that had fought in Playa Larga were already in Playa Girón because they had run out of ammunition. He said he didn't need their congratulations; he needed ammunition, medical supplies and support. Then he asked to speak directly to the American task force commander. The commander came to the radio and this is how Pepe remembers the conversation:

Task Force Commander: *"Hello, Pepe, how are you? . . ."*
Pepe: *"Where have you been, you son of a bitch? Where the hell have you been? You have abandoned us."*
Task Force Commander: *"I know that you have your problems, but I've had mine."*

Then Gray, the American frogman, came on the air and said: *"Hello, Pepe, I want you to know that we will never abandon you, and if things are very rough there we will go in and evacuate you."*

Pepe's exact words, both as written down and as recorded on tape at that time, were: *"I will not be evacuated. We will fight to the end here if we have to."*

Gray asked what Pepe needed and Pepe replied, "Weapons, bullets, communications, medicine and food." He elaborated and specified the kind of ammunition and supplies most urgently needed.

Gray said, "We will get you all those things tonight. We will go in tonight."

"That's what you said yesterday and you didn't come," Pepe said.

But this time, Gray answered, they were coming for sure. In the next sentence Gray uttered the words that Pepe cannot forget: "Jets are coming." Gray said six jets and several B-26s would be arriving within two hours to support the Brigade; and before the ships returned that night, C-54s would drop supplies. Gray warned that the jets would not bear any United States insignia or identifying marks and he cautioned the Cubans not to fire at them by mistake.

Pepe turned to the men around him and gave the good news.

"Now we will hit them!"

Everyone was happy, everyone except Oliva. "I myself felt ashamed that I left Playa Larga because I thought that if they were coming maybe I could have lasted that much longer. So I felt very bad in that moment." Oliva also chastised himself for suggesting a retreat to the Escambray. It was never suggested or discussed again.

From Pepe's conversation with Gray stems the controversy over the use of United States air power in the Bay of Pigs invasion. Since Pepe immediately informed his battalion commanders that jets were coming and ordered them to place panels to mark the front lines for the planes, everyone in the Brigade soon learned the news. Many soldiers mistakenly interpreted that promise for an even greater commitment and assumed—understandably, but incorrectly—that the United States had pledged its air power from the beginning. In time it came to be accepted as fact that the United States had withheld its power and reneged on its promises. In fact, there is no way of determining by what authority Gray made such a promise: the highest authority holds that it did not come from Washington.

When Pepe turned from the radio, Oliva got in a jeep with Manuel Penabaz and returned to where the Second Battalion was resting. Along the way they talked about the fighting and the jets that were coming.* Oliva told his men the good news. They cheered. "I told them to rest because maybe that afternoon we would go back to fight."

By eleven o'clock Pepe received a messenger from Del Valle at San Blas: the enemy was attacking heavily and the para-

* Penabaz, who escaped in a rubber raft, was rescued by a freighter and taken back to Miami after the invasion, contributed a great deal to the air cover controversy in his book *Girón 1961*, published in 1962 in Spanish, and in an article published under his name entitled, "We Were Betrayed," in the January 14, 1963 issue of *U.S. News & World Report*. In the article Penabaz authoritatively wrote of assurances of United States support and of what was said and promised by the Americans—both in Nicaragua and at the Bay of Pigs.

To quote Pepe San Román, who is among those misquoted by Penabaz: "Penabaz was a lawyer who did not know anything about the operation, how it was going. He was not close enough to the radio to hear what I said to anybody. He was not in on the preparation of the plan. He was not present at the briefing. He didn't know anything at all about the operation. He was there as a lawyer to take care of any courts martial. Now he knows more about everything than anybody else."

troopers needed support. The Third Battalion, in position on the right flank to the east, was ordered to San Blas and the Fourth, back from Playa Larga, took up the position on the road to Cienfuegos. (The Sixth Battalion already had been sent to the west of Girón to defend the road from Playa Larga.) It was good news for the Third Battalion for the men had not yet been in combat. They moved out, singing Cuban songs, on the road to San Blas.

At ten o'clock the 4.2 mortar unit defending the road to Covadonga was ordered back to San Blas, and the retreat on the northern front began. "At that time we were in the hands of God," said Roberto San Román, who was twenty-six years old that day, "because we had only one gun protecting the road."

But Castro's troops, numbering nearly twenty thousand men, did not attack. Their failure to act saved the lives of many and prolonged the fighting.

The failure of Castro's large force to deliver the decisive blow was due to a curious coincidence. Two paratroopers, in the advance guard at Covadonga, were captured that morning and immediately questioned about their strength. One man, Carlos Onetti, bravely said that he was part of a force of more than one thousand men holding the road from Covadonga to San Blas. The other, less brave and more practical, told the truth: the invaders' positions had been defended by only nineteen men. A militia captain cursed the second paratrooper as a liar trying to lead them into a trap. It was impossible for nineteen men to hold that outpost for more than twenty-four hours, the captain said. To soften up the "large" force ahead of them, four batteries of 122-mm. artillery began pounding San Blas, but the troops were withheld.

At Yaguaramas the same opportunity for a knockout blow was missed. There, it would have been even easier because no mortars defended Néstor Pino's position. Pino, still under constant attack, waited for reinforcements from San Blas until shortly after ten o'clock when he heard a .50-caliber machine gun firing from behind him. This was his support, he was certain; his men were told to prepare for a counterattack. But instead of support, it was an armored car from Del Valle, ordering retreat. In the absence of effective communications, the paratroopers got the orders mixed up and many went all the way back to Girón, only to turn around and head back for San Blas. It was another opportunity for Castro which, like the others, slipped away.

Del Valle himself moved out of San Blas and took a new position several hundred yards south of the town. By midafternoon he had placed a third of the paratroop battalion and the entire Third Battalion in position. The terrain was rocky and many men were unable even to dig shallow trenches. By then Roberto San Román remembered, "The men were asking 'What are we going to do? How are we going to get out of here?' It was very difficult for me to answer."

The United States press reported the war from the comfortable confines of Miami, aided by the cheering communiqués of Lem Jones. At 1:20 P.M. in New York, Jones released Bulletin No. 4. "Peasants, workers and militia are joining the freedom front and aiding the rapidly expanding area already liberated by the Revolutionary Command," it began. For the first time, however, the Bulletin conceded attacks "by heavy Soviet tanks and MIG aircraft * which have destroyed sizeable amounts of medical supplies and equipment."

In Miami that afternoon the *News* was continuing to report its informed rumors. The paper quoted one source as having received a "completely confirmed" report that Santiago de Cuba —Cuba's second largest city—had fallen to the freedom fighters while fighting continued to rage in four of the six provinces. And, the *News* informed its readers, "leaders of the rebel party who still are in the United States claimed that the main invasion force [of five thousand to eight thousand, the story said later] had struck half way across the narrow island and was in Colon, on the Central Highway which runs the length of Cuba." While the invaders were pressing forward, the paper said, Miró and his council were in a ship off Cuba.

Apparently there was misinformation in official quarters also. In Guatemala, in Homestead Air Force Base outside of Miami, and in Key West, additional Cuban recruits were told that the Brigade was winning and that they were to prepare and wait to join the victorious fight.

* Even this was incorrect; Castro then had no MIG jets.

At Girón they were waiting, too.

The men of the Second Battalion lay on mattresses in the large tourist homes, their clothes off, eating canned fruit, and trying to ignore the sound of artillery coming closer. Some men, too keyed up to sleep, too tired to talk, too tense to relax, nervously strolled along the shoreline.

One of those soldiers, Felipe Rivero, sat down near a concrete pier and began to think about what would happen when they won. "I was trying to feel interested and I wasn't. Then I met a Brigade officer with a bottle of Scotch and we toasted to victory sitting in the sand. I felt like a tourist. I continued walking and then the plane came. So I ran to a small store with an old man and two peasants." The strafing was intense and he ran out and got under the pier. Three soldiers were already there. "The faces really had panic there. Their faces said what was going on and I suppose mine did, too." The shooting stopped and Rivero went back to the store, asked for a beer, told the owner he would pay him in Havana and continued walking down the beach drinking the beer. "So I felt all right again and then I heard a plane open its motors." The plane had cut its engine and dived. "And then I saw a B-26 behind me and the belly open and the eggs dropping." He crawled to a house and huddled under a bed for protection. The attack over, Rivero went back to the beach to pick up his bottle of beer. "It had been stolen and I was very mad."

Since his first conversation with Gray that morning, Pepe had been on the radio constantly, asking for his promised support. "I did not send dispatches," Pepe said, "it was a continuous conversation, and a continuous argument over the radio, as if we were talking by phone. Everything was so disorganized and we were so disappointed that we were raising hell, sending everybody to hell and asking for things. We said we need support from coordinates number such and such. An enemy battalion is in that position. We will mark the zone for you."

About three o'clock in the afternoon the awaited help seemed to arrive. Two F-86 Sabre jets, with no identifying marks on the body or wings, came roaring over the front. They flew first from southwest to northeast, and then came back from the east to west, dipping their wings in salute and glistening in the sun. For a moment the fighting stopped along the entire front as men leaped out of positions, threw their weapons in the air and cheered madly. "They were beautiful," one soldier said. "Arrrummmmmmm! They go flying over. We never saw them again."

Neither at San Blas nor at Girón did anyone see the planes fire. But to the west, on the road to Playa Larga, where Enrique Ruiz-Williams was then placing his 4.2 mortars in position for the coming attack, immediately after the jets flew over there was an explosion about five miles ahead and black smoke rose into the air. "I don't know if they did that or some of our B-26s did it," Williams said, "but I saw the explosion and the big smoke and in fact I got up in a tree to find out what happened." He was unable to see far enough. Castro has stated that on Tuesday afternoon United States jets, flying from a great height, attacked a column advancing from Playa Larga and caused "a lot of casualties."

Whether the American planes attacked or not, Pepe's information was that they did not. He immediately took the radio again and told Gray the jets did not support them. Gray replied, "The planes are there to give you support against enemy aircraft. They are not going to give you land support."

Pepe exploded. "How in hell are we going to get land support? We have nothing to fight with on the ground."

While he was talking a messenger arrived from Del Valle, giving exact coordinates of a large enemy concentration. Pepe gave the exact position to Gray. "And then Gray came on the radio and said that the planes were overhead at that moment. I don't remember how many C-54s, how many C-46s, how many B-26s, how many F-51s. Lots of planes, about twenty all together. They were coming to us, some loaded with ammunition and supplies, and the others carrying bombs."

Two years later, Pepe said, "I am still waiting for them."

Throughout the afternoon planes swept over Girón—but they were Castro's. Then, at six o'clock, artillery began to hit the small town and on the east and west advance guards of Castro's troops began to engage the Brigade. At San Blas, where the enemy was attacking heavily, only two tanks and acts of individual heroism saved the Brigade from annihilation. The perimeter was narrowing and the pressure was expanding. Without supplies, it was only a matter of time before the end came.

Late in the afternoon a C-54 arrived and the first supplies from the air were dropped over the Girón airfield. Pepe's words, as written down and relayed by Gray to Air Command at Puerto Cabezas, told of the frustration: "Plane dropped supplies on air-field and wind blew them away. Drop on roads in town from low altitude. Need planes to land air field and take off wounded before morning. Pepe." A C-54 arrived but the wind blew the parachutes into the sea and the Cuban frogmen, led by José Enrique Alonso, got in rubber rafts and headed out under air attack to rescue them. "Those frogmen did a good job," Pepe said. "They were very brave."

Equally brave were the fifty to sixty peasants who had volunteered to work at Girón. One of them, Manuel Almagro, whom Roberto Pertierra, the Brigade's supply officer, called "the toughest man I ever saw," drove his truck into the midst of the firing to pick up two badly wounded soldiers. When he reached them, they had died. He buried them and went back to work.

By twilight Pertierra had organized a group from the Second Battalion and the civilian volunteers to pick up the supplies that had been carried by the wind into the jungle. For hours they worked in the darkness, guided only by flashlights, trying to find the supplies. Very few were found.

In the meantime, Oliva had volunteered to take charge of the western defenses facing toward Playa Larga after the Sixth Battalion commander, Francisco Montiel, was wounded slightly. At eight o'clock Pepe dispatched the Second Battalion to the front after receiving word that the attack was coming. When the Second Battalion moved forward Máximo Cruz, the courageous company commander, tried to go with them. Badly wounded, still bleeding, Cruz had been lying in the infirmary at Girón. Artime found Cruz trying to walk away from the infirmary and told him to return. Cruz replied: "Please don't give me that order, because I don't want to be insubordinate to you, but my boys are being killed and I want to die with them." Then Cruz passed out.

For some reason, however, the attack did not come and the Second Battalion withdrew into Girón where the men slept fitfully by their weapons, denied even one night's sleep because of the land crabs that swarmed over the ground where they lay. The crabs seemed a particularly bad sign: they were black and red, the color of Castro's 26th of July flag.

The fighting that Tuesday night at Girón was limited principally to skirmishes with infiltrating militia. The relative quiet gave Oliva and Ferrer an opportunity to study the maps and plan their defenses while Pepe continued speaking over the radio with Gray. Late that night Pepe again lost contact with the *Blagar*. "Maybe they turned the radio off in order not to hear my complaints," he said.

At four o'clock in the morning Oliva lay down to rest. An hour later Pepe woke him up and ordered him, with Ferrer's assistance, to prepare a map containing the latest combat information. A transport plane was scheduled to land at Girón within the hour to pick up wounded and Oliva was to fly back to Puerto Cabezas and report the critical situation personally to Frank. As Pepe said, "If any person could get Frank to support us, that person was Oliva. He would have raised hell at the rear base."

"I told Pepe that I was not going," Oliva said, "that I could not leave Cuba knowing the position our troops were in. He told me it was an order, that I was the only one that could go back there as the second in command of the Brigade and impress the people there of the situation. I told him to send Ferrer, Yayo [José R. Varona, the G-2 or intelligence officer] but that I was not going. He insisted. Then I told him to give me the order in writing."

Pepe wrote: "Frank. Oliva presents himself to you to tell you that our situation is desperate and we need your help badly. Pepe."

Oliva, sick at heart, began to prepare the maps.

When Pepe lost communications with the *Blagar*, he assumed the Americans had given up trying to help him. In actual fact, the *Blagar* and *Barbara J* were working frantically against a number of formidable obstacles: the reluctance of the crews to go back; time itself; lack of air support to cover the unloading of equipment at the beach; and uncertainty in Washington about what could be done to save the operation. The ships—the *Blagar*, the *Barbara J* and the *Atlantico*—were at the "Zulu" reunion point, fifty miles south of the Bay of Pigs, where tons of ammunition and weapons were being loaded into three LCUs.

"A lot of the crew didn't want to help in the loading," said Andy Pruna, who was aboard the *Barbara J*. "So we were loading and almost dying from the heat and the exhaustion in the hold of the ships. One of the guys, I remember, lost a finger and we also had some wounded aboard. In our ship they were demanding some kind of protective air cover, especially since the only protection we had were the .50 calibers."

Air cover was again a key. The messages from the *Blagar* to Nicaragua that night succinctly spelled out the problem. One read: BARRACUDA, MARSOPA (code names for the *Barbara J* and *Blagar*) AND LCUS CANNOT ARRIVE BLUE BEACH DISCHARGE AND LEAVE BY DAYLIGHT. REQUEST JET COVER FOR US IN BEACHHEAD AREA. Two hours and thirty-eight minutes later: MARSOPA PROCEEDING BLUE BEACH WITH 3 LCUS. IF LOW JET COVER NOT FURNISHED AT FIRST LIGHT BELIEVE WE WILL LOSE ALL SHIPS. REQUEST IMMEDIATELY REPLY.

The granting of such a request could come only from one man: John F. Kennedy.

It must have been a day of frustration and anguish for John Fitzgerald Kennedy. The news from the front continued to grow blacker. Not a single element of the invasion plan had proved successful, and now the total disaster that he and his top officials had been assured could not happen was imminent. Moreover, there was the threat that Russia might act. Khrushchev had made that clear in a special message to the President that morning. Written, the Premier said, "at an hour of anxiety fraught with danger to world peace," it stated the Soviet position in chilling terms. "It is not a secret to anyone that the armed bands which invaded that country have been trained, equipped and armed in the United States of America. The planes which bomb Cuban cities belong to the United States of America, the bombs they drop have been made available by the American Government. . . . As to the Soviet Union, there should be no misunderstanding of our position: we shall render the Cuban people and their Government all necessary assistance in beating back the armed attack on Cuba. We are sincerely interested in a relaxation of international tension, but if others aggravate it, we shall reply in full measure."

The President himself dictated the reply. It was temperate but firm, and clearly and precisely worded. The Premier was under a "serious misapprehension" about Cuba, for there were "unmistakable signs that Cubans found intolerable the denial of democratic liberties and the subversion of the 26 of July Movement by an alien-dominated regime." The President had stated before—and he stated again—that "the United States intends no military intervention in Cuba." But should an outside force intervene "we will immediately honor our obligations under the inter-American system to protect this hemisphere against external aggression." The President trusted that the Premier would not use Cuba as a pretext "to inflame other areas of the world," for he hoped the Soviet Union had "too great a sense of responsibility to embark upon any enterprise so dangerous to general peace." The President's message ended with a statement of principle: "I believe, Mr. Chairman, that you should recognize that free peoples in all parts of the world do not accept the claim of historical inevitability for Communist revolution. What your Government believes is its own business; what it does in the world is the world's business. The great revolution in the history of man, past, present and future, is the revolution of those determined to be free."

Before seven o'clock at night, less than ten hours after Khrushchev's message was received, the President's reply was handed to Mikhail A. Menshikov, the Soviet Ambassador to the United States.

The principals had spoken, and the minor actors took their cue. Tito asked the United Nations to act against the aggression; Nasser wired Castro his support; Nehru was dismayed. And in New York Adlai Stevenson quipped that he wasn't sure who was attacking Cuba, but he was sure who was attacking us.

Neither the words nor the jokes were of any comfort to the President. Until nearly ten o'clock he lingered in his office, ignoring the reminders of his staff that he had to prepare for the reception for his Cabinet and members of Congress and their wives and guests. At the last minute he put on white tie and tails and at 10:15 he and Mrs. Kennedy walked down the main stairs into the entrance hall. As the Marine band, resplendent in red dress uniforms, played *Mr. Wonderful,* the President and First Lady whirled around the ballroom, the picture of youth and confidence. For an hour and a half the President mingled with his guests, a gracious host and charming President.

Shortly before the clock struck midnight, the President left

the reception and went immediately to his office. Rusk, Mc-
Namara, Bissell, Lemnitzer and Burke were present. Bissell,
quietly and calmly, presented the case and the request: the
Brigade had only one hope left—United States airpower.
Of those hours of deliberation from midnight until 2 A.M.,
there have been several accounts. It can be stated from the highest sources, however, that the essence of the debate was this:
Dean Rusk vigorously opposed the use of American power;
Arleigh Burke strongly backed Richard Bissell; and John Kennedy ruled out any *major* use of American arms. The President
did, however, for the first time, alter his policy on the use of
United States forces. In a compromise, but one with a reasonable
chance of success, he gave the authority for jet fighter planes
from the carrier *U.S.S. Essex*, on duty in the Caribbean off the
Bay of Pigs, to provide an "air umbrella" Wednesday at dawn
while the B-26s from Puerto Cabezas struck hard at Castro's
forces and the *Blagar*, the *Barbara J* and the three LCUs unloaded the vital supplies at Girón. The military order went out.
It clattered over the teletype machine in the small operations
room at Puerto Cabezas. ON D+2 (WEDNESDAY) FROM 0630 TO
0730 THE SKY WILL BE CLEAR. The jet air cover request was
granted.

His decision made and the orders given, Kennedy walked
alone into the White House garden.

CHAPTER 3

WEDNESDAY: "FAREWELL, FRIENDS"

Since Sunday night the Cuban B-26 pilots had been flying around the clock on what had become virtual suicide missions. By Wednesday morning nine of the sixteen B-26s had been shot down, and several of the remaining planes were in poor flying condition. When the pilots were called to the briefing room at Puerto Cabezas early that morning to receive their missions, some of them refused to continue flying without the assurance of air support. Oscar Vega was one of them.

"They gave the orders to Captain Zúñiga and me to fly over Playa Girón," Vega said. "I said No, if I didn't have the air support promised. The American chief of operations * told me that he would give me his word of honor that we would have air support, that they were just waiting for the word from Washington. I said we would go, but said that if we did not have fighter cover by the time we flew over Grand Cayman [175 miles due south of the Bay of Pigs] we would return to Nicaragua, and he said 'O.K.'"

Four American advisors, knowing that the order had been received pledging United States jet support, volunteered to fly for the exhausted Cubans. Riley W. Shamburger, Jr., Wade C. Gray, Thomas Willard Ray and Lee F. Baker were casual and confident as they got into two of the B-26s—two in each plane —wearing tan shorts. Their planes, and two others flown by Vega and Gonzalo Herrera, took off for the three-hour-and-twenty-minute flight to the Bay of Pigs. Vega's right engine developed trouble and he had to turn back. The others flew on.

In the first light of the day, the B-26s were approaching their target—nearly one hour *before* their jet support was supposed

* Billy Carpenter.

to arrive at 6:30. Why they arrived at Girón an hour early is not clear, but the result was disastrous: the U.S. jets were still on the carrier deck when the planes flown by the Americans were attacked by Castro's jets. One B-26 was shot down and crash-landed in flames on the air strip at the Central Australia sugar mill.* The other fell into the sea enveloped in flames and smoke. The four Americans died. By the time the mournful word was passed to the carrier, the bombing mission had ended.

Gonzalo Herrera, who had heard his American comrades vainly calling the distress signal "Mad Dog Four! May Day! May Day!" to get carrier support, proceeded on to his target: enemy troop and artillery concentrations massed in front of San Blas. The Brigade troops had been under heavy artillery fire all night and Castro's forces were ready for a massive attack when Herrera's plane dived, strafed the position with machine guns, turned, made a second pass and dropped two napalm bombs. After the tremendous explosion, there was deep silence.

Herrera headed toward the sea but was attacked and hit. With one engine out and thirty-seven hits in his fuselage, he skimmed low over the water all the way back to Nicaragua and landed safely at Puerto Cabezas. His was the last shot fired by the Brigade air force. Since their mission was to provide an "umbrella" for the Brigade B-26 bombers, after the bombers were shot down the American jets never left the *Essex*. Without the protective air cover, the supply ships did not hazard the unloading at dawn. And no more bombing missions were scheduled.

At ten minutes to six a C-46 piloted by Manuel Navarro, carrying 850 pounds of rockets and ammunition, maps, mes-

* This crash landing has led to a number of accounts among the Brigade soldiers and pilots. That the plane did land on the strip is certain. From civilians who lived in that area came a story that one of the Americans ran from the plane with a pistol and fought a fierce but brief battle with militia until he was shot to death. The other American, either wounded or dead when the plane landed, remained inside and was also shot. One Cuban claimed to have seen a photograph showing two Americans lying on the ground with bullet holes in their heads. The accounts cannot be verified but it is interesting that Castro, so quick in every other instance to prove and gloat over American involvement, however slight, never mentioned the death of the Americans. That story was not made public until March 3, 1963—and then only in the United States press. President Kennedy later acknowledged, at a news conference, that the men died in the service of their country. He did not say how they died or for whom they were working.

sages and complex communications equipment, landed on the Girón air strip. Navarro had been told in Nicaragua that his mission was very important and very dangerous. Whatever happened, the communications equipment must be delivered—if not on the ground, then by parachute. Navarro also had been told to pick up wounded prisoners if he could. He and his American navigator, "Bob," who volunteered to fly with him that morning, were finishing unloading the plane when Oliva drove up in a jeep.

"I told him that I had been ordered to go to Nicaragua," Oliva said, "and he told me he was ordered not to take anyone except wounded, but he could take me the same as he was taking Farías [a wounded Brigade pilot whose B-26 had crash-landed there Monday]. I told him the last order was the one he had to obey. I gave him the maps and my message, but I did not go in the plane because I had an excuse not to go."

As Navarro was preparing to take off, Dr. Juan Sordo arrived. Sordo and Navarro are not in agreement on what was said. Sordo, who had been treating men without rest for two days, said Navarro "refused to take forty wounded men out." Navarro said, "I don't remember exactly what he told me, but he said it would take some time for the wounded men to get there. Then I took the decision, as the captain of the plane, that it was too much risk to stay any longer. So I didn't have time to wait for the wounded men. If I stayed longer I would lose the plane, the crew and our mission." He took off with Farías, the wounded pilot, and the messages and maps Oliva had given him, and flew back to Puerto Cabezas. It was the only time during the fighting that a plane landed and took off from Girón.

Oliva reported back to Pepe. "Pepe was very angry with me and told me that I had to go; that a C-54 was going to land later in the morning. I didn't want to disobey him, but he had to know the way I was feeling at that moment. Then I think that God wanted it to happen my way because a messenger arrived from the Sixth Battalion." Castro's troops were advancing from the west. Pepe sent Oliva to take command of that front.

In a deserted house at the abandoned airfield of Opa-Locka outside Miami, the leaders of the Cuban Revolutionary Council were being held under armed guard until they could be flown

THE BAY OF PIGS / 157

to Cuba to establish their provisional government. Since Monday, when they first learned of the invasion by radio, they had been hearing and reading communiqués issued without their knowledge in their names. They were men with sons, brothers and cousins in the Brigade and by Wednesday morning, when they knew the invasion was not succeeding, they threatened to leave despite their guards. Arthur Schlesinger, Jr., and A. A. Berle were dispatched by the President to Opa-Locka to see the Cubans, arriving at 7:30 A.M. Schlesinger then telephoned the President that he should see the Cubans. Kennedy agreed. Soon the Cubans were on an air force plane bound for Washington.

Twenty-two years old, handsome, blond, athletic and cocky, Alejandro del Valle was an inspiration to his men. When, at about 6 A.M., Gonzalo Herrera's plane flew away from the San Blas front, Del Valle took advantage of the confusion Herrera's attack had created among the enemy. He organized a counterattack with his paratroopers and the Third Battalion. Standing on top of one of his two tanks, Del Valle signaled for the attack. The men moved forward under a heavy artillery barrage, some walking dazedly, others running, but all going ahead. To the forward observers, watching through binoculars, it was like a picture: the lines of men, the bright blue sky and the early morning sun, the puffs of smoke and earth rising from the craters, the flash of small arms fire and the blue uniforms of the enemy. Del Valle was hit and knocked from the tank. He immediately climbed back and the tank moved ahead in the vanguard of the troops.

It was a gallant, forlorn, even foolhardy attack—and yet it was succeeding. Castro's vastly superior forces broke and ran. Some enemy soldiers tore off their shirts and waved them in surrender. That moment marked a crest for the Brigade. For a few fleeting seconds the liberation army felt victorious. And then the attack faltered and stopped, first with the Third Battalion on the right flank, and then on down the line, and men began moving to the rear. They were running out of ammunition.

The Third Battalion retreat became disorganized. A few of the paratroopers joined their ranks and the retreat threatened to become a rout. In rage and with tears in his eyes, Del Valle ran among the men trying to stop them, shouting: "All paratroopers back to the line and die there." He repeated it over and over. His men regrouped and formed a line on the sides of the road, placed their bazookas, and waited, two miles south of San Blas, at a junction called Bermeja. As they were forming their position, the paratroopers were astonished to see a jeep driven by a captain in Castro's militia come racing straight into their lines. Sitting beside the captain was Major Félix Duque, one of the top enemy commanders. The major had been in charge of the troops at Yaguaramas, and in the mistaken belief that the forces coming from Covadonga already had taken San Blas and moved south, he took a short cut—straight into the lap of the Brigade.

The captain was frightened but Major Duque spoke up boldly: "Men, you don't know what's coming toward you. I have five thousand men and fourteen tanks. You'd better surrender. You know you're going to lose this war."

Cocky as ever, Del Valle snapped back, "You don't know what Del Valle can do with a hundred paratroopers."

A Brigade soldier called out, "Let's hang these Communists."

The major, still unperturbed, answered, "I am a Socialist, but I am not a Communist. You are Cubans and you are harming your country."

With that, Del Valle personally took the major back to Girón and reported to Pepe San Román.

Del Valle told Pepe the Third Battalion was retreating in a disorganized manner and the commanders were not in control of the men. Pepe immediately ordered the first- and second-in-command, Noelio Montero Díaz and Dagoberto Darias, relieved of duty, and sent word by Del Valle to his (Pepe's) brother Roberto to assume command of the Third Battalion and "fight until you don't have anything left to fight with."

When he received the news, Roberto San Román appointed Arturo Comas in charge of the Heavy Gun Battalion; then Roberto went to find Noelio Montero. "I am very sorry," Roberto said, "but I have to take your place."

"I wish you luck," Montero said, "but there is nothing else to do here."

At ten o'clock Castro's troops entered San Blas, and by eleven o'clock were approaching the last defenses blocking the road to Girón.

The first tank, an American-made Sherman T-34, turned the bend in the road and Valdés knocked it out with his bazooka. "I hit it! I hit it!" he shouted, jumping up and down. A second tank, a Stalin, approached, and Valdés destroyed it. A third tank came and a .57 recoilless rifle shot struck the turret, killing the tank commander. The tank retreated and small arms fire began between Castro's militia, in their blue uniforms, and what was left of the Brigade on the San Blas front. Step by step, the paratroopers, the Third Battalion and the two Brigade tanks were beaten back. Their ammunition was nearly expended. By two o'clock Castro's tanks had formed a solid line and were firing straight into the Brigade position. It was flat land and the only shelter was mangrove trees.

"They hit so many men we knew we had to leave," said Roberto San Román. "Some men had already left and we only had about forty men left. So we decided to retreat."

As Roberto turned back to Girón, he saw Benito Blanco, a truck driver from the Heavy Gun Battalion. "The truck is here," Blanco said, motioning to the trees. Blanco had followed his commander in the truck when he saw Roberto leave to take charge of the Third Battalion. All during the fighting, Blanco had waited, sitting on a rock, as calm as if he were watching television. The men jumped aboard the truck—a Russian truck, captured at Girón—and Blanco drove off. In turning south onto the road, the truck met one of the Brigade tanks which, thinking it was the enemy, fired. The shell hit the front of the truck, instantly killing Blanco and another man. Roberto was hit in the legs, chest, neck and face by shrapnel. The truck veered out of control, smashed through a fence and came to a stop among the mangroves. One of the soldiers made a tourniquet with his belt for Roberto and told him not to worry, that God would take care of him. "And, really, God helped me," Roberto said, "because he gave me the aid that I needed."

He and the others walked through the woods to the highway, searching for the 4.2 mortar position. They found it but no one was there. Then they began walking down the road fifteen miles back to Girón. Before long a jeep came moving fast down the road from behind them with eleven or twelve men packed on so that the jeep itself was hardly distinguishable.

It was Del Valle. Roberto was pulled onto the jeep and they drove on, passing Brigade soldiers trudging toward the beach. In the distance they could see smoke and flames rising from Girón.

At Girón Pepe San Román resumed his radio contact with Gray on the *Blagar* that morning while his communications officers assembled the equipment flown in by Navarro that would enable him to send messages directly to Nicaragua. Until midafternoon, when the equipment was ready, Pepe sent his battle reports through Gray. Better than anything, the stark words sent out over the airwaves to the *Blagar* told the story of the disaster that was overtaking the Brigade. The radio log kept on the *Blagar* reads as follows:

5:00 A.M. *Do you people realize how desperate the situation is? Do you back us or quit? All we want is low jet air cover. Enemy has this support. I need it badly or cannot survive. . . .*

6:13 A.M. *Blue Beach under attack by B-26. Where is promised air cover? Pepe.*

6:42 A.M. *C-54 dropped supplies on Blue Beach. All went into sea. Send more. Pepe.*

7:12 A.M. *Enemy on trucks coming from Red Beach are right now 3 km. from Blue Beach. Pepe.*

7:50 A.M. *We are fighting in the west flank of Blue Beach with tanks. Pepe.*

8:15 A.M. *Situation critical left flank west Blue Beach. Need urgently air support. Pepe.*

8:40 A.M. *Blue Beach is under air attack. Pepe.*

9:14 A.M. *Blue Beach under attack by 2 T-33 and artillery. Where the hell is jet cover? Pepe.*

9:25 A.M. *2000 militia attacking Blue Beach from east and west. Need close air support immediately. Pepe.*

9:55 A.M. *Can you throw something into this vital point in the battle? Anything. Just let jet pilots loose. Pepe.*

I. PRINCIPALS

April 12, 1961, Press conference:
"There will be no Americans in-
volved inside Cuba . . . no inter-
vention by American forces."—
John F. Kennedy.—*N.B.C. White
Paper*

Allen Dulles, Director of the CIA.
In the spring of 1961, he said the
time to invade was at hand.—
A. P. Photo

Admiral Arleigh Burke, Chief of
Naval Operations at the time of
the invasion.—*A. P. Photo*

General Lyman L. Lemnitzer,
Chairman of the Joint Chiefs of
Staff. The chiefs approved the
battle plan.—*Wide World Photo*

Richard M. Bissell, Jr. He was the CIA mastermind behind the U-2 flights and the chief architect of the Bay of Pigs operation.—*Wide World Photo*

General Charles P. Cabell, Deputy Director of CIA at the time of the invasion.

The target: Fidel Castro, harvesting crops prior to the invasion. He knew it was coming and told his people to prepare.

José Miro Cardona and Manuel Ray, two of the leaders of the Cuban Revolutionary Council in whose name the CIA mounted the invasion.—*N.B.C. White Paper*

The Brigade forces in Guatemala. *Left to right*, Manuel Artime, civilian leader; José Pérez San Román, military commander; Antonio Maceo and Manuel Antonio de Varona, leaders of the Cuban *Frente*.

Erneido Oliva, second in command of the Brigade, at Base Trax, Guatemala.

Alejandro del Valle, commander of the parachute battalion (he died on the fishing boat after the battle), with Artime in Guatemala shortly before the invasion.

José ("Yayo") Varona, Intelligence Officer of the Brigade, at Base Trax.

The Brigade, training in the Guatemala mountains.

Training in skirmish formation
before the invasion.

(*Above*) Spring, 1961. Brigade airstrip built by the U. S. at Retalhuleu, Guatemala. Base Trax was high in the mountains in the
background (*Below*) Adlai Stevenson, before the UN and before
the world, claims that the planes which bombed Havana before
the invasion were Castro's own. In fact, which he apparently did
not then know, they were from CIA's Brigade air force bases in
Nicaragua.— *N. Y. Herald Tribune Photo by Ted Kell*

(*Left*) Puerto Cabezas, Nicaragua, point of embarkation for the Bay of Pigs. (*Right*) Unidentified American "advisors" in Nicaragua.

At sea on the weekend of the invasion, a Brigade soldier prepares for the days ahead.

The invasion begins. Aboard the flagship *Blagar,* sunset, Sunday April 16, 1961, off the coast of Cuba. Pepe San Román, second from left, and Manuel Artime, second from right, salute as the Cuban flag is raised, signaling the beginning of combat. Artime cried, "I thought it was the beginning of the liberation of Cuba."

A Cuban frogman on the way to the Bay of Pigs with a censored American friend.

The first morning — disaster. Castro's "nonexistent" air force sinks the Brigade supply ships, the *Rio Escondido* (a Castro photograph) and the *Houston* (an eyewitness painting by Brigade frogman, Andy Pruna).

Castro militia on the Playa Girón front.

Castro counterattacks on the Playa Larga front.

Castro's peasant *militianos* remained loyal.

(*Left*) A Brigade B-26, shot down by a Castro jet. (*Right*) Fidel takes personal command of the battle. — *N.B.C. White Paper.*

IV. DEFEAT

Brigade prisoners captured in the swamps (a Castro film).

(*Left*) Manuel Artime captured after thirteen days in the Zapata swamps. (*Below*) Pepe San Román in prison in Havana, shortly after his capture. — *UPI*

Interrogation. José Andreu, a Brigade officer, is interrogated on television by a panel of Castro officials.

The defeated Brigade in the Havana sports palace.

Fidel's triumph. He berates the Brigade "worms" in the sports palace.

V. AFTERMATH

A study in responsibility. Dwight Eisenhower, who authorized the CIA to create a counterrevolutionary force, and John Kennedy, who inherited and executed the plans, confer on April 22, 1961, three days after the final defeat. — *A. P. Photo*

VI. THE TRIAL

The Trial. One of the largest mass trials since Stalin's in the '30's. Captain Pedro Luis Rodriguez of Castro's forces testifies against the Brigade in the Principe prison in Havana, March 30, 1962. — *Wide World Photo*

VII. LIBERATION

Alvaro Sanchez, Jr., President of the Cuban Families Committee, a key figure in the liberation negotiations.

Freedom. A wife greets her liberated husband at the airport in Miami. — *Wide World Photo*

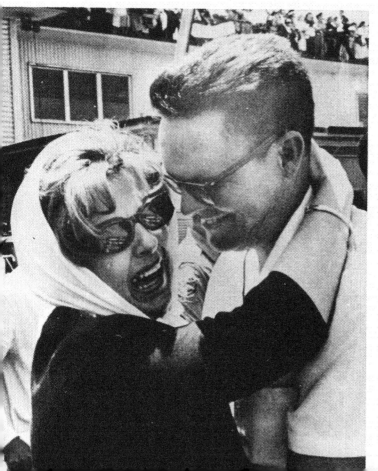

President Kennedy accepts the Brigade's banner at the Miami Orange Bowl, December 29, 1962. He promised to return the banner to the Brigade in a free Havana. — *Wide World Photo*

Jacqueline Kennedy, speaking in flawless Spanish, at the Orange Bowl, calls the Brigade "a group of the bravest men in the world." — *Wide World Photo*

(*Above*) Three who were vital to the liberation effort: Left to right, Attorney General Robert F. Kennedy, Enrique Ruiz-Williams, and James B. Donovan. — *Tony Rollo, Newsweek.* (*Below*) Brigade leaders present Robert F. Kennedy with a medal of gratitude for his role in their liberation. *Left to right*, Roberto San Román, Manuel Artime, Ramón Ferrer, Mr. Kennedy, Enrique Ruiz-Williams, Pepe San Román, and Erneido Oliva. — *A. P. Photo*

Toward the end messages came quickly: "In water. Out of ammo. Enemy closing in. Help must arrive in next hour." "Fighting on beach. Send all available aircraft now."

Through all the chaos and despair of defeat, Pepe retained the calm that was his hallmark. Even his anger was quiet; he was not a pounder or a shouter. Those who heard him on the radio that day, and many on the convoy off the Bay of Pigs did, heard the quiet voice, sounding more tired, edged more with anger and bitterness but still determined and still calm. By eleven o'clock in the morning, Pepe's only direct contact was with the *Blagar:* the batteries on the portable radios had run out and he had lost all voice communications with all his battalion commanders. He was forced to rely on messengers and the messengers were not always reliable.

"When the troops started getting demoralized they saw things as worse than they were and they made them bigger," Pepe said. "For example, about twelve o'clock I was told the enemy had crossed over Oliva and Oliva's units were scattered and killed, and they were coming into the beach, into the town and they were fighting in the town. I ordered everybody there to assemble with the weapons we had—pistols, carbines, M-3s—to stay in the trenches we had opened there. We got in position to fight. We were in that position for about half an hour, and another messenger came and Oliva was asking for reinforcements and his situation was difficult but he had held his position. So we were in the trenches and I told everybody to dismiss and sent Oliva back a message that I had no reinforcements to send. I told him to hold his position by any means, because as long as that position was held everything was all right."

Only once that day did Pepe completely lose his temper. It was when he discovered that the first message to Nicaragua in the afternoon had been sent, without his authority, saying PLEASE SEND HELP. PLEASE DON'T LET US DOWN. "That was the message they sent without my authorization signed by my name. I went there and I told them not to send any more messages, that I just wanted military messages. That this and this is going on, but not asking 'please.' If they [the Americans] wanted to send anything, send it, and if they don't want to they can go to hell."

It was then about 3 P.M. and the men began preparing a second message in code to be sent to Nicaragua. But time was running out. From the north, the west, the east and from the air, the Brigade was under heavy attack. To the south, at their backs, was the sea—both a barrier and the last hope. Gray kept saying to hang on, that help was coming from the sea.

Messages filtered back through the military chain of command, from Girón to the *Blagar,* from the *Blagar* to the American destroyer operating under the code name "Santiago," from *Santiago* to the Washington command group and then to their final destination, the White House. For the President, who was also commander-in-chief, those must have been searing hours. There were conferences with his military and civilian advisors, a brief spoken apology to the Cuban Revolutionary Council, in which he assumed the full blame for failure and promised to do what he could for their sons,* and there were the final decisions to make. The nature of John F. Kennedy's personal feelings is reflected in part by the orders that went out from Washington that day. They indicate how close the United States came to a total commitment.

First, CINCLANT (Commander-in-Chief, Atlantic) was instructed to fly reconnaissance missions over the beach and to send two destroyers to positions off Playa Girón to determine the possibilities for evacuation. Two hours and fifty-two minutes later, in midafternoon, CINCLANT received these instructions: "Have destroyers take Brigade personnel off beach to limit capture. Navy use Brigade boats and craft as practicable and provide air cover. Destroyers authorized return fire if fired on during this humanitarian mission."

"All of a sudden we get the order that we're going in and this time we get no opposition from anybody," Andy Pruna said. "When the final order comes that we're going in, even the ones that were trying to mutiny were ready to go."

The *Blagar,* the *Barbara J,* the *Atlántico,* the three LCUs formed a line. Moving up alongside them came the American destroyers. "So now we know that we are going in. These destroyers are not going in for nothing. And they are going full speed ahead right beside us. And it is a wonderful sight. Everybody is ready to die. Everybody is ready to go." *Santiago* asked for instructions: describe the Brigade uniforms, describe those

---

* Both Miró Cardona and Tony Varona had sons in the invasion.

of Castro's troops. Overhead in the cloudless sky came the planes, heading toward Playa Girón, fifty miles away. The destroyers pulled away and the slower merchant ships followed in their wake.

The last battle had an epic quality all the more tragic because it was so hopeless. It did not affect the outcome or even add a footnote to history. It was merely another moment when men tried against great odds and failed.

What the Cubans call "The Last Stand of Girón" actually began on Tuesday night when a forward observer named Gabriel Gómez del Río put his ear to the ground and heard "something big coming." He had driven out earlier that afternoon with his commanding officer, Enrique Ruiz-Williams, to place the 4.2- and 81-mm. mortars in position to the west of Girón on the road to Playa Larga. By night they had selected a curve and concentrated their fire on it. By 4 A.M. Gómez del Río had heard the enemy approaching from far away. He called Williams on the radio and Williams replied: "I want you to go to the front and make sure of your direction of fire because we are going to put in the history of Cuba how many men we kill today."

"And that's what happened," Gómez del Río said. "He directed the fire good and we really hit them."

The first trucks approached the position about six o'clock. In the lead was a truck carrying ammunition and men. A mortar shell landed directly on it. "Green smoke, green smoke, and nothing, no truck, nothing," Gómez del Río said. Militiamen ran into the palm trees by the bend in the road—and the mortars hit them. "This I'll never forget: those palm trees just go up in flames." Men ran out screaming, their clothes on fire. The Castro column was stopped.

After 7 A.M. Oliva had taken command of the front.

"When I arrived there," Oliva said, "I found out that there were about seven bazookas, and with the experience we had at Playa Larga against the tanks I made a battery of bazookas." He placed them pointing straight toward the curve in the road, where Castro's men had to come. In front of the bazookas he stationed the 170 men from the Sixth Battalion. Oliva then told Pepe by radio that a heavy attack was coming and he needed help. Fifteen minutes later the Second Battalion arrived, and ten minutes after that three Brigade tanks. Oliva placed the tanks in steps to the left, also pointed toward the curve, and held the Second Battalion in reserve.

At 9:45 A.M. the enemy began to move forward again and the Brigade 4.2s opened fire. This time Castro's troops, despite their losses, continued to advance and at ten o'clock the first tank came through the curve. "We cut his head." An armored truck came next and Enrique Garcia destroyed it with a bazooka. Another tank came around the curve, advanced fifty yards more than the other and then it, too, was hit and blown up. A third tank came and was destroyed. "We didn't see any more movement," Oliva said.

From across the road, in the dense underbrush, came soldiers. An aide at first told Oliva they were from the Brigade. "This would sound illogical in the middle of a war," Oliva said, "but they were dressed like militiamen and they called from there, 'Friends. What's happening? Friends,' and I was confused. We were dressed in camouflage and standing in the open and they were *milicianos;* they saw us and shouted at us."

Oliva took advantage of the confusion and waved and shouted for them to come over. The militia crawled under a fence and ran across the road.

"Ay! They are the mercenaries," one militiaman shouted.

They were part of an advance group of 150 men who had been attempting to infiltrate the lines and attack. "Pancho" was the name of their commander. Oliva told the men to shout, "Pancho, come over, Pancho, come over," and another group came running toward them and surrendered. "This was very funny," Oliva said, "in the middle of the road we were dressed in camouflage and we called them and they came over. I think they went crazy. Then the famous Pancho came out of there and he was running toward us and the thing was getting dangerous. Now we had about one hundred men running toward us." Pancho recognized the enemy and the firing began. Pancho was one of the first to die. "It was Dantesque."

It was only the beginning of the infantry assaults. As he had done at Playa Larga, Oliva called for white phosphorus. For an hour the tanks, the infantry and the mortars fired continuously. In Julio Díaz Arguelles' 81-mm. mortar squad the men

were firing so rapidly the mortars actually began melting.*
When the enemy retreated it was 12:30 P.M. and Oliva had lost
radio contact with Pepe. A truck with bazooka and .50-caliber
ammunition arrived from Girón. Shortly after that a car came
from the enemy lines with two militiamen who wanted to surrender. They told Oliva their commander had betrayed them
by sending them into slaughter and that Osmani Cienfuegos
was leading a column of three thousand men toward them. And,
they said, Fidel Castro was already in Playa Larga.

Oliva brought the Second Battalion into position. It was
1:30 P.M. By two o'clock artillery shells were landing behind
them. Then one struck the second tank in line. Elio Aleman,
the second in command of the Brigade's tank company, died
instantly. Gonzalo Carmenate, the commander of the first tank,
shouted that an enemy tank was concealed between the three
destroyed tanks in the curve. He fired his own gun and knocked
out the enemy with one shot. But Aleman's tank was in flames,
between the two others loaded with ammunition. A disastrous
explosion was imminent.

The boys got fire extinguishers from the tanks but it wasn't
sufficient," Oliva said, "I shouted to the tank crew that someone
had to take the tank out of there."

Jorge Alvarez, called the "little egg" by his comrades, ran
from his own tank, climbed into the burning vehicle and drove
away, with flames shooting up from the back and smoke pouring
from the top.

"I thought that man would never come back," Oliva said,
"but fifteen minutes later he came running into the line and
back to his own tank. I told him he was promoted to captain.
It was illogical but in a moment like that it was the only thing
that I could tell a man who had done such a thing."

The infantry was now upon them in hand-to-hand combat.
Their small forces were almost overwhelmed. Oliva called for
Pedro Avila's Company G of the Second Battalion to counterattack on the left flank. Company G advanced into woods
and tangled vegetation so thick they could not see the enemy
in front of them. They moved forward into intense fire from
machine guns and Czech grease guns. "You could see the

---

* This has been attested to by a number of soldiers interviewed at different
times and places.

branches break and the sap falling down and imagine what it was if it was your arm or leg," a soldier said.

A running battle began, a battle with shadows who shouted "Fatherland or Death!" and seemed to be everywhere and nowhere. "They had guts," a Brigade soldier said of the enemy, "they really had guts. They made themselves as if dead and when we passed they shot at us. So we had to shoot at everything we saw."

In a stupor of weariness, tormented by thirst and the heat of the day, the men fought on. The cries of the wounded rose in the woods, along with the shouts for water. "The only thing that you could hear in the air was bullets and more bullets," another soldier said, "and you holler to hell and nobody answers. In the battle you are not you, you are something else, you are an animal. You kill or you get killed. That's what they told us in Guatemala and that's the way it was."

"They were very brave," Oliva said, "and they stopped the advance."

Later, Oliva was criticized for sending Company G as a sacrifice and he himself said: "In a way they were right, but I tried to save the others."

Company G was cut off in the woods. Oliva ordered Rodolfo Díaz, the commanding officer of the tank company, to move forward toward the curve and support Company G. "After I repeated it twice, he went."

Avila, the Company G commander, called Oliva desperately. "Where is the tank you sent? I don't see it."

"I told Avila to throw a grenade to the place where the tank should go and I gave the order to Díaz again, and I told him what he should do: he should go over there and fight until all the company is out. So the tank went to the front again. I saw the explosion of the grenade, and the tank accomplished his mission well, and Avila's company could come out."

Oliva ordered his men to fall back two hundred yards into trenches. But by this time the mortars were out of ammunition; calamity seemed inevitable.

Williams had sent some men to Girón for more ammunition, but they said they could not find any. Certain he had seen boxes of mortar shells in a house at Girón, Williams himself walked back to the town accompanied by two men, a potato farmer called the *guajiro* and Oscar Vila. When Williams went back to Girón, he tried to find Pepe San Román to tell him the situation.

"I was coming back in the middle of the road there in Girón," Williams said, "when the *guajiro* told me, 'look at the blasting.' I heard the blasting two or three times and then it stopped so he said, 'This is very close, very close, Williams,' and I said, 'Which one?'" As Williams turned to look, a shell exploded next to him "and I was blown up in the air and there was a truck there. I was so high in the air I saw the .50-caliber machine gun on the truck below me. So I landed. When I came down I started looking for Vila, and he was almost dead, but I saw some movement in him. I could not move one side because I was hit in the neck." He called out to ask if his men were all right, and the *guajiro*, although badly wounded, said he was "O.K." Williams had been hit with more than seventy pieces of shrapnel. Both feet were smashed. He had a hole near his heart and a large one in his neck, he was unable to move his left arm and he had two broken ribs.

A jeep carrying a message for Pepe came by and picked up the men—Williams insisting that his men be taken first—and they were driven to San Román's post.

"I found him in front of me in the jeep," Pepe recalled, "lying there bleeding all over, as if he had exploded inside. He was lying there as a person that is going to die very soon. His eyes were still brilliant and he had the courage to tell me, 'I may not see it but I am sure we will win.' And then he shouted and I will never forget it, 'Beat them! Beat them!'"

Williams himself, seeing that Pepe was looking sadly at him, tried to reassure him and told San Román not to worry, that "*bicho malo nunca muere*" (a bad insect never dies). Then he was carried to a small concrete house on the beach where he was placed on a cot beside his two wounded comrades and several others.

LAST MESSAGE FROM PEPE. TO 2AW FLASH.

1. QUOTE. AM DESTROYING ALL MY EQUIPMENT AND COMMUNICA-
TIONS. TANKS ARE IN SIGHT. I HAVE NOTHING TO FIGHT WITH. AM
TAKING TO THE WOODS. I CANNOT WAIT FOR YOU. UNQUOTE.

The message clattered into Nicaragua by Morse code at 4:32 P.M.—the second message sent directly to the rear base. As soon as it was sent, Pepe took to the radio to talk for the last time with Gray on the *Blagar*.

"Gray, the enemy tanks are already into our position in Girón. Right here very close to us. You can hear the guns. I am ordering the retreat."

Gray begged him not to—"Hold on, we're coming, we're coming with everything."

"How long?" Pepe asked.

"Three to four hours." (The merchant ships would have arrived about 7 P.M.)

"That's not enough time. You won't be here on time. Farewell, friends, I am breaking this radio right now."

A sailor said: "I remember that the Americans started crying."

"Everyone was completely heartbroken, everybody was crying," Andy Pruna said. "Nobody talked." The merchant ships turned around and headed out into the Caribbean.

The end had come shortly after four o'clock when Rafael Torres Jiménez, the commander of the last tank defending the road north to San Blas came rumbling into Girón, saying the enemy tanks were five or six kilometers behind him, coming fast. Pepe dispatched messengers to Del Valle and Roberto in the north, the Fourth Battalion on the east and Oliva on the west, ordering them to separate and go into the woods and fight as company units until reinforcements came. Then he sent his formal messages, destroyed his equipment and with Artime, Ferrer, other staff officers and forty-six men headed into the Ciénaga de Zapata swamps.

Until the end they did not know they were beaten. They had walked back toward Girón, dirty and tired, throwing away their packs and shovels in the heat, but still hoping that something would happen. Some say they even believed this, too, was a part of the plan—a last maneuver to draw Castro's forces toward the beach where the airplanes would wipe them out.

"When I saw Girón it was the first time I realized that we had lost the war," a soldier said. "People without morale, people who didn't know what to do, people who were trying to get away." To another the sight of the shattered buildings and stripped trees—"as though a hurricane had passed"—and the confusion on the beach resembled "that picture you call Dunkirk. You ask where you are going. 'We don't know. We don't know.' We go to see the chief commander and we don't see anybody there." Castro's artillery still was pounding Girón. Shortly before five o'clock Del Valle, Roberto San Román and the paratroopers arrived at the beach in their jeep. They quickly learned of the order to disband but they didn't see Pepe. It was precisely at that moment that they saw two American destroyers, three or four miles away, approaching Playa Girón. "Let's get in that boat," Del Valle yelled, pointing to a fishing sailboat anchored offshore. The men took off their shirts and pants and swam to the boat. With twenty-two men aboard, they began paddling furiously with their hands. The boat did not move. In their desperation they had forgotten to cut the anchor rope. They cut it and then they moved out slowly toward the American destroyers.

Oliva had waited in his last lines of resistance for the final attack. But strangely there was a sudden unnerving calm on the battlefront. The minutes dragged by until at 4:15 Oliva left to go back to headquarters to talk to San Román.

What Oliva did not know was that Castro's forces had spotted the American destroyers coming fast toward Girón and had halted their advance on all fronts, not daring to move ahead if the Americans were going to land. From the beginning, too, Castro had miscalculated the Brigade forces. He assumed, from the casualties his men had suffered and from the continued fierce opposition, that the Brigade was still solidly entrenched and able to give battle. He also thought he was facing from five to eight thousand men. Not until 6 P.M. did his troops enter Girón. Had they gone forward at four o'clock San Román is convinced that at least 60 per cent of the Brigade would have died, "60 per cent, you can be sure of that." But Castro waited and once more enabled the Brigade to escape.

When Oliva left for Girón, he also did not know another vital fact: the messenger that Pepe had sent with the order to retreat had never reached him. (Later that messenger, Ramón E. Machado, said he tried to reach Oliva but the enemy barred the way.) At 4:30 Oliva was walking the mile and a half back

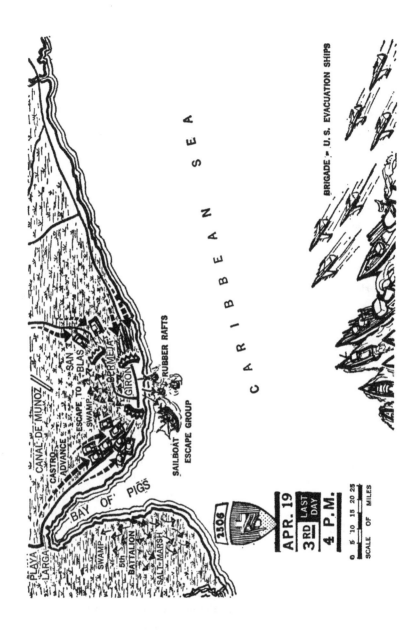

PLAYA LARGA

CANAL DE MUNOZ

CASTRO ADVANCE

SWAMP

5th BATTALION

SALT MARSH

BAY OF PIGS

ESCAPE TO SAN BLAS

SWAMP

SAN BLAS

PERMEJA

GIRON

RUBBER RAFTS

SAILBOAT ESCAPE GROUP

C A R I B B E A N   S E A

BRIGADE – U. S. EVACUATION SHIPS

2506

APR. 19
3RD LAST DAY
4 P.M.

0 5 10 15 20 25
SCALE OF MILES

to Brigade headquarters. When he was halfway there, he was picked up by a jeep. Something was wrong, he could tell—it was too quiet along the beach. A young radio operator named Humberto Cortina brought the first word of defeat. He came running toward Oliva, saying the headquarters staff had left. "That's impossible," Oliva snapped. He ordered the jeep driver to go faster.

He arrived at the command post and saw the equipment destroyed and the maps burned.

"Where is San Román?" Oliva asked. In the confusion someone said that San Román was escaping on the sailboat. (It was Roberto San Román in the boat, not Pepe.)

Thinking that he and his men had been betrayed by the Americans and abandoned by his own Brigade commander, Oliva, surrounded by three hundred of the Second and Sixth Battalions, tore off his shirt, shook his fist toward the sea and shouted that *he* would not abandon them; that they would die there like men facing the enemy. "I can still see Oliva standing there, shaking his fist," one said long after.

Young Amado Gayol, who had fought magnificently on the San Blas front, drew a pistol. He was going to shoot himself "because I didn't want my parents to suffer knowing I had been tortured and then executed."

But Oliva yelled at him, "No. You are a man. Not like those at sea."

Several yards down the beach the wounded Máximo Cruz crawled out of the infirmary and saw the American destroyers still moving toward the coast. He yelled to Padre Lugo who was walking away, "Father, Father. Don't leave. Here are the Americans. They have come to save us." As he was speaking, two artillery shells landed in front of the ships. The ships turned and left.

The frustration and rage poured out. Soldiers ran to a tank to try and shoot at the destroyers. Their hatred spilled over onto their own men. Brigade soldiers fired rifles trying to hit the men on the sailboat and also those who were leaving on rubber rafts. They were the final shots in the Bay of Pigs invasion. A soldier * watching the last American ship said: "In the wake of that ship goes two hundred years of infamy."

* Whose name is withheld at his request.

Oliva and his men blew up their tanks, shot their truck tires and destroyed their heavy equipment. Then they began marching in a column to the east. They had walked only five hundred yards when two T-33s and a Sea Fury attacked them. When one of the planes dived low, a soldier saw the Cuban flag on its wings. He felt, horribly, like an outlaw in his own land. The column broke and the men ran into the jungle. It was every man for himself.

Bulletin No. 6—the final one—was issued at 9 P.M. in New York.

"The Revolutionary Council wishes to make prompt and emphatic statement in the face of recent astonishing public announcements from uninformed sources. . . . The recent landings in Cuba have been constantly although inaccurately described as an invasion. It was, in fact, a landing of supplies and support for our patriots who have been fighting in Cuba for months and was numbered in the hundreds, not the thousands. . . . [Today's action] allowed the major portion of our landing party to reach the Escambray mountains. . . ."

In Miami, the closing markets edition of the *News* was still on the stands: "Rebel invaders claimed today to have driven 80 miles and linked up with guerrillas in the Escambray mountains to score their first big victory in the battle to topple Fidel Castro."

CHAPTER 4

THURSDAY: "DEFEAT IS AN ORPHAN"

When the battle was over, what Churchill calls the "terrible Ifs" began to accumulate. *If* the underground had been alerted in time and had launched a major sabotage campaign; *if* Nino Díaz had landed and fought his diversionary action in Oriente; *if* the second bombing raid on Monday had not been canceled; *if* the landing area had been explored and charted in advance; *if* military landing craft had been used instead of boats with outboard motors; *if* the military experts had recognized how damaging an unopposed T-33 jet trainer could be when armed with rockets; *if* fighter planes had accompanied the B-26s; *if* the Brigade had been trained to take alternative action as guerrillas; *if* the landing area had been adaptable for guerrilla action; *if* President Kennedy had not publicly stated that the United States would not intervene; *if* clouds had not obscured the target over San Antonio de los Baños Tuesday morning; *if* the B-26s had not been an hour early at Girón Wednesday morning; *if* so vast a majority of the mandatory supplies had not been loaded on the lost *Rio Escondido;* *if* the ships had succeeded in unloading the supplies; *if* the convoy had not fled so far and had been in time to land help; and the final, tantalizing "if"—*if* all these had taken place, would the Brigade have won?

At the moment of defeat there were no answers—only questions. President Kennedy's immediate concern after the final news from Girón was to make a public reckoning, to rally support at a time of crisis, and to make clear to the world the intentions of the United States. He and his advisors, principally Theodore C. Sorensen, began working on a speech at eleven o'clock Wednesday night. The final draft was not completed until an hour before it was delivered at noon Thursday to one thousand members and guests of the American Society of Newspaper Editors at the Statler-Hilton Hotel in Washington.

The speech marked a major change in United States policy. In the era of the Cold War, it stands in importance beside a very few documents and decisions: George Catlett Marshall's commencement address at Harvard University in 1947 inaugurating the Marshall Plan for the reconstruction of Europe; Harry S. Truman's decisions to send supplies to Berlin by air in 1948 and later to send troops into Korea in 1950; and John Foster Dulles' doctrine of "massive retaliation" throughout the 1950s in the Eisenhower years.

Ironically, the President spoke from the same rostrum in the same hotel before the same group that Fidel Castro had addressed two years earlier. (Castro had been conciliatory then and had spoken of democracy as the aim of the Cuban revolution.) When the President began, he appeared determined and rather grim as he explained his decision of the last twenty-four hours to discuss "the recent events in Cuba."

"On that unhappy island," he said, "as in so many other areas of the contest for freedom, the news has grown worse instead of better." While the United States had made it repeatedly clear that its armed forces would not intervene in Cuba, "let the record show that our restraint is not inexhaustible." The United States would not hesitate to intervene—alone, if necessary—to safeguard its security. And, "should that time ever come, we do not intend to be lectured on intervention by those whose character was stamped for all time on the bloody streets of Budapest. Nor should we expect or accept the same outcome which this small band of gallant Cuban refugees must have known they were chancing. . . ."

Cuba, he said, "was not an island unto itself" and "our concern is not ended with mere expressions of non-intervention or regret." He remarked that Castro had said the invaders were mercenaries and quoted Pepe San Román who, when asked if he wanted to be evacuated, said, "I will never leave this country."

"That is not the reply of a mercenary," the President said. "He has gone now to join in the mountains countless other guerrilla fighters who are equally determined that the dedication of those who gave their lives shall not be forgotten and that Cuba must not be abandoned. And we do not intend to abandon it either." The President turned to the future. "There are from this sobering episode," he said, "useful lessons for us all to learn. Some may be still obscure and await further information. Some are clear today."

Three main points were inescapable: *First*, "The forces of communism are not to be underestimated in Cuba or anywhere else in the world . . ."; *second*, the United States and the nations of the hemisphere "must take an ever closer and more realistic look at the menace of external Communist intervention and domination in Cuba"; and *third*, "it is clearer than ever that we face a relentless struggle in every corner of the globe that goes far beyond the clash of armies or even nuclear armaments."

It was also clear that "out of the rising din of Communist voices in Asia and Latin America" that "the complacent, the self-indulgent, the soft societies, are about to be swept away by the debris of history." Then the President laid down the new guidelines which would shape United States policies for the remainder of his administration.

"Too long we have fixed our eyes on traditional military needs; on armies prepared to cross borders; on missiles poised for flight. Now it should be clear that this is no longer enough: that our security may be lost, piece by piece, country by country, without the firing of a single missile or the crossing of a single border. We intend to profit from this lesson. We intend to reexamine and reorient our forces of all kinds; our tactics and our institutions here in this community. We intend to intensify our efforts for a struggle in many ways more difficult than war, where disappointments will often accompany us."

He closed dramatically: "History will record the fact that this bitter struggle reached its climax in the late Nineteen Fifties and the early Nineteen Sixties. Let me then make clear as the President of the United States that I am determined upon our system's survival and success, regardless of the cost and regardless of the peril."

The eloquent words and the fighting stance did not alter the embittering fact that the Bay of Pigs had been a devastating defeat for the United States. And for Kennedy, who hated to lose even more than most, it also was a deep personal defeat. As the President remarked ruefully to reporters later, "There is an old saying that victory has one hundred fathers and defeat is an orphan." The orphan was on his doorstep.

Defeat came in different forms. At Homestead Air Force Base, the Cubans were told not to lose faith—in fifteen days they would be called again. Then they got on trucks and left the base. At Base Trax in Guatemala the Americans assembled the men and spoke with what Jose Quintana called "great emotion." "They were very sorry they had lost the war and they said that they were willing to go over there. Almost they cried. It is my personal opinion that they love those people in the Brigade."

The men lingered at Base Trax until days later when Miró Cardona and Tony Varona came and said they must return to Miami. At Key West, Jimmy came on Thursday and told Llansó and the other Cubans the invasion was a failure. Bill and Max had tears in their eyes when they helped the Cubans unload the weapons from the boats used by infiltration teams. At Gesu Catholic Church in Miami candles were burning and women were kneeling silently in prayer while blocks away other Cuban women were kneeling in front of the statue of Martí in Bayfront Park, chanting, praying and waving placards demanding that the United States act. To the few remaining underground radio stations still operating inside Cuba came the last message from Carl on Thursday: TRY TO SURVIVE.

While the survivors struggled to comply, pundits began their post-mortems. Even then some could not accept the result. Widely printed throughout the country that Thursday was a story by William L. Ryan, the Associated Press's foreign news analyst, which implied that Castro had been killed. "What has happened to him?" Ryan asked on the front pages of the nation's papers. "Is he just playing it safe, cagily staying in the background until the smoke clears? That would be unlike him. Has he been shoved aside by the Communists? It is possible. Is Castro still among the living? He was reported to have been fishing in the Bay of Cochinos area when the first anti-Castro guerrillas hit the beach over the weekend and may have been in the area of fragmentation bombing. Whatever the answer to these questions, it seems likely that something has happened to change the status of Fidel."

Something indeed had happened. Fidel was stronger than ever and exulting in his triumph. And he was not so difficult to find. Since Wednesday night he had been in Playa Girón where, in fact, someone *had* tried to kill him.

In the house near the sea where Enrique Ruiz-Williams lay, the wounded were suddenly confronted by the person of Fidel Castro. Williams, carrying seventy wounds, both minor and major, recognized him at once. He groped under his thin mattress and tried to reach a .45 pistol he had concealed there earlier in the afternoon. Williams does not know whether he really drew the gun and pulled the trigger and the pistol did not go off, or whether he simply made the gesture and failed to get the weapon. Those lying there with him are certain only that he made such a gesture. All agree, however, on what happened next.

Castro said, "What are you trying to do, kill me?" and Williams replied, "That's what I came here for. We've been trying to do that for three days." Castro was not angry.

A militia police captain reached down and patted Williams and said, "Take it easy. Take it easy. You're in bad shape."

Castro asked, "Is there an American here?" and snapped a flashlight into the faces of the wounded men in the room. The door had been blown off its hinges during the bombing that afternoon. He reached down, picked it up and uncovered Oscar Vila who had been standing next to Williams when the shell exploded. "This man is dead," Castro said. He dropped the door. Then Castro gave orders: "These men can't stay here. Take them to Covadonga and put them in the hospital."

Even in his hour of glory, his time to boast of crushing in less than seventy-two hours an invasion prepared, as he said, "by all the sages of the Pentagon and of the Government of the United States," Castro was unable to sit back. After the President spoke, Castro told his people on television that "now they threaten direct intervention. . . ." Castro's words that day were perhaps the most revealing he had uttered since assuming power. Triumphant, and yet marked by fear of what might be coming, they conceded a great deal that he later tried to conceal.

"Are we going to be frightened because we hear that the United States Marines are going to come?" he asked. "No, we are not going to be frightened. The soldiers of imperialism are also made of flesh and bones, and bullets go through them, too. . . . Look, even if they dropped atomic bombs here, there would always remain part of the people to go on struggling. That is: we must fear nothing, nothing at all; we must have no fear, maintain our serenity, because the events that will be unleashed as a consequence of an aggression against Cuba will definitely not end in Cuba. . . . Our duty is to resist; to resist is to plant ourselves on the ground and fight against any enemy that comes with whatever he brings. Do you understand? To resist is to prepare our spirit and our mind to resist whatever may come; the bombs they drop, the planes that come; in that case they would have a total superiority in the air, so that what we have to do is build a lot of trenches, a lot of foxholes to defend ourselves, because after all, they can't have a bomb for every man in every trench."

While, in Marxist rationale, Castro was certain that "imperialism is . . . historically condemned to vanish," nevertheless "we don't want imperialism to commit suicide at our expense. I mean to commit suicide by attacking us."

Castro also disclosed how drastically his overwhelmingly superior forces had suffered. (Much later, he attempted to show that his men suffered only slight casualties. He gave that same report to all observers, newsmen and government officials. But before his own people, that day immediately after the invasion, he was more candid.)

"As for the casualties, our forces suffered a lot of casualties. These casualties are due, in the first part, to the fact that on the first day they parachuted forces in the rear of our forces that were defending the beaches; they had to struggle to prevent being surrounded, and had a lot of casualties. In the second place, the battalion from Matanzas, that was advancing to reinforce the men who were fighting at the beach, also suffered casualties as a consequence of their air force, of their air attack. The attack on Playa Larga also caused casualties, because it had to be carried out on a road that was completely covered by the fire of enemy mortars and cannons. On the day we attacked, that we marched from Playa Larga to Playa Girón, the attack of the

United States 'Sabre' jets caused a lot of casualties in the column. During the attack on Girón on the 19th there were also casualties, because it was an attack that had to be carried out on very rough ground, and they had dug very good trenches there, and our people continued the attack, and had casualties. And also in the area of San Blas; wherever our forces attacked, they had to attack against the heavy fire of automatic weapons, mortars and anti-tank cannons. . . ."

His own analysis of the fighting indicated that "This experience shows the need of attaching the greatest importance to the question of training of the units, and the training of the officers." On balance, he said, "it is possible that the same thing [victory] could have been achieved with less casualties, had our troops been more experienced. . . ."

Those were concessions that Fidel Castro never made again about the Bay of Pigs invasion.

The exact number of casualties is, at best, a guessing game. But a conservative estimate places Castro's losses at 1,250 dead on the battlefield. Approximately four hundred more died later as a result of wounds and lack of medicine and medical equipment. More than two thousand were wounded.*

It was important for Castro to discredit those who had inflicted such losses. They must not be thought of as patriots, even misguided ones. From that time on he repeatedly indicted the Brigade as mercenaries, war criminals, thieves, smugglers, "immoral and shameless people that plundered this country in a criminal manner . . ."

In another way, Castro revealed more than he intended when he attempted to justify the acts of terror his government had instituted during the invasion. "The need was felt to arrest all suspects, all those people who for one reason or another could be active, or could act, or would make moves to aid the counter-revolution. When such a measure is taken, naturally, some injustices are always committed, but it is unavoidable. . . . I repeat that there could have been cases of injustice, and even cases of some revolutionary arrested by mistake, but that is understood by those who are revolutionary. . . ."

---

* This estimate is not based on any official information or documents; it comes from Castro's doctors who were in the combat zones and who treated the wounded in the hospitals.

The battle was over but, Castro said, it must not be forgotten. "Those comrades who have fallen in the combats of Playa Larga, Playa Girón, San Blas, Yaguaramas, in all those places, deserve the most beautiful monuments, and they deserve that right there, some place in the Zapata Swamps, a great monument be built for the fallen. . . ."

As he spoke, the Brigade was going through its ordeal in those swamps.

CHAPTER 5

THE SWAMPS

"It was very curious, that swamp. It had no water."
"It was very difficult to move in. It was full of thorns."
"I saw Coke bottles dancing before me. I was going mad."
"I remember thinking, 'I'm going to fill myself from here to here.' I had a thing in my mind about the water."
"Every day we were getting weaker and dizzier."
"I caught a snake but I couldn't eat it. It made me sick."
"When you are hungry, you eat anything."

Each man had his story. For three days they had fought without rest and with little food or water. Then, in small groups, afraid to stop, almost too tired to go on, numb and bitter from defeat, they crawled through the swamps—trying to get through to the mountains, to a town or finally to firm ground. A very few made it.

Time itself became a haze and the hours of daylight and darkness blurred into one. The more religious prayed constantly. Some said their prayers were answered. Others tried and gave up in despair. For the lucky ones, water was found—under a smooth white stone or in a small pond. The maddening thirst and gnawing hunger drove the rest to desperation—to drinking urine, to eating insects from under the bark of trees, to chasing lizards and snakes and eating them raw and drinking the blood.

Constantly overhead was the whirring sound of Castro's helicopters and the monotonous and continual burst of his machine guns firing aimlessly into the woods, everywhere and anywhere. Artillery shells raked the area and the few roads through the swamps were swarming with patrols. Castro's men made no effort to go after the Brigade; the Brigade had to come to them.

Tormented and tortured, slowly dying, many remember suddenly losing their senses: a man cut into a cactus for the soft, spongy substance that contained the precious moisture and discovered he had cut off the head of a frog. He began worrying about the frog and then thinking, "Am I going mad? How can I be worried about a frog after all I have been through?" A son was seen to stand up suddenly in the night and fire his submachine gun toward his father. He has never remembered doing it.

At first there was always the fear of being detected. Birds flew by and the men argued about whether to shoot them or throw stones at them. Most threw stones—and seldom hit their targets. If they were fortunate enough to catch a bird or a reptile or even a chicken, they ate it raw rather than risk a fire. Some tried to escape by swimming along the coast line at night and resting during the day. One group even succeeded in getting to an island and surviving for a week on weeds and birds until they made a smoke signal and Castro's militia arrived the next day.

Each man was certain he would be shot if captured. But as the days passed, even that fear changed until many didn't care what happened. Their camouflage uniforms had hidden them well, but eventually they were forced to the roads where they stumbled into the arms of enemy patrols. Some tried to hide along the beach. "We found two cans of Russian meat. It was like Santa Claus being there. We ate this in the sand." They heard voices from the north. They ran to the south and heard voices coming that way. They tried to cover themselves with sand. They were captured. Some decided to surrender—often suddenly and without logic. "I saw a man beside his teenage son. I saw two brothers. All normal men, all of a sudden in this mess. So I said, 'This is it. I'm going to present [surrender].'" Others were willing to face the firing squad—anything but the terrible thirst.

In the act of surrender the fear of the unknown—of death or perhaps torture—soon gave way to astonishment. "Militiaman, militiaman. We surrender! We surrender!" and the militiaman screamed in terror and called for help. "I saw they were simple little men involved in this thing just like me. I wasn't afraid any more."

A Brigade soldier cried out, "Shoot us but, in the name of humanity, give us water first!"

One of Castro's men replied, "There isn't going to be any shooting here," and he handed over his canteen. On the trucks and station wagons, on the way back to Girón, some militiamen threw them oranges, laughing and saying, "You threw bullets and we throw oranges."

By their looks and by their manners, however, the militia made it clear that Castro's forces actually believed the Brigade was a mercenary force. The prisoners were stripped of their personal belongings—watches, pens, wallets, wedding rings, pictures, belts—for souvenirs for the militia. Some handed over their belongings without comment. But there were cases of stubborn bravery. A militiaman asked for a soldier's boots. "No," the soldier said, "I gave you the watch, my pen and my chain, but not my boots." He couldn't explain it later—but he would rather have died than give up his boots. The militiaman shouted and cursed. "He said his boots were torn and mine were new. Then I said, 'That's why I came back to Cuba, to put some new boots on you.'"

Girón was a scene of confusion: long lines of soldiers, jeeps and trucks and buses; nurses and officers; newspapermen, television cameramen and photographers; and Chinese, Czechs and Russians in civilian clothes—all moving about with a sense of importance. The center of attention, the objects of scorn and shouts, were the prisoners. Dirty, disheveled, gaunt, unshaven, most wearing only the T-shirts and pants their captors had left them, they came into the town in long lines, bound together, poked by bayonets. They were silent and grim.

"I knew when I saw Girón that it was something historic," a soldier said.

They were approached by European and Asian newspapermen and women. A tall, blonde French girl asked a prisoner why he had come and he replied: "To fight Communists." After more questions, the girl remarked in disgust that he had been completely brainwashed by the imperialists. Stung, the prisoner spoke back: "I'm glad I came in the invasion." "You're crazy," the girl said and turned and walked away.

The prisoners were taken to the unfinished tourist houses

where they slept on the floor amid the oppressive smell of toilets that had no water. When they spoke at all, their words were bitter. "Everybody was very resentful of the U.S. government," said Dr. Juan Sordo. "Everyone thought we had been stranded and left to die, for Fidel to kill us all and have a piece of Hungary for himself. I myself felt resentful and very bitter, because of the lost opportunity of freeing Cuba. I took it for granted I was going to be shot. But I was so disconnected from the reality of the situation that I didn't care. I was nearly starved and I only wanted to sleep." Rest was not easy. The militia shouted insults during the night and warned the prisoners they would be shot —not then, but later—always later.

They ate and drank and for the time that was enough. Occasionally, there were moments of joy when a son was reunited with a father, brother with brother or simply friends with friends. One of the strangest and most touching of the many reunions occured when Roberto and Adrian Maciá, who had been captured during the day, were thrown into a house on the beach at night. It was dark inside and the Maciá brothers—members of one of the most respected families in Cuba—woke up two prisoners asleep on the floor. Incredibly, the two turned out to be their brothers-in-law, Luis Entrialgo and Francisco Rodríguez. "It was a crazy chance," Roberto Maciá said. "They had been taken that day, too. We started yelling and shouting and embracing each other, and outside they must have thought that we were crazy because we stayed up all night talking." They did not talk of a missing brother, Jorge Maciá, who had been on the *Río Escondido*. All were certain he was dead. Not until months later did they learn that Jorge had been picked up by a ship and taken back to the United States.

Of all the prisoners, Negroes received the worst treatment. Their presence in the invasion force infuriated Castro. It was contrary to the impression of a united, happy Cuba that Castro was assiduously trying to cultivate.* Ramón Quintana's experience as a prisoner told of a different Cuba.

* After the invasion Castro claimed that the Brigade had contained almost no Negroes. Without attempting to check, many writers believed him. One of the most notable examples was a *Look Magazine* article by Laura Bergquist in March, 1963. After talking to Castro, Miss Bergquist wrote that the invasion was doomed from the start because the Brigade was composed of *Batistianos,* the privileged, "and almost no Negroes."

Quintana, twenty-three years old, small and so black that he was nicknamed "Lumumba" in the Brigade, was captured with two others, one of them white, after eleven days in the swamps. The white man was brought back to Girón, but Quintana and the other Negro were tied to an orange tree with thistles. Their tongues were so swollen from drinking urine and from lack of food that they could hardly speak. For nearly three hours they were kept tied to the tree in the heat of the day while the militia shouted insults and called them "niggers." "Niggers. Why do you come? Why do you come with the Yankees when they treat the Negro no good?"

Finally, they were taken to Girón where Castro himself questioned them. Angrily Castro told them they were guilty of treason on two counts: they had betrayed their country and betrayed their race.

After Castro left, Osmani Cienfuegos said they were going to be shot. Quintana and two other Negroes were taken outside, lined up and told: "We're going to shoot you now, niggers, then we're going to make soap out of you." After more curses and more pointing of rifles, they were taken back inside. Throughout their imprisonment, the Negroes in the Brigade suffered most at the hands of their captors.

Girón became a propaganda show, carefully staged and enacted under the eyes of the cameras. Militia, draped with remnants of camouflage uniforms and dangling loot, waved the captured weapons of imperialism for the cameras. Anyone who in any way could be considered important was taken to be interviewed.

One of the first was José Antonio (Pepito) Miró, the son of Miró Cardona. Miró, thirty-three years old, a lawyer with three children, was captured along with others in the Second Battalion one day after the fighting ceased. When he was brought to Girón, he was photographed and then questioned by Carlos Rafael Rodríguez. (Rodríguez, one of the earliest Communists to join Castro in the Sierra Maestra, later the editor of the Communist paper *Hoy*, then the President of the INRA, ranks with Raúl Castro and Che Guevara in the ruling Cuban hierarchy.) He startled young Miró by asking him first, "How is Frank?" And then, in turn, how were Pat, Jimmy and Seabee —all of the top Americans at Base Trax. Miró said he didn't know any of them. Rodríguez asked Miró his position in the Brigade. When Miró answered, "I am a private," Rodríguez did not believe him. Surely, he had to be one of the leaders. Miró refused to give any other information and he was sent to rejoin the other prisoners.

Castro and his men were looking for the top prizes, the leaders. The first break came on the fourth day, Sunday, April 23, when Oliva was captured.

Oliva had tried to reach the Escambray, but his luck had been even worse than some. "In the four days we did not have any water," he said. "We didn't find anything to eat. I had very bad luck because we never found snakes or anything." At the end he was reduced to drinking urine. The day before he was captured, he took his pistol and almost shot himself. "Then I thought of my family and I thought I was a coward for doing that, because my family would never know if I was dead or alive. So it was better to go on and see what was going to happen." He was taken prisoner when he was spotted trying to cross the road in the vicinity of San Blas with a small group. A large patrol flushed them out and they gave up. "There was no use shooting there; we didn't have a chance."

At Girón, Major Fernández, the military commander who had fought against Oliva at Playa Larga, took him aside. They had served together under Fidel and Fernández was kind. He asked how Oliva had let "those people" get him mixed up in the invasion. "I made a decision at that moment," Oliva said. "I was sure that they were going to kill me. So I thought that I should keep a straight line in front of the enemy and die with dignity. I told him that I would always fight communism and the only reason they had captured me was because I ran out of ammunition."

When a Russian newspaperwoman tried to interview Oliva, Fernández told her that all Oliva had to answer was his name, rank and serial number. She left. On Tuesday night Che Guevara and his staff came to see him. Why did he leave Cuba? Because they were Communists. Did he know what treason meant? Yes, death and the *paredón*. Wasn't he afraid of death? "Yes. I was also afraid of the dentist when he took out four teeth."

They left Oliva alone and waited for Artime and San Román to turn up. Besides, Oliva was a Negro and it wasn't in Castro's interests to publicize that fact. Oliva's picture was not printed along with many other prisoners and he was not taken before the television cameras.

Pepe and Artime had separated after several days and each continued with a group of ten men. Pepe's group had separated again—and still again—until by the sixth day Pepe had only one man with him. Unlike Oliva, Pepe had found both food and water. He and his men had eaten a raw chicken, bones and all, and killed a cow and eaten it until the meat spoiled. Ramón Ferrer had first discovered the possibility of water. Under rocks they dug until the ground became moist. They continued digging for an entire afternoon, taking out dirt with a canteen, carefully scattered it so as not to give away their position, until at last they struck water. For two days they stayed by the waterhole and then separated into smaller groups.

Pepe was captured while trying to get back to the water. He walked straight into a militia patrol that was lost in the woods on Tuesday afternoon, April 25. When the militiamen asked who he was, Pepe gave them another name. He was certain he was going to be executed, but when that time came he wanted everyone to know how he died, rather than being shot and left deep in the swamps, his death a mystery to his men and to his family. But to his surprise the militia were kind.

"Oh, my brother, now you are in good hands. Don't be afraid! You will see how good we are."

"They gave us sardines and beans and tuna fish and things like that and we ate as if we were dogs after a hunt," Pepe said.

The prisoners were lined up in a single file late in the morning and waited until their names were called to get aboard a large trailer truck for the trip to Havana. Standing beside the truck, in charge of the operation, was Osmani Cienfuegos, the Minister of Public Works. Calling the names was Fernández Vila, an official in the INRA. The truck was American-made, the kind used on express highways—aluminum, plywood stripping inside and only two doors, one on each side in the middle of the truck.

Cienfuegos was taunting the men as they got aboard: they were cowards, *latifundistas* (large land owners), *Batistianos*, mercenaries. When Oliva's name was called Vila said, "This is the second-in-command."

"What have you got to say?" Cienfuegos asked.

Oliva said he would only give his name, rank and serial number. Vila shouted that he was insulting Cienfuegos and Oliva snapped back, "Keep your mouth shut. I remember you as the thief in the INRA."

In the midst of the argument Cienfuegos ordered Oliva taken away. It may be that Cienfuegos thus saved Oliva's life. San Román was not among those in the first group and he, too, was spared what followed.

By the time one hundred men had been packed into the truck the prisoners were shouting, "No more. No more. We can't breathe." Cienfuegos was unmoved. Máximo Cruz' name was called and now even Vila was concerned by the shouts from inside the truck.

"Sir," Vila protested, "we can't put any more in. They will die."

Cienfuegos' reply is burned into the memory of those men. "Let them die! It will save us from shooting them."

He waved his arm and ordered "forty more pigs" put on the truck.

When there were 149 men on the truck, the two doors were closed and bolted and the trip began. It was one o'clock of a hot, sunny afternoon. In the total darkness inside there was panic: men shouting, packed solidly against each other, desperately struggling for air. "It was the terrible heat," one man said. "Sweat ran like a river."

Terrified, the men ripped off their clothes and beat on the walls with their fists and rocked the truck, vainly trying to turn it over—anything to stop it. From everywhere came shouts and screams: "Oh, my god! I have no air! I have no air! I am going to die!" To one man, it was "like Dante's inferno"; to another, "it was an enemy you couldn't fight. I'd much rather be shot." With belt buckles they scratched and clawed on the aluminum walls until they succeeded in making a few holes, measuring from a quarter of an inch to two inches long. They fought for the chance to reach these holes and the air. "When you are going to die," one said, "the first is a very deep sleep. If you sleep, you die." When a man began to pass out, he was grabbed and placed in front of one of the holes until he revived and then another would take his place. On and on the truck drove, never stopping. From time to time, when the driver applied his brakes, the sloshing of sweat on the floor could be heard. When the sun went down, moisture on the walls and ceiling condensed and "it began to rain for us." Men began to die.

Eight hours after they left Girón the truck stopped. When it did the pounding and shouting increased. From outside the prisoners heard voices ordering them to be quiet or the doors would not be opened. For what seemed an eternity they were quiet. Then the doors were opened. The prisoners staggered out, falling "like leaves," stumbling over their comrades, their faces turned black, yellow, gray. Nine men were dead. Another died after he was taken outside.

The Brigade had reached Havana.

Castro had ordered the militia not to shoot the prisoners. His reasons are a matter of conjecture. Yet it seems clear that he acted, not out of humanitarian instincts, but out of self-protection; for he had warned in advance that the invaders would be killed and certainly his record of approving mass executions for "enemies of the people" had revealed how little he valued human life or public opinion. There is no question, as shown in his own words, that after President Kennedy spoke Castro feared United States intervention. It also seems apparent that he did not want to give the United States any excuse to invade. The execution of the prisoners might have presented such an opportunity. To make sure that Castro understood his words were not a bluff, the President kept two United States Navy task forces, each including an aircraft carrier, on patrol off Cuba with several thousand Marines in battle gear aboard LCNs (Landing Craft, Navy). And immediately after the President's speech, two British navy frigates were ordered to prepare to go to Cuba.

Although the survivors of the Brigade had every reason to think they had been forgotten during their ordeal in the swamps, the United States took steps that stopped just short of intervention to try to save them. On Wednesday night, CINCLANT was notified that the order authorizing air cover and the right to return fire if fired upon was rescinded. Instead, CINCLANT was instructed to maintain a safe haven for the Brigade ships fifteen miles offshore. On Thursday and Friday, the destroyers were ordered to patrol the shore at night to evacuate any survivors they could find—and commanders were authorized to *ground their ships and use air cover if necessary.*

Even these measures were not enough. To carry out the evacuation, landing parties would have had to go ashore.

On Saturday morning the Cuban frogmen from aboard the *Barbara J,* along with the Americans, Rip and Gray, were taken to the carrier *Essex* for a conference with an admiral. The admiral told them that Navy reconnaissance planes had spotted many men still in the swamps who would die if they were not rescued. He asked if the frogmen would be willing to go ashore, and pick up the men. They agreed; then they left to talk to the pilots who had made the flights.

The pilots had no insignia, rank or identification, and their planes were painted black and also carried no identifying marks. They explained where they had sighted the men—principally on the west coast of the Bay of Pigs, and among many small keys at the southwestern entrance to the Bay.

Early the next morning the frogmen and Gray and Rip headed for the shore. Three hundred yards from the coast they saw a naked man floating, holding on to a large piece of wood. It was Jorge Tarafa of the Fifth Battalion, who had been a classmate of Carlos Font. They pulled him aboard and Jorge began yelling, "Please don't shoot me!"

"Jorge, don't you know me?" Font said. "I am Carlos from school."

Tarafa didn't respond at first. When he recovered, he explained that he was trying to reach the destroyer with his piece of wood. He was the first of more than thirty men rescued by the frogmen.

As soon as they got to the beach they found two more men, who said there were others back in the swamp. They went into the swamps and found three more men, naked except for T-shirts. The frogmen were shocked at their appearance.

"It's amazing what those men had lost in such a few days," Andy Pruna said. "They looked like skeletons. They were full of cuts from the mangroves. The roots are very sharp and their feet were cut and infected. They didn't have any water or anything to eat. They looked very bad. Their eyes were sunken, their skin gray and cracked from the sun and the sea." One of the rescued men, from the Second Battalion, said that he had fought until he was the only man in his unit left alive and then, out of ammunition, he had taken to the swamps.

Frogmen searched the shore line while navy planes flew overhead trying to spot survivors and six American destroyers stood by offshore. After carrying survivors back to a destroyer, the frogmen returned late in the afternoon. They found a wounded man lying on the shore, unconscious, battered by the waves. They revived him with oxygen and then began giving him a transfusion. Thinking they were taking blood from his body rather than giving it to him, he became hysterical and begged them not to kill him. In his delirium, the man believed he had been taken prisoner by Castro—and he had heard that before a man was shot the militia took blood for plasma for the revolution.*

Through the night and into the next day they searched for survivors. Along a canal they found two men, one dead and the other unconscious. When the latter came to, he whispered so faintly that they had to lean over to hear him, "Did we win? Did we win?"

Everyone stopped and looked at each other.

"What did he say? What did he say?" Gray asked. They told him. Gray also became quiet. Then he said, "Tell him that we are going to win."

They carried the survivor to the whaleboat and returned to bury the other. He was a young man. They took off his wedding ring and began digging a grave. When they tried to bury him, the feet wouldn't go in. They dug the hole deeper and tried again. There was a pause. "Nobody wanted to put the earth on his face. It was a kind of quiet face. Finally we didn't look and we put the earth on his face." Rip made two sticks for a cross, Carlos Font said three Hail Marys and they went back to the destroyer.

On the ship they learned that radar on another destroyer had detected a small sailboat farther out in the sea.

---

* Other Cubans contend this actually has been done.

CHAPTER 6

THE BOAT

They were twenty-two men on a twenty-two-foot sail-boat. In the few hours before dark they sailed toward the American destroyers, away from Girón and away from the sound of battle. The wind was south and they were heading straight toward the larger ships on the horizon. Night came. They never saw the destroyers again.

Most of them were paratroopers who had followed their commander Del Valle aboard the boat; but there were also men from the headquarters company, from the Third Battalion of infantry and from Roberto San Román's Heavy Gun Battalion. Thrown together by chance in the desperate moments of defeat, they were representative of the Brigade: they ranged in age from eighteen to forty-three; they were humble men, educated men and one of them had been an Ambassador. Only one had had experience with a sailboat.

That first night, Wednesday, April 19, they entered shallow water and ran aground close to the lighthouse of Cayo Guano, south of the Bay of Pigs. An argument broke out: some wanted to go to the lighthouse, kill the occupants and take what food there was; the others were opposed. Del Valle and Roberto San Román, as the principal leaders aboard, decided against an attack. The men jumped into the water and pushed until the boat was free, and they sailed on.

In the morning they examined the boat more closely: they found a small water tank about a quarter full and a storage bin filled with fish. The three or four on top were edible, but underneath the fish were rotten and had to be thrown overboard. With a cigarette lighter and the few pieces of charcoal on board, the fish were cooked, cut into small pieces and divided. They drank the water and ate the fish. It was the nearest thing to a meal they had while on the boat.

On the second day, Friday, they caught two small fish with a hook tied to a lighted flashlight as bait. José García Montes, thirty-seven years old, who had been Cuba's Ambassador to Japan, a thoughtful, quiet man whom everyone respected, was appointed to cut the fish. While they stood watching silently, he carefully cut the fish into twenty-two tiny pieces, and took the last piece himself. They ate the fish raw, including its intestines. That night a storm came up and the boat was tossed about so severely they were certain it was their last moment. All night long they bailed with small tin cans, fearing they were about to capsize. Roberto San Román was so convinced it was the end that he pulled a piece of shrapnel from his face "just to see how big it was. We were thinking it was the last day on earth." The boat weathered the storm and on Saturday they were greeted again by bright sunshine.

Their first two days served as a pattern for the others. They took turns at the rudder and keeping the single sail to the wind. And always they talked—about the battle, about the hated Americans, about what fools they had been to let themselves get in such a trap. Del Valle and Roberto tried to steer the conversation away from the invasion—not out of loyalty to the Americans, but in an attempt to maintain morale.

There were quarrels about what they should do. Some, especially those with relatives in Cuba, wanted to go back and land on the western coast of Cuba in Pinar del Rio Province, but Del Valle and Roberto convinced them to go with the wind. By now the coast certainly would be heavily patrolled. So they sailed on.

The sun was a punishment. On the first day, someone had suggested they lean over the boat close to the water and let the waves refresh them. Soon, when they were not attending to the boat, everyone was leaning overboard, splashing water over their bodies. It became almost an obsession: some even tried to put water in their ears, in their nostrils, anywhere that it might possibly soak into their body and save them. They would use the tin cans to dip up the water and pour it over one another. When a man would drop his can and lose it, violent accusations would be made. Because of the size of the boat, they had to sleep in layers—a head on someone's stomach, feet on someone else.

When they lost sight of the destroyers they planned to sail due south toward Grand Cayman Island, a British possession. But after the storm on the second night the wind changed from south to southwest, and they knew it was going to be a long trip.

"The thing that mattered then was to get someplace," Roberto said, "because after the second day we knew that nobody was looking for us."

For four more days they sailed southwest. Occasionally, they would see ships far off, and occasionally planes, flying very high. Each time, no matter how far off or how high, everyone started yelling, climbing the mast and waving furiously. Those who still had shirts held them into the wind and waved them back and forth. Each time, when the ship or plane was out of sight, everyone slumped back into the boat and began cursing the United States again.

On the fourth full day, Raúl García Menocal, twenty-one years old, the scion of a family that had produced presidents of Cuba, said he remembered reading that if you placed a cork over a bottle of urine and dropped it in the ocean the salt water would filter through the cork and the urine would become sweet and purified after an hour. Many men urinated in bottles, put the corks on and dropped them into the sea, tied by a string. Before half an hour had gone by, Menocal could not wait. He pulled up his bottle and drank. The experiment had not worked. He was so angry that he threw the bottle down, and from that time on as soon as he urinated he drank.

Each day they had been dropping their line overboard with the flashlight, and on the fifth day a shark nearly as large as the boat itself grabbed the bait and was hooked. For more than an hour, Del Valle and Armando López-Estrada, one of his airborne officers, fought to land him. Three or four times they succeeded in bringing the shark alongside, only to have it rush off with the line. At one point, Del Valle said he was going to jump overboard and kill the shark with a knife, and his men had to restrain him. When the shark was pulled close the last time, Del Valle hit it over the head with a paddle. The shark

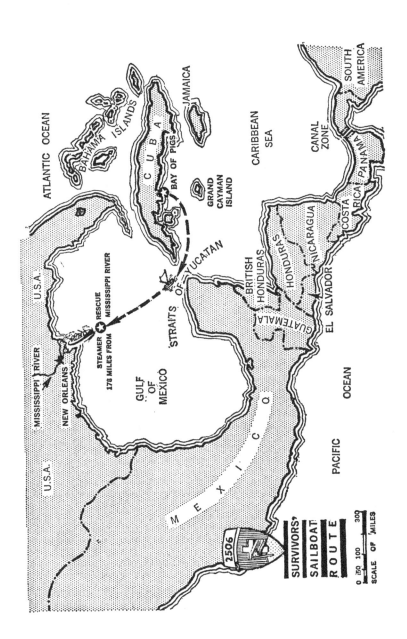

ATLANTIC OCEAN

BAHAMA ISLANDS

JAMAICA

CUBA

BAY OF PIGS

GRAND CAYMAN ISLAND

CARIBBEAN SEA

CANAL ZONE

SOUTH AMERICA

COSTA RICA

PANAMA

U.S.A.

MISSISSIPPI RIVER

NEW ORLEANS

STEAMER RESCUE 178 MILES FROM MISSISSIPPI RIVER

STRAITS OF YUCATAN

BRITISH HONDURAS

HONDURAS

NICARAGUA

EL SALVADOR

GUATEMALA

U.S.A.

GULF OF MEXICO

M E X I C O

PACIFIC OCEAN

2506

SURVIVORS' SAILBOAT R O U T E

SCALE OF MILES

0   50 100   300

got loose, the paddle was broken and the flashlight was lost. For one long day that shark followed the boat.

On the crude chart they were making they traced their course: from south to southwest. Then a wind shift forced them to turn northwest and it became apparent they were not going to reach even Central America. Although morale was steadily getting lower, it was not until the sixth day that they received their first great shock.

Inocente R. García, a quiet man, called the "uncle" by everyone, at forty-three was the oldest man on the boat. He knew something about a fishing boat, and he had helped to distribute the men so their weight would be better balanced. Since the beginning he had been coughing and by the end of the fifth day had become worse. He was lying in the boat, half conscious, calling for water and talking incoherently—about his mother, his friends or the war. He turned almost yellow and, to their horror, the men saw green pus coming from his eyes. When they awoke in the morning he was dead.

Del Valle seemed even more shocked than the rest: García had been one of his men, he had trained him and led him. A bitter argument began over what to do with the body.

"He didn't want to bury that man in the ocean," Roberto said. "I told him that his corpse was destroying our morale. Del Valle said, 'Let's wait a few hours to see if we are rescued and we can deliver his body to his family.'"

The rest of the men were equally divided. In the end Del Valle agreed to the burial. Someone spoke a brief eulogy, they knelt and said the rosary and the body, heavily weighted, was thrown into the sea.

García's death was a heavy blow. As they became weaker, they began talking constantly about food—the food they had thrown away in Guatemala, the food they were going to eat when they got back—and always about water and juices. They began making resolutions: they were going to be better husbands and fathers; they were going to work hard and make their families proud of them. Del Valle, who was single, told Roberto, who was married and had children, that he was going to get married and go to New York with him and forget about the war.

After García died the boat ran into a dead calm. For twenty-five hours they drifted under the broiling sun with the sail hanging slack. The cursing increased. In the midst of the calm a ship passed—close enough, it seemed, to see them. Again men climbed wearily up the mast and waved their tattered clothes and shouted. While they tried to attract attention, the rest laboriously cut part of a spar in two with dull combat knives until they had two rough paddles. Then they took turns paddling toward the ship. Some of the men were so weak that they were unable even to lift the paddle when their turn came. The ship disappeared, but they continued paddling. Now they could see sharks gathering around them.

García Montes, bleeding from the mouth, and so weak he could hardly move, was told to rest. He replied, "No, as long as I'm alive I won't be a burden for you," and he took his turn. Most maddening of all during the calm was the sight of fishes beneath the boat; but there was no way to catch them. At night the wind came up, and they picked up speed under shortened sail.

In the afternoon of the next day one of the men went berserk. He began screaming and shouting curses, blaming all of them for what had happened. He collapsed in the bottom of the boat, still screaming, but staring wildly and fixedly ahead. From those terrible, staring eyes they saw green pus coming. He was placed beside Raúl Menocal, who was also delirious and showing the fatal sign of green pus. The men bathed their sick companions as well as they could, but late in the day Menocal died. A quarter of an hour later, as it was getting dark, the second man died. García Montes, a lawyer by profession, had also studied medicine, and was asked to certify the deaths. With great effort he crawled across the boat until he reached the two men. He held Menocal's wrist to check his pulse and then called back, "I'm sorry, but I'm not sure if he's dead or not."

He was not feeling well himself, he said, and would wait until the morning to verify the deaths. In the morning all three men were dead, with García Montes still holding Raúl Menocal's wrist.

This time the service was brief. It was a great effort to throw the three bodies overboard and the men were exhausted when it was done. Nothing was left to weight the bodies and for nearly twenty minutes they could see them, floating.

At some point—no one knows exactly when—they had passed through the Straits of Yucatán and entered the Gulf Stream. In the Gulf the water was wonderfully clear, and the sky a brilliant blue. Very deep below them they could see large schools of fish. To the tormented men it seemed as though the fish were taunting them; swimming close and then deliberately moving away. Men dived into the water trying to snatch them, but it was no use. They had been eight days without food or water. Each day they took turns cooling their bodies in the water, holding onto the rope they had cut in escaping from Girón.

Among the men were two brothers, Joaquín and Isias Rodríguez. Twice Isias had thrown himself into the sea, saying he was going to kill himself. Both times the others had pleaded with him to come back, and both times he had swum back. But on the third time he refused. His brother called out that their mother was waiting, but Isias said he wasn't going to die as the others had. On the boat they began discussing whether they should swim to bring him back. The life of another man had become of such little value by then that Roberto San Román said, "I will go if you reserve that place for me." (It was a special place in the front part of the boat, that only one man could occupy.) The men agreed and Roberto swam to Rodríguez and convinced him by saying they were already in the Gulf and soon would reach the coast. "Well, he came back. But after I got to the boat that place had been taken by somebody else, and they didn't give it to me." The others spoke harshly to Rodríguez and told him that the next time he jumped no one was coming for him.

Some already had lost forty or fifty pounds. Their hair was long and matted, their skin was burned and cracked and their bodies were covered with blisters and boils. On each fingernail and toenail there was a distinct white mark, showing the place where the nails had stopped growing. They all had continual violent stomach cramps. Some had taken to raking in seaweed and eating it. From the second day, when they had caught the small fishes, they had nothing to eat until the ninth day.

Roberto was dozing on the front part of the boat that day when a seagull landed on his leg. Holding his breath and trying not to move his body, he edged his hand slowly toward the bird—but it flew away and perched on the mast. With the infinite patience born of desperation he climbed up until he reached out and caught it.

"When I caught the bird I was the important man on the boat," Roberto said. "Everybody came to me. I was so weak that I made a little pressure on the bird's head to kill it, but it's funny, I was not in a hurry to eat it. After that I put the bird in the water and started cleaning it."

Slowly, feather by feather, he cleaned the bird and then held the prize for all to see before dividing it. "Some of my friends took a leg, another the head. What I took was the chest and the heart."

That afternoon they again sighted ships on the horizon and again yelled and waved, and again fell back in despair. Each man reacted according to his personality—some with prayers, some with blasphemies, some with silence. No one showed the strain more than Del Valle.

With the death of the first man, Del Valle had changed. He was still the recognized leader of them all, the one everyone turned to for the final decision and the one who, more than anyone else, maintained discipline. Yet the death of García had unsettled him. Already weakened from fighting with the shark, he seemed to fail rapidly and became weaker and weaker. Whether he lost his spirit or his faith, no one can say—but he was obsessed with dying. After García's death, he told Roberto that if he ever died he didn't want to be thrown overboard, and he didn't want to be buried at sea. "You must hang me on the mast or do something to take me to land." Every day he asked Roberto to inspect his eyes and every day Roberto told him he was all right.

On the night of the tenth day Del Valle became delirious. He was lying next to the mast, with Roberto's head on his stomach, calling out messages to the American advisor of the paratroop battalion. With his hand on the mast, he tapped out imaginary telegraph messages. He shouted out the coordinates of their position at sea and told the Americans to come and rescue them. The messages had a certain horrible logic: "We are weak and sick and dying"; then he would pause for a few moments and act as if he were receiving a message. The last thing they heard him say that night was: "We are saved. They are coming in a ship." In the morning he was dead.

"When Alex died it shocked all of us," Roberto said, "because he was the leader. He wanted to do everything. I didn't work on the part of throwing him over because he was my very best friend and I didn't want to touch him or see him dead."

The twelfth day at sea began with five men dead and seventeen dying. That afternoon Jorge García Villalta died, with the familiar green pus coming from his eyes. He was thirty-three years old and they felt his death deeply, for he had led them from the beginning in saying the rosary five or six times a day. He had been the kind of man who thought of others and who tried to make them forget their situation with a kind word or a smile or an expression of faith. With his death following closely after Del Valle's, it seemed that all faith was a mockery, and to hope was futile. For the next day they sailed on in silence.

Then, when there was no hope, the skies darkened and the night of the thirteenth day it began to rain. Momentarily they forgot their weaknesses and jumped up. There were brief fights over who would hold the two or three remaining cans to catch the water, and whether to drink it or save it. Some men opened their mouths as the rain beat down. They drank as much as they could catch. But in the morning they felt worse than before: the taste of the water had tantalized them and made them crave more. Their throats were swollen and they felt as if they had no air in their lungs. To make it worse, they had found another man dead when they woke up. Marcos Tulio, a very strong man, was the seventh to die.

That fourteenth day, the day after the rain, was hot and clear without a cloud in the skies. Suddenly, in the middle of the morning, they saw a sail coming closer. It was a two- or three-masted sailboat, and they could see people walking the deck. The boat spotted them and circled around them three or four times.

They put down their sail, beat on their tin cans, waved their clothing, shouted and tried to climb the mast once more. But the ship did not come closer. They waited and then someone said, "We must be close to land. That is why they don't pick us up." They raised the sail again and continued on. For some minutes the ship followed them; then it turned away and the Cubans moved on, straining to see the land they were sure must be ahead. The day passed and in the night one man called out, "Land!" He saw the lights of a village. They tried to alter their direction and sail toward the lights, until they realized they were the lights from a ship far in the distance.

Thursday, May 4, the fifteenth day at sea, dawned bright and clear. The fifteen men lay in the boat, barely able to move or talk. "I remember that morning," Roberto said, "I was getting a little out of my mind. It is very difficult to explain. I don't know if I was crazy or not. It's like being dizzy. I remember I caught some seaweed and showed it to the men and said it had water inside it and I ate it."

In the middle of the afternoon he dived out of the boat and went as deep as he could into the water to try to get cool. When he came up he began drinking salt water—as much as he could hold. About four o'clock he lay down beside three others who were covering their eyes with canvas. López-Estrada joined them. Roberto pulled out his combat knife, handed it to López-Estrada and said, "Kill me. I don't want to die as the others." López-Estrada refused.

About 5:30 o'clock in the afternoon, when the sun was beginning to set and the water was very dark and the horizon very bright, Cuélla went to the mast and tended to the sail. He said the sail looked like the gown of the Virgin. He knelt down before it and began praying to the Virgin de la Caridad del Cobre, the patron saint of Cuba, who guards over men in distress at sea.

Joaquín Rodríguez, who was steering the boat, shouted across to him, "Don't pray to the Virgin any more. We have been praying for days. Only Satan can save us." And he began summoning the devil in a loud voice.

At that moment someone shouted, "A ship! A ship!" and the next thing they remember they were in the water, swimming toward a black ship.

The Atlantic Seaman, an American oil freighter bound from Venezuela to New Orleans, picked up the Cubans in the middle of the Gulf of Mexico, 178 miles from the mouth of the Mississippi River.

On the sailboat one man was found dead—he was the youngest of them all, Miguel Cosío, a marvelous guitar player who used to entertain the troops during the days in the training camps and on the way to the Bay of Pigs invasion. Despite transfusions, two others died on the freighter shortly after they were rescued. The survivors were transferred to a Coast Guard cutter and were taken to New Orleans—twelve barely alive out of the original twenty-two. Somehow, word had reached reporters of a rescue at sea and they were waiting when the cutter docked. The Cubans were told not to talk to the reporters as they were carried, with their faces covered, to waiting ambulances. Their account of what happened on the boat has never been printed until now. In the Naval Hospital in New Orleans they were nursed back to health.

While they were in the hospital a CIA agent interviewed Roberto San Román for more than four hours about the invasion. When the interview was completed, he handed Roberto newspapers and magazines containing accounts of the invasion. There, for the first time, Roberto saw a picture of his brother Pepe, unshaven, staring straight ahead, holding onto the bars of a cell.

BOOK FOUR

Prison

CHAPTER 1

"YELLOW WORMS"

Captivity began with twenty days that were centuries. Tired, angry, bitter, uncertain of the future, the prisoners were brought to *El Palacio de los Deportes* (the Sports Palace) in the center of Havana. There in the amphitheatre they sat in rows on hard, small chairs for more than twenty-one hours a day, one thousand men from the demoralized Brigade. It was the low point.

Throughout night and day loudspeakers blared out the names of the prisoners, ordering them to come forward. Each man was questioned about the invasion and the role of the North Americans. Tape-recorded statements were taken and the men were asked to sign "confessions." Paper and pencils and envelopes were passed through the stands and the voice on the loudspeaker suggested that if they wanted to "rehabilitate themselves" it would be wise to write letters to the Secretary-General of the United Nations condemning President Kennedy and the United States. Approximately 10 per cent of the Brigade wrote letters. Perhaps one might consider this a small proportion under circumstances which they understood as betrayal by the United States.

They were separated by battalions, each sitting apart. While the food was adequate, they were not permitted to move or even stretch their legs. They sat in the chairs, some wounded, covered by the filth of battle and the days in the swamps. They had to beg for permission to go to the toilets. There was an outbreak of dysentery and there were only twelve toilets for a thousand men. They were not permitted to bathe or shave.

"I know these are many little things, but they work on your

mind," one man said. "Even though they were not insulting us and not physically mistreating us, we began to understand the monstrosity of being a Communist prisoner. They knew about our rumors, they knew about our morale, they knew we were craving for sleep, and they knew that Cubans sometimes take two or three baths a day and it is a form of torture not to take one."

Already exhausted when they were taken prisoner, the continued lack of sleep made them numb and dizzy. From three until six in the morning they were permitted to lie on the floor on dirty mattresses, where they could look up at the bright lights on the ceiling. In their fevered, dispirited state, some of the men felt as though they were in a vast operating room. What plagued them most was their own sense of stupidity, their shame at betrayal and abandonment. While they never lost their sense of humor, no amount of joking and laughing could conceal the deep hatred they felt toward everyone who had contributed to their defeat. Many believed the Americans deliberately had abandoned them to the executioner in order to provide an excuse for intervention.

"I thought," Amado Gayol said, "that the Americans wanted a cemetery to pass over with their tanks and one of the graves had to be mine."

Their captors played on their fears and bitterness and planned an extravaganza that would prove to the world the duplicity of the United States. Carefully selected prisoners were to be questioned before a television panel. Some were weak and had promised to say whatever their captors wished; others were chosen to prove Castro's thesis that the Brigade was composed of the sons of the rich and war criminals. The wealthiest among the Brigade—three young brothers, Lincoln, Omar and Santiago Babún—as well as the sons of Tony Varona and Miró Cardona were selected to indicate the Brigade's political leadership. Castro's greatest triumph, however, came when he was able to put three genuine Batista war criminals before the cameras, Ramón Calviño, Rafael Soler Puig and Jorge King Yun. The most notorious was Calviño, who had tortured and raped a woman and murdered two men. Calviño was in the group of sailors that swam ashore when their ships were sunk. Although Calviño was *not* in the Brigade, once ashore he had fought until he was wounded and captured. More than anything else, his presence with the invaders permitted Castro to damn the Brigade as a mercenary force.

For four nights, the parade of prisoners on television continued, until thirty-seven men had been interrogated at length. Despite the staging and selection, the propaganda show proved to be a mixed blessing for Castro. Some of the prisoners were abject, as the Communists expected, and some conceded their mistakes. "I am completely sorry for what has happened," Father Segundo de las Heras said, "and I ask the Cuban nation to accept my sorrow. I am ready to do anything I can to make up for what happened."

But others spoke up bravely. "If you have so many people on your side, why don't you hold elections?" asked Carlos Varona, Tony's son.

And Fabio Freyre, a cattleman from Oriente, when asked why he came to fight, replied, "Because I want in my country the establishment of the 1940 Constitution, a democratic government with free press and elections so the people can choose their own government."

But the most notable interrogation involved Felipe Rivero. The manner in which he was chosen for the panel, and the more than fifty pages of transcripts from his interrogation, reveal a great deal about the nature of the Brigade and its captors.

Rivero, thirty-seven years old, was an aristocrat and a dilettante—and, like many of his class, had never had to work for a living. He had married a niece of one of Batista's ministers and had once held a minor post in the Batista government. Thanks to the income from bonds in a mine, he had been able to live comfortably in Cuba and could have continued to do so in exile. However, unlike many in his circumstances he had recognized that "the high classes in Cuba were not only corrupt: they were apathetic and incapable of understanding." He had enlisted in the Brigade as a private, "to do something for my country."

Rivero seemed exactly the type of person for Castro to parade before the world: he was a wealthy man with Batista connections and a perfect example of the complacent and corrupt aristocracy in contrast to the nobility of the revolution's workers. Rivero deliberately contributed to this impression by acting fearful and implying that he had been enticed by Yankee propaganda. He was questioned three times and then told he had been recommended highly for a TV appearance. At night he was taken to the Labor Confederation building, where he waited with other prisoners on wooden benches in a gloomy cellar. The prisoners were not permitted to speak to each other. One by one, they were taken before the panel.

Rivero was one of the last to appear. When his name was called he was taken to the backstage of the theatre and led through the velvet curtains. "A militiaman said 'this way' and I saw the lights and knew I was going to appear in public." The ten-man panel sat at a table behind a large sign reading: FATHERLAND OR DEATH. WE WON. The prisoner sat at a smaller table in front.

The panel members soon discovered they had been mistaken about Rivero. Instead of a pliant prisoner, they were confronted with a man who behaved candidly and courageously. Why had he come in the invasion? they asked. Because "this country has been dominated by a series of foreign powers, and has come out of one form of imperialism to fall into another." When asked how he could have joined "the sons of the murderers from the Batista regime . . . the sons of the rich people . . . the sons of the people that misapplied funds . . ." he replied, "The majority of the men that are in this, they answer to different ideas and to different political parties and different groups. . . ."

His answer angered the panel and they hammered back at him, "No, no. It was not different groups. There were not the Cuban people."

Rivera calmly said, "I am telling you that in this group we have all different social classes and different ideologies."

Again, the panel maintained, "There were no workers, and laborers and Cuban farmers . . . those were not with you. With you were the older owners of the factories, the older owners of the *latifundium* . . . the murderers . . . not all of the Cuban people, just one part, the reactionaries."

"I saw many laborers there," Rivero said.

"Where are they? So far we haven't seen any here."

"They are in the Sports Palace."

Over and over during that long interrogation, each of the ten members of the panel tried to get Rivero to admit that the Brigade was composed of mercenaries and murderers. He never would; the Brigade, he said, "believed in an idea."

If that was so, they asked, why did the Brigade lose?

"Man! We lost for a simple reason."

"Which?"

". . . one thousand men against five or ten thousand or thirty thousand men. It had to be with this result."

Rivero said sharply, "If you think that I am going to attack my comrades here because I am a foot from being shot, you are wrong. . . . We went on fighting knowing we were going to lose. We had resisted for five days—and you should know the history of No. 2 Battalion; you should know who were in Battalion No. 2—under grenades, under the constant attack of the air force, under mortars. You will understand that at this moment the most that I can feel about being executed is sadness for my family, but it is not a thing that makes me afraid or terrifies me."

Finally, Carlos Rafael Rodríguez could stand it no more and said, "I think that you are a little confused between, let's say, heroism and cowardice. . . . Surrendering after fighting for only five days, that is not heroism, my friend."

Rivero said, "Well, in the Sierra Maestra you had water, at least."

After more of the same, Rodríguez shouted, ". . . You have been trying to present Battalion No. 2 like a battalion of heroes and the Second Battalion is a battalion of cowards. Nothing more than that."

They tried to elicit from Rivero the admission that the United States had trained, supplied and directed the invasion. They asked about the American planes and ships. Rivero said he had seen a warship but was unable to identify it.

Q. What made you think it was a warship?

A. It could have been the Barracuda, some people said. (That was a small ship that we had.) Or it could have been a destroyer, or it could have been a pocket battleship, a German ship that was not sunk in the Second World War that was around there. I don't know what it was.

Toward the end of the interrogation, Rodríguez inadvertently made admissions that he and the panel had been denying all along. He conceded that "in your group some people came that had worked once, and it could be that there also came workers that had mistaken ideas . . ."

The Communists had seriously misjudged a man like Rivero, and they repeatedly made the same miscalculations about the Brigade as a group. Their strategy was the tested and, in the past, successful Communist one of dividing the enemy by instilling hatred and pitting class against class. They believed, for example, that Rivero had come back to regain his property. What they failed to understand was that Rivero, as well as the potato farmers in the Brigade, was a nationalist first and foremost. As Rivero said, "I am not going to resign from my country where I have my grandmother that is eighty-seven years old" and "I have not come to get back some miserable bonds from a mine." No matter how embittered the men of the Brigade were toward the Americans or toward each other in private, as Cubans they resisted all attempts to divide them.

In another way Rivero's interrogation was revealing. He expressed the belief of the Brigade that Cuba was ripe for revolt.

"Tell me one thing, Rivero," Carlos Rafael Rodríguez asked. "All your companions have said here—I don't know if you think the same way as they—that you were expecting an uprising."

"Exactly," Rivero said. "That is why we came, because of course we did not want to commit suicide. We also thought that the whole island was in flames and that the militia was going to join us."

Rivero was taken back to the Sports Palace where the final act of the show took place. From 11:30 on the night of April 26 until after three o'clock the next morning, Castro stood in the center of the amphitheatre under the kleig lights and gloated over the defeated Brigade. It was his supreme moment of triumph. He said he had every reason to shoot them all, but the revolution was going to be kind to them. He would spare their lives—except for those who had committed war crimes under Batista; they must pay the penalty. Some in the Brigade cheered him wildly and one man shouted that he would fight beside the great Prime Minister against the Yankee imperialists.

Others stood up and faced Castro. Carlos Onetti asked directly, "Dr. Castro, are you a Communist?" Fidel ignored him.

At one point Castro singled out Tomás Cruz, of the paratroop battalion. "You, Negro, what are you doing here?" Castro outlined the gains Negroes had made under his regime and said that Negroes were even permitted to go swimming with white men.

Cruz quietly replied, "I don't have any complex about my color or my race. I have always been among the white people, and I have always been as a brother to them. And I did not come here to go swimming."

Despite the prisoners' hostility toward the Americans, despite the fear of what was to come, Castro's long harangue before the Brigade backfired. He had overplayed his hand. As one man said later, "I admired Fidel in many ways before that, but when I heard him making such a propaganda show with the lives of our men I realized what a monster he was—I lost my admiration. We were in the hands of a maniac and I knew that man must be fought with everything we had."

No one in the Brigade felt more embittered about the defeat than Pepe San Román. When his turn came to make the trip to Havana, Pepe was crowded into a bus filled with prisoners. At the Central Highway of Cuba, running east and west the length of the island, he remembered the words of Frank in Nicaragua. As the bus made a left turn onto the highway, "I put my left hand out like Frank told us to. I put my hand out and we went straight into Havana."

He had been in the Sports Palace only minutes when militiamen began searching him. They said they were looking for pills; they were certain he would try to kill himself. "I am not that kind of man," Pepe said.

He was then taken by car to G-2 headquarters and thrown into a cell. A large crowd gathered; everyone wanted to see San Román, the commander of the mercenaries. One militiaman made a sign with his hand, indicating they were going to cut Pepe's throat. Photographers took pictures. Guards passed and shouted insults: they were going to kill him; he was going to be taken to the *paredón*.

Pepe remained indifferent. "I didn't care about anything," he said. "I was discouraged with everything."

Only once did Pepe reply. When one of the guards called the invaders cowards, Pepe said, "It's very easy for you to be talking so brave to a prisoner. I would like to have seen you in combat."

He was returned to the Sports Palace and taken to a private office at the top of the building. A woman brought coffee and he was offered a cigar; then the door to the next room opened and in came Fidel Castro, Osvaldo Dorticós, the president of Cuba, and several other high officials.

Castro began to talk: President Kennedy was responsible; the President was a madman; the President had betrayed them; the President was the enemy of all true Cuban patriots.

"How can it be that you are involved in this, San Román?" he asked.

"All I have to say to you is my name and my serial number and my unit."

Pepe said later, "Castro got mad as hell. He threw something that he was holding in his lap and said, 'How in the hell can you come here attacking your own country, helped by our enemies? You are a traitor to your country. You have gone against all the rules and all the laws of the world. And now you say you are not going to talk.'"

After shouting and raging for several minutes, Castro abruptly became friendly. "Let's talk, San Román," he said. "Don't feel that you are the Brigade commander and that I am Fidel. Let's talk like two people. Why did you come back to your country this way? Why did you do it? Explain it to me."

Pepe said he wouldn't argue. "I don't know how to speak very well. I know that you will beat me on that field. The only thing I know is weapons and that is the field I took."

Castro did not appear angry. He talked at length again about President Kennedy, the United States and Guatemala. They all had betrayed the invaders. When Castro was finished, Pepe was taken to another building and put in a small cell, alone. After several days Castro came to see him. He ordered chairs brought to the cell and offered Pepe a cigar.

"We sat there," Pepe said, "and he was very kind, as if he was my father. He stayed about an hour, explaining everything about the revolution and asking me the reasons why I had come to fight him, asking about my background. He said that he had all my records and he knew that I had been in Fort Benning and Fort Belvoir, and he said, 'Do you think that is the reason the U.S. picked you to be the commander of the Brigade?' I told him nobody had picked me; it had happened that way. Then he left and he told them to bring me something to read and to make me comfortable because he knew I was bored."

During those days alone Pepe brooded. He was certain his brother Roberto had been killed; he didn't know what had happened to Oliva or Artime or Ferrer or to the others close to him. He kept going over what had happened: what they had been told and what they had found; what had been promised and what had been delivered. In a letter to his father he put down some of his thoughts: "The war? How was the war? All the incalculable and the unexpected that you can imagine in a military operation were all together in this battle of Girón, that was about sixty-four hours of fighting without rest, of heroic acts from both sides in this battle." He wrote of the decision to order the retreat: "I had to order the troops to retreat, what was left of the Brigade, and go into the woods. God help them, I told myself, what right do I have to order my men to sacrifice their honor? What right do I have to order my men to go on building Cuban widows, only for honor? What right do I have to order the enemy with his cannon to destroy all those beautiful new houses? Could we win the war with that? It was already lost. No. Our presence in there didn't have any value, because our purpose was not to kill Cubans, our purpose was to win a war that will bring peace and happiness to all Cubans, and this war was lost to us. All this comes to my mind that afternoon of the 19th of April."

And much later he said:

"I hated the United States, and I felt that I had been betrayed. Every day it became worse and then I was getting madder and madder and I wanted to get a rifle and come and fight against the U.S. Sometimes the feeling came very strong to me that they had thrown us there knowing that they were not going to help us. Many times I had the feeling that we were thrown there to see what happened, because they were sure that Fidel was going to capture us and put all of us in the firing squad and we would be killed and there would be a great scandal in the whole world. Sometimes I felt like that. And sometimes I felt that they changed their minds at the last moment, and they didn't have time to give us the order to come back. But anyhow I felt that if they had organized us and taken us through a whole year of that training, even if the world was going to fall to pieces, they should not have forgotten us. That was an engagement that they had with us."

He thought about Frank and Gray and their promises. "They had all wrong information. Even the attack of the airplanes [on Saturday, April 15]. How could they say that all the planes were destroyed? They didn't have proof of that. Intelligence cannot work like that."

The more he thought, the more bitter he became.

Helicopters flew over the swamps. The news was broadcast over loudspeakers that Artime had surrendered and had given the order for the troops to do the same.

Actually Artime was not taken until his fourteenth day in the swamps. Like some of the other men, he had eaten small birds and he had found some water early. Toward the end, however, "The feeling of thirst was very strong and we could not move our tongues to talk.

"Up until the moment I was captured, I always had thought that they needed me for the liberation of Cuba. But at that moment when I was taken prisoner, the thought that came to my mind was that the Lord wanted my blood; that I needed to die for the liberation of Cuba."

His captors did not recognize Artime, but they confiscated a diary he had kept since he had gone into exile. At Girón he was given something to eat and drink. A man named Oscar Fernández, a Castro doctor whom Artime had known in school, saw him and said, "Artime! So you could not escape. You are very unlucky." He was immediately separated from the others, bound and thrown on the floor and left alone. An old militiaman quietly spread his own coat over Artime's shoulders, and Artime slept until he was awakened by a kick. "When I opened my eyes, what I saw made my hair stand up."

Manuel Piñeiro, a big man known to Cubans as "Barbarroja" because of his long, bristling, bright red beard, was standing over him, along with Pedro Luis Rodriguez and Ramiro Valdés, the chief of Castro's G-2. All three were Communists from the old guard.

Barbarroja was the first to speak. "Artime, you are the son of a bitch that has caused us more trouble and made us more harm than anyone else. Now you are going to pay for everything you've done to us." He said Artime's movement, the MRR, was destroyed, there was nothing left of the Brigade and Artime was going to die. He could die in two ways: quickly, by a bullet, or slowly, in misery. "If you cooperate with us you will die, shot, but like a hero. If you don't, we are very sorry, but you are going to suffer deeply."

First, they asked about "the people that betrayed you, the Americans." Second, they wanted to know about the MRR. And third, they wanted Artime to sign a declaration. Artime refused to talk. Barbarroja grabbed him by the neck and shouted, "Artime, you've failed the test. You're going to be sorry." They took him by car to Havana.

In the Sports Palace he was put in a separate cell, questioned briefly and left alone. In the middle of the night Pedro Luis Rodríguez and Osmani Cienfuegos took him away in a car. When it stopped "we went down some stairs that looked like they were to a basement. We went into a room that had mattresses all over the walls. There was a chair on the floor and in front were three rocking chairs and I saw a couple of spotlights, but they were not on. To impress me there were two guys that had no shirts, big and fat." They took off Artime's shirt and strapped him in the chair—by the legs and around the shoulders and waist. His hands were tied behind him. The spotlights were turned on in Artime's face and the interrogation began.

Artime does not know how long he was kept there. He thinks it might have been as long as three days, but he is not certain. However long, his was by far the most difficult and barbarous interrogation of any man in the Brigade. This was perhaps not surprising, for Artime was the only prisoner who had led an underground organization, and he was the only one in the invasion who had dealt directly with the Americans in the United States. His captors wanted to know who those Americans were and what they had said. During those hours of interrogation Artime was not permitted to sleep. He was given black coffee and when he slumped into unconsciousness ice water was dashed in his face. Because of the lights he was unable to see those who were questioning him; but he knew there were various men. One voice, gentle and kind, would say that the revolution understood Artime's mistake and wanted to treat him with compassion if he would cooperate; another, harsh and loud, would maintain, "No, this man is a beast. He is responsible for all the deaths." At one point, Artime was grabbed by the hair and forced to look at the wall where photographs of mounds of dead men were projected. The voices and the questioners alternated —the gentle followed by the harsh. Once the two voices spoke together.

Gentle voice said, "Get out of here. Put that pistol up. Get out of here."

Harsh voice answered, "I'm not leaving. I have as much right to be here as you."

After more argument a door slammed and only the gentle voice spoke. "Look, I want to help you, Artime. That man who left, he is so excited because his brother was killed at Girón. The only way to save yourself is to recognize your errors and admit that you are a traitor to the revolution."

The interrogation droned on until Artime almost lost his senses. For the first time, he prayed to God to kill him quickly. Twice his captors said they were going to shoot him. The muzzle of a pistol was placed in his mouth and the trigger pulled; the hammer fell on an empty chamber. The other time they placed a pistol against his temple. Once Artime begged for water and a voice said, "Yes, I'll give you some water," and he was slapped hard across the mouth. When he passed out, he was brought back to consciousness—by ice water or with lighted cigarettes. He carries scars with him today.

Finally it was over. Artime awoke to find himself in another room, untied, lying at the feet of Cienfuegos and Pedro Luis Rodríguez.

"Cienfuegos kicked me on the shoulder and he said, 'Get up, you son of a bitch. Now is the time.'"

They put a shirt on him and took him to a car. Cienfuegos told the driver, "to the Laguito" (a small lake where some people were murdered during Batista's time). In the car Cienfuegos told Artime this was his "last chance to come through." Artime repeated what he had said throughout the interrogation: he wouldn't sign anything; he didn't know anything. "Cienfuegos put his gun on my head and told me he was going to count three before shooting." When Artime remained silent, Cienfuegos put away his gun and the car continued until it reached the Sports Palace. Artime was taken to a cell and again left alone.

Within half an hour Ramiro Valdés, the G-2 chief, came to the cell. "Artime," he said, "what have they done to you?" Valdés appeared quite concerned and asked if it were true they had hit him and burned him. He explained that the government was not responsible; that Pedro Luis Rodríguez and Cienfuegos had found out what had happened and brought him back to safety. Tell us who attacked you, he said. Describe their faces and we will put them in jail. If Artime wanted, Valdés would even take him to the G-2 and let him try to pick out any of the men. Those responsible would be treated severely—they were fanatics, not true revolutionaries.

Artime said, "Commander, let's forget about it, because I never saw their faces." Then Valdés ordered guards to bring food and drink and he and Artime ate dinner together—a typical Cuban feast of chicken and rice and black beans. Valdés kept apologizing for what had happened and promising that the revolution would punish the guilty.

After the prisoners had been in the Sports Palace for two weeks, a militia girl with a dark skirt and small fur-lined Russian boots passed among the Brigade, handing out T-shirts and saying, "Yellow, yellow, yellow," the color of the shirts. The guards took up the chant. The men were, as Fidel kept saying, "yellow worms," and the shirts were a symbol of their cowardice.

Along with the T-shirts they were given towels—one towel for each ten men—and were permitted to take showers. Soon the towels were so soiled that they were useless. But, as one prisoner said, "After that long without a bath we were happy."

One night the loudspeakers commanded the men to stand and they were divided into groups according to social class. Those who were members of social clubs went to one group, those who owned factories or large amounts of land to another, and to still another group went the former soldiers and teachers and on down to the workers. When they had been catalogued and questioned about their occupations, they were told to return to their battalions. They continued to sit on the small chairs under the bright lights.

For the first few days Oliva was held apart from the Brigade, with other battalion commanders and staff officers. Then he was transferred to a cell occupied by more than thirty men—civilians, members of the Brigade's infiltration teams and soldiers. There he learned of the inquisition that had begun with the invasion. A doctor told how he had been arrested by his barber because he had once spoken critically of Castro; a man was taken to prison by a friend after he said, casually, that he thought the invaders might win if they had planes and tanks; a teenage boy was arrested without explanation while milking his cows.

With bars from a bunk bed, they began making two holes in the back of the cell. A young, blond man, whose pregnant wife was in another cell and whose screams could be heard throughout the day, was, as Oliva put it, "like a human drill, out of his mind trying to make that hole." They worked for seven days, covering the holes with newspapers. Then on May 4 Oliva and six others of the Brigade headquarters staff were told they were going to be shot. Instead, they were taken back to the Sports Palace.

"It was very emotional when they took us there," Oliva said, "because all the people of the Brigade stood up and started applauding us. A militiaman took me to an upper room and there I met Barbarroja and Pedro Luis [Rodríguez], a captain that was in charge of our case." He was questioned about the invasion and about why he had left Cuba, but was not mistreated. When the questioning was over, he was taken to a small cell, similar to Pepe's. Later a Castro officer came with pen and paper and told Oliva he could write a letter to his wife. It might be his last one, the officer said.

"I explained to her that I was not a mercenary, as they were saying, and that what I had done I did for my daughter and that my conscience was at peace with God." (Oliva's wife never received the letter.)

On the seventh day of solitary confinement, Oliva asked if he could go to a toilet (until then he had had only a bucket in the cell). The request was granted. As he went down the corridor, he saw Manolo Artime in a cell similar to his. On May 14 Oliva was taken from his cell and down an elevator to the first floor. When he stepped out he saw that the Sports Palace was empty —not a member of the Brigade was left.

CHAPTER 2

THE COMMITTEE

May Day, 1961:

In Havana, the parade began and continued throughout the day: tanks and trucks and planes and rockets and banners bearing likenesses of Karl Marx, Fidel, Raúl and Che Guevara. After nearly seventeen hours of continuous parading, Castro began his address to the Cuban nation. Cuba, he proclaimed, was a Socialist nation and there would be no elections.

In Matanzas, in the hospital, the militia rolled in television sets before the most seriously wounded Brigade prisoners and kept them tuned to the display of Communist Cuban might; a display, the militia constantly reminded the prisoners, indicating the invincibility of Castro and the revolution. Many of the wounded felt like Enrique Ruiz-Williams, who said, "Until that day I just wanted to die. But on the first of May I made the decision to show these bastards that I was not going to die. I started fighting again."

In Washington, Dean Rusk was testifying about the Bay of Pigs invasion before the Senate Foreign Relations Subcommittee on Latin American Affairs. Rusk, Senator Wayne Morse told reporters later, said the decision to attack had been made by Cuban refugees and the attack conducted by Cubans.

In Gettysburg, Pennsylvania, Dwight David Eisenhower held a press conference. "Don't go back and rake over the ashes," he said, "but see what we can do better in the future. To say you're going into methods and practices of the administration—I would say the last thing you want is to have a full investigaton and lay all this out on the record."

A full investigation *was* under way, but not for the benefit of the public.

On April 23 the President had appointed his brother, Robert F. Kennedy, and General Maxwell D. Taylor to head a committee to find out what had happened at the Bay of Pigs. Allen Dulles and Admiral Arleigh Burke were the other members of the committee. They began working immediately, going back into the documents in existence and talking to the men who had planned the operation. It was an investigation of far-reaching significance, and it came at a time when United States prestige had dropped to its lowest point in the Cold War era. (Two days after the committee was appointed, the United States attempted to hurl an unmanned Project Mercury space capsule into orbit. After thirty seconds of flight the Atlas booster rocket exploded, putting the United States even further behind the spectacular feat of Russia's Yuri Gagarin only two weeks before.) Failure in space and increasing East-West tension lent an even more urgent note to the investigation.

It has never been reported to whom the committee talked or what its findings were: everything was conducted in secrecy. The investigation was not a means to develop political careers. Also, there was no attempt to find a convenient scapegoat, for the President had stated firmly, both publicly and privately, that he assumed full responsibility for the invasion.* That something was seriously wrong, and that the nation's very survival might depend on uncovering and correcting weaknesses, was apparent to everyone involved. Yet from the outset the investigation was handicapped by one crucial lack: few of the invaders were available, and none of the top leaders.

---

* On April 24, for example, a statement was issued at the White House which read: "President Kennedy has stated from the beginning that as President he bears sole responsibility for the events of the past few days. He has stated it on all occasions and he restates it now so that it will be understood by all. The President is strongly opposed to anyone within or without the administration attempting to shift the responsibility."

In the second week of May Roberto San Román was released from the Naval Hospital in New Orleans and taken back to his family in Miami. A day or two later two CIA agents came to his house and said they wanted him to go to Washington with four other Brigade members—two paratroopers, one man from the Second Battalion and one frogman. They had been called by the special committee.

"When we got to Washington there were two more CIA men waiting for us, Jack and Joe, very nice people," Roberto said. "They took us to a house near McLean, Virginia, where we had everything we wanted. That morning I saw Frank and Seabee and people from the camp. Frank was very mad for what had happened. In his own words he said, 'Don't you ever accept any job from the CIA again.' He said that, and I don't know why, because I don't think all the blame is to the CIA.

"He said he had gone before the committee already and that he had been rough. He said everything he had on his mind. He told me this would be my only chance and that I should say everything—feel free to talk and to ask. And that is exactly what I did!"

The five Cubans were taken to the Pentagon by "Jack and Joe." Gray and Rip, the two American frogmen, preceded them. Roberto was the first man in the Brigade to be called. General Taylor and Robert Kennedy were leading the questioning. Behind them was a large map with the area of operations at the Bay of Pigs.

"They wanted to know," Roberto said, "the reaction of the enemy, how soon they reacted with tanks and artillery. How much did they fire and how much did we fire? How many did we kill and how many men of ours died? The reaction of the population—and this was a question of Mr. Kennedy—he wanted to know the reaction of the people. They wanted to know if we thought we could have won the battle. What did we need to win the battle? I told them we needed only three or four jet planes, that's what we needed to win. Three or four jet planes that could knock out the little air force that Castro had at that time. I told them I didn't know how they could do this to us. Our troops were so good—because they involved people from every class, rich and poor, rebels and soldiers and everybody together against the common enemy—and they didn't answer those questions.

"General Taylor was very interested in the steps of the combat. He wanted to know when we advanced, when we retreated, why we retreated and how many men joined us from the civilian population. I think it was Robert Kennedy who asked what we were promised during the briefing in Nicaragua. I think he meant support, what kind of support. And then I said that we were never told by any uniformed man of the U.S. armed forces that we would have this battalion or this air force squadron supporting us but that during the briefing, as in the training, they let us believe things."

Roberto spoke at length about what Frank had said to them and how "we thought if we needed air fire support, we would have it." When he first mentioned Frank, General Taylor asked, "Who is this Frank?" and Allen Dulles said, "Colonel Frank ———."

For several hours Roberto told his story, and by the time he was finished a number of colored pins had been placed on the big map, indicating the combat lines. Robert Kennedy asked personal questions: how Roberto felt, how he had recovered from his ordeal at sea, how his family was, and what his plans for the future were.

The other Cubans were called in one by one, but for much briefer periods of time. When Blas Casares, a frogman who had been on the flagship *Blagar*, was questioned, the committee seemed particularly interested in the Cuban fleet. "They asked me if ships had gone back any time," Blas said. "Apparently that had been worrying them. And I told them that we had started going back to resupply the people on the beach when they said they didn't have any ammunition. We did start back, of course, and in one of our messages that we sent we asked for support, for the *Santiago* and the *Tampico* [code names for American destroyers] to escort us, because if they didn't we believed we would lose all our ships. But we turned back when they [the Americans] gave us the order to turn back. They [the committee] were very interested in that.

"At the end," Casares said, "they asked me if I wanted to say anything of my own, and at that moment I felt very bitter and I told them I didn't know who planned the invasion, but whoever planned it, I believed he was crazy. They laughed a little bit, all except Dulles. He just looked right through me. That is the only way I can describe it."

The next morning the men were taken to the White House and into President Kennedy's oval office. Roberto San Román spoke for them all and gave the President a short account of the battle. The President was gracious, considerate and apologetic. He wanted them to know that he was taking all the blame for the failure, and he talked about the future of Latin America and the contest for democracy and freedom in the hemisphere. The next ten years were going to be the decisive ones in that contest, he said; and he left them feeling that the battle had been lost, but not the war.

That night the Cubans were invited to a party in their honor at Hickory Hill, the country home of Robert Kennedy in Mc-Lean, Virginia. Everyone was solicitous and friendly. But the most lasting impression, at least on Roberto San Román, was made by Ethel Kennedy, the Attorney General's wife.

"I thought they took us there to forget about the invasion," Roberto said, "but she was the one that talked about it. She kept asking me questions and putting Mr. Kennedy in a very rough situation. She said she had read about the invasion and she asked me if it was true that with some planes we could have won. I told her yes and explained. I thought they were going to avoid this point, but that was the point that she talked about first. She is a wonderful woman."

From the Cubans and from the Americans who had been on the scene, the committee quickly determined that Brigade 2506 had fought with extraordinary courage under extremely difficult conditions. Yet the very courage and determination of the men tended to obscure some more basic aspects of the invasion. The deeper the committee delved, the more apparent it became that the entire operation had been poorly planned. Two of the most glaring miscalculations concerned Castro's air *and* ground forces. Castro's army was far stronger and fought more fiercely than anyone had anticipated. Consequently, the Brigade would have needed many more men—perhaps ten thousand, perhaps twenty thousand—to accomplish its mission. Added to this was the erroneous belief that the Brigade B-26s would control the air and enable the men to operate at will on the ground. Another miscalculation was obvious: there had been no uprising, no mass defections from Castro's forces. And the CIA's alternative plan for the Brigade had not been employed.

None of the Cubans knew anything about an alternative plan. It was discovered that the plan had not been given them at their briefing in Puerto Cabezas. At the time of the investigation in May of 1961, the CIA contended that Pepe and Oliva had been told privately by Frank about the guerrilla option just before the ships left. Since Pepe and Oliva were then in prison, the committee had no way of establishing the real facts in the case. Examination *did* show that the CIA had shied away from any talk of guerrilla warfare or alternative action because it might weaken the resolve of the Cubans to keep fighting.

In any event, the committee's investigation led to a further conclusion: that even if the Cubans *had* been given an alternative plan and even if they had been trained as guerrillas, as the CIA claimed *before* the invasion, the invasion site itself was totally unsuited to guerrilla warfare. It was completely unrealistic, given the terrain of the Zapata Swamps, to think the Brigade could have reached the Escambray Mountains eighty miles away. Yet, from the beginning, that guerrilla alternative and the escape valve in the Escambray had been a key element in the planning, and of great influence in the President's decision to approve the invasion.

Upon closer scrutiny, other aspects of the planning that once had seemed so plausible were seen to be faulty. An operation that had started out as a clandestine covert action had changed drastically to a full-fledged overt military campaign. This was such a basic change in concept, that if it were to succeed, the entire plan would have had to have been altered. Launching an invasion is quite different from putting ashore some guerrillas in the middle of the night. The military plans, nevertheless, remained the same. Incredible as it seemed in retrospect, no one appeared to have recognized the implications of this change in operations. "It started out a duck and became a chicken, or whatever figure of speech you want to use," one man said, "but no one realized it."

There were other serious handicaps: messages from the fighting zone at the Bay of Pigs took too long to reach the top level at Washington; the ships provided for the invasion were inadequate; the number of planes was inadequate; the Bay of Pigs itself was inadequate.

These points were fairly easily determined; but there were deeper, even more important, considerations. How was it possible that such a plan could have been approved by the leading military minds of the country? How was it possible that some of the most intelligent men in the executive department failed to spot and counsel against such obvious shortcomings? The implications were grave.

Everywhere President Kennedy turned he could find those responsible: the military had failed, his own advisors had failed and he himself had failed, after only ninety days in office.

Throughout the entire planning for the Bay of Pigs invasion there had been an air of unreality, of vagueness, of unjustified confidence. The desire to conceal the fact of United States support led to a number of compromises: the landing at night, the canceling of the second air strike on Monday, the reluctance to act decisively when disaster approached and an apparent refusal to recognize how disastrous a defeat would be—not only to the cause of Cuban freedom and democracy in the hemisphere, but to the United States and its role as the leader of the West. One of the harshest and most accurate judgments was made immediately after the defeat when one of the leading participants told Stewart Alsop: "The trouble was that we were acting like an old whore and trying to pretend that we were just the sweet young girl we used to be."

The question for the President was not so much what we used to be, but what we were going to become and what had to be done to insure the right course. And that called for a new, hard look at the cumbersome machinery of decision-making in the government—the agencies, the bureaus, the departments and the men who ran them.

The Bay of Pigs has been surrounded by so much partisan controversy that a number of assumptions have come to be accepted as fact by otherwise responsible citizens. Depending on the point of view, the failure has been attributed to left-wingers in the State Department, to the young professors and amateurs in the White House, to a weak President, to the CIA or to the military. Each of these explanations misses the point.

Sometimes a more sinister explanation for the failure is given: "someone" wanted the Cubans to fail and deliberately scuttled a good plan with a good chance of success. This assumption is equally spurious for, if anything, the Bay of Pigs was a classic tragedy of good intentions. No one wanted the invasion to fail —from the Eisenhower administration to the Kennedy administration, from the Cubans to the Americans who trained them and ardently believed in them. Yet fail it did. The fault was shared by all who had a hand in it.

In the assignment of responsibility for the failure the military, and specifically, the Joint Chiefs of Staff carries a heavy burden. They selected the Bay of Pigs-Zapata Swamp area for the invasion, and they did so taking into account the alternative plan for guerilla action. If that area was unsuited to a guerilla operation, and it most certainly was—they must take the blame for the blunder. They blundered, too, in failing to recognize how devastating the T-33 jet trainers could be in battle when armed with rockets. The result of that failure led to the virtual destruction of the Brigade airforce and the loss of the supply ships. But in the larger sense the military bore less responsibility in the overall Bay of Pigs operation than the CIA. And, finally, the responsibility must rest with the CIA.

The CIA, by its nature, remains in the shadows: it lends itself to the role of the villain, however frayed the cloak and however bent the dagger. Even this is not a fair generalization: the CIA has brilliant, dedicated men and women who perform thankless and dangerous jobs throughout the world that help to safeguard the United States and the free world. It is a cliché of the agency that its successes never get reported and its U-2 flights and Bay of Pigs invasions become *causes célèbres*. The CIA is necessary to the survival of the United States and it shall remain necessary for as long a time as can be anticipated. Acknowledging these as truths, however, does not make the CIA sacrosanct, nor does it relieve the agency of its responsibilities or hide the dangers that are inherent in such an organization.

The gathering of intelligence, with all that is implied in that general term, is the lifeblood of the agency. However, in the Cuban invasion the CIA went far beyond this function. The CIA's men in the field tended to take matters into their own hands, to cross over the line from intelligence to the formation of policy. They did this in Miami when they picked and groomed men and then dictated to the *Frente*. They acted for the United States—or implied that they did—when dealing with the Cubans and led them to believe much that was not true. Later there was no way for the Cubans to prove they had been promised anything. In American terminology, they were left holding the bag.

"You begin to understand what it is like when they run the show," a Cuban said. "They say, 'Meet me at the corner of Thirty-second and Flagler in a car.' They say, 'My name is Bill, my number is Pl-6-9945. Call me.' When they want you, you come, you call. When you want them, they are gone; you never see them again. So what happens? Who has the responsibility? So someone says, 'What are you doing here?' You say, 'Bill sent me.' 'Bill. What Bill? What is his last name? Where does he live?' And you say, 'Bill, Pl-6-9945.' There is no Bill at that number. To hell with them, I say. That is no way to run anything."

The same tendency to act independently, to make decisions that influence policies, was exhibited to an even greater and more damning degree in Guatemala. For there the agency—or again, at least its agents—was acting at times contrary to established United States policies, and *even* contrary to the wishes of the President of the United States. The agents came dangerously close to taking things into their own hands. When Frank told San Román, Oliva and Artime about the plot to take the Americans prisoner and proceed with the invasion despite the opposition from Washington, he was exhibiting, at its most extreme, the potential threat of a powerful organization with virtually unlimited funds, accountable for its actions only to a few, and operating beyond established guidelines in sensitive areas throughout the world.

Some of these implications became clear during the Washington investigation; some, apparently, did not. For instance, the special emissary of the President sent to Guatemala just before the briefing was supposed to make certain that no Americans participated in the invasion. Then the committee discovered that the first men to land at Playa Girón and Playa Larga were Americans. While the committee learned about that particular lapse, the most startling disclosure about the invasion—the plot to take the Americans prisoner—apparently was not known.

Nevertheless, enough facts came to light to precipitate a re-evaluation of policy.

Out of the wreckage of the Bay of Pigs came invaluable lessons. Perhaps the most important dealt with the subjective analysis of facts leading to decisions. No matter how great the advisor's previous reputation in the Pentagon, the State Department or in the White House itself, his opinions should no longer be accepted at face value. "If the President asked ten questions before, now he asks sixty-two," said a man close to him. When the time came for a decision on Laos or some other crucial area, the advice of the military and of the State Department was examined with a cold eye. A shift in policy, subtle but significant, began. President Kennedy surrounded himself with those who asked the tough questions: the Bob Kennedys, the Maxwell Taylors, the Ted Sorensens, the Robert McNamaras, the Paul Nitzes. Emphasis was shifted to guerrilla warfare and paramilitary operations and away from what the President had called "traditional military needs." A searching re-examination of policies in diplomacy and defense began. In the process an inevitable ruffling of feelings occurred and there were bitter, but subdued, protests from within the Pentagon and the Department of State. Quietly, older men were eased out or transferred.

In the long run, the lessons of the Bay of Pigs probably saved the Administration from making potentially more serious mistakes later, and might even have saved American lives. In that sense, Joseph P. Kennedy, the patriarch of the Kennedy clan, was correct when he told his son, the President, after the invasion, that Cuba was the best lesson he could have had. But for the Cubans in exile, and for 1,199 members of Brigade 2506 languishing in prison, it was, at the very least, an end to their dreams.

CHAPTER 3

TRACTORS FOR FREEDOM

"History recounts that on a certain occasion the Spanish people exchanged Napoleon's soldiers against pigs. We, on this occasion, are going to be a little more delicate: we will exchange with imperialism the soldiers against tractors."

Fidel Castro was speaking before the National Association of Small Farmers on the night of Wednesday, May 17, 1961. He was quite specific: "If imperialism does not want its worms to work, let it exchange them against tractors and agricultural machinery! Of course, those among such blackguards that may have committed murder, we cannot exchange against anything. Those that have assassinated are not subject to exchange. All others, all others, we will exchange with imperialism, against five hundred bulldozers, if it is interested in rescuing them."

In some manner, Fidel said, the United States "must compensate the Republic for the damage they have caused it." Furthermore, he added, "the tractors must be caterpillar type, not those with rubber wheels, no. They have to be good, so that they may be used to clear brush and jungle, to open roads, to make constructions by tractor."

Four days before this proposal, Brigade 2506 had been transferred in the middle of the night from the Sports Palace to the Naval Hospital, a five-story building, still uncompleted, on the other side of Havana. Here, by contrast, the treatment of the men was vastly improved. They slept twenty to a room on mattresses on the floor and were given soap and toilet articles. Their spirits rose and when the news came of Castro's speech, rumors of release began to circulate.

On May 18 there was a sudden commotion in the corridor of the Naval Hospital where the Brigade leaders were kept in isolation in separate rooms. A crowd of *milicianos* stopped in front of Pepe San Román's room and the door was opened. In walked Castro, surrounded by his guards.

"Hello. How are you, San Román?" Castro asked.

"I am all right, Major," Pepe said, getting up from his mattress.

"San Román, are you sure that your brother is dead?"

"Yes, Major, I am sure."

"Well, then I have good news for you. Your brother is alive." He handed Pepe a letter from his wife and parents in Miami saying that Roberto had been rescued by boat.

"I have some more good news for you, San Román," Castro said. "You and all your men are going back to Miami." He explained his proposal to exchange the prisoners for tractors and asked Pepe what he thought.

"Well, Major, I don't know what to say after what's happened to me."

Then Pepe asked Castro if he didn't think it might be dangerous to free the Brigade. Fidel answered quickly, "None of you will come back. But if you do, I don't care if a thousand more come with you. It wouldn't make any difference."

Castro's soldiers then announced the news to the Brigade and instructed each battalion to vote for representatives—excluding the leaders—to go as a commission of prisoners to the United States. Ten men were chosen, and on the 19th Castro met for the first time with the commission. The men were given new clothing and taken on a tour of Havana; their guards pointed out the advances made under Castro, such as new housing for laborers, and commented upon the improved level of morality in the city—many prostitutes had reformed and become dedicated militia women. "See what the revolution has done for Cuba," the prisoners were told.

"Fidel talked to us quite friendly," said Hugo Sueiro, the commander of the Second Battalion and a member of the commission. "He had our records and knew all about us, and called us by our first names. We discussed the kind of tractors he wanted. He said he knew the United States press was going to ask a lot of embarrassing questions, and he said we shouldn't talk bad about America because they would get mad and we shouldn't talk bad about him because *he* would get mad and the negotiations would be broken. He said we should stay in the middle. He said there were a lot of guilty people in the invasion and the Americans were to blame—all those politicians and the press had done this to us—and only we and our relatives were suffering. He said the revolution was generous and was going to let us go free."

The next day the commission left for Miami by plane.

At the same time a committee was being formed in the United States to deal with the Brigade commission. Ostensibly, the "Tractors for Freedom Committee" was a private organization. Actually, it was formed at the personal request of President Kennedy. As Dr. Milton S. Eisenhower wrote later in his book, *The Wine Is Bitter*, "I became involved in this strange affair quite suddenly." At seven o'clock on the evening of May 19 Dr. Eisenhower's phone rang. It was President Kennedy.

"I want to ask you for some help," the President said.

Milton Eisenhower replied instantly, "I'll do whatever I can."

The President explained that Castro was sending a commission of ten prisoners to the United States and that the government felt a moral obligation to help bring about the release of the Brigade. The government, however, could not deal directly with Castro because it had severed diplomatic relations with Cuba that January, in the closing days of Dwight Eisenhower's administration. The President proposed establishing a committee of private citizens to raise the money to buy the tractors. Mrs. Franklin D. Roosevelt and Walter Reuther, the labor leader, already had agreed to serve, and President Kennedy hoped that Dr. Eisenhower, a Republican, would become a member along with another Republican, thus making the committee completely bipartisan. According to Dr. Eisenhower's account, the President said he would explain the matter publicly the next day. Dr. Eisenhower accepted immediately and began what he described as "the most exasperating, frustrating and enervating six weeks of my life."

Everyone concerned felt the same frustration. The entire episode of the Tractors for Freedom Committee is, in retrospect, one of the sorriest in recent American history. It was marked by political partisanship of the lowest sort, by expediency, cynicism and hypocrisy. The committee found itself in the middle. But in the end the ones who really suffered were the prisoners: their cause became lost in the mass of rhetoric and charges issued from Capitol Hill and echoed on the editorial pages of many newspapers.

The attacks began almost immediately after the formation of the committee. It was clear from the beginning that the committee was backed informally by the government. (Milton Eisenhower announced to the press on Saturday, May 20, that the committee's work "is sanctioned by the government." The press reported that fact and opponents in Congress used the information to discredit the President.) Coming as the exchange did, right after the Bay of Pigs disaster, the moment was opportune for enemies of the administration.

When the Senate met on Monday, May 22, Senator Homer Capehart, a Republican from Indiana, said that he thought the operation was "illegal" unless "authorized directly by the President." Yet, Capehart said, if the President *did* authorize it, that "constitutes an unforgivable sin." President Kennedy was damned if he did and damned if he didn't. "If we accept the operation," Capehart went on, "we will become the laughing stock of the entire world."

Members of Kennedy's own party—Senators Wayne Morse of Oregon and J. W. Fulbright of Arkansas—called on the administration to make clear its position. "If our government approves, it should say so," Morse said. Senator Karl E. Mundt, a Republican from South Dakota, rose to whip an old enemy, the State Department: the department, Mundt said, was following a policy of "pacification" toward Castro because of "its silent cooperation" with the Tractors for Freedom Committee. Senator Styles Bridges, a Republican from New Hampshire, had something to say: "How much more humiliation and disdain must be taken from this Communist dictator?" . . . And Capehart broke in: "[Castro's] only purpose [in the exchange] must be to kill American youths, and who will trade tractors for them?" On that same Monday the man who would lead the attack against the exchange made his first comment. Senator Barry Goldwater, the Republican from Arizona, said that if the United States sent the tractors to Castro, American prestige "would sink even lower."

Meanwhile the Brigade commission arrived in Washington for its first meeting with the committee at the Statler-Hilton Hotel. Ulises Carbó, a former newspaperman in Cuba, who was the most fluent in English, presented the case for the prisoners. The meeting was cordial and the committee listened quietly as Carbó outlined Castro's demands. When he finished, there was a long discussion about the kind of equipment Castro wanted. Why that point seemed to need clarifying is uncertain, for Castro had stated exactly what he wanted: five hundred bulldozers, Caterpillar type. Another point bothered the committee: Carbó had said that Castro was irritated because the United States referred to his proposal as an exchange or a trade; Fidel himself was demanding indemnification. When Carbó explained Castro's view, Milton Eisenhower felt "the whole affair began to take on ominous overtones." Again, it is difficult to understand why Dr. Eisenhower suddenly was struck with misgivings, for Castro had been clear on that point also. In his first speech, and in every speech thereafter, he stated emphatically that the United States must pay; and the word he used was indemnity, a compensation for wrongs committed.* Distasteful as it was to accept his demands, Castro's proposal was consistent and the entire negotiations hinged in Castro's mind on an admission of responsibility by the United States.

Despite the initial misgivings, the meeting concluded optimistically with both prisoners and committee members confident the negotiations would succeed.

"It was a nice interview," Hugo Sueiro said. "Everyone was in accordance with the idea that we would get the tractors."

The prisoners were taken to their suite of rooms at the Statler-Hilton and there they met Richard Goodwin, a twenty-nine-year-old advisor to President Kennedy who was acting as the official-

---

* On Friday night, May 19, for instance, Castro spoke at a large rally staged to honor him for having won the Lenin Peace Prize, and referred to the pending negotiations in these words: ". . . we are willing to send them back, in exchange for an indemnity for the damages caused to the nation, represented by five hundred bulldozer tractors. It can be considered as an act of peace, to give such opportunity to their friends to pick up again the men they sent on the Zapata Peninsula adventure."

unofficial liaison between the President, the committee and the prisoners. Goodwin, a brilliant man, first in his class at Harvard Law School, was one of the most highly regarded men in the inner circle around Kennedy. The President was relying on Goodwin as a principal advisor on Latin America, even though Goodwin had no particular background in the field.

Goodwin's role in the tractor negotiations is controversial. Undoubtedly well intentioned, he nevertheless irritated both the prisoners and some on the committee (notably Dr. Eisenhower). At his first meeting with the Cubans, they felt he insulted them. According to Sueiro and Carbó, Goodwin greeted them by congratulating them because they had "won the propaganda war and shown Castro to be inhuman." Goodwin said that the President was extremely interested in what was happening; that he, the President, was sorry for what had happened and was going to do everything he could to help. To strengthen the point, Goodwin picked up the phone and called the White House, giving the men the impression he was talking directly to the President.

"I asked Goodwin specifically if we were going to get the tractors," Carbó said, "and he said, 'Without the slightest doubt,' which I'll always remember. We were sure the thing was resolved."

Then the men were taken, one by one, to another room in the hotel where Roberto San Román questioned them about the battle. Roberto, who had testified only days earlier before the administration's special investigating committee, had been asked by the Pentagon to gather more facts about the areas in which he himself had not fought: particularly Playa Larga and Girón. When he had finished his interviews, he personally gave the information to high officials in the Pentagon.

By the end of the day, Castro had replied formally to the State Department's initial statement that "The United States would give its most attentive consideration to the issuance of appropriate permits for the export of bulldozers to Cuba, for the rescue of the prisoners." Castro was furious, as Ulises Carbó had indicated to the committee he might be, because the negotiations were being interpreted in the United States as an exchange instead of an indemnification. Castro now acted threateningly: he warned that all of the prisoners might be shot. "The mercenary prisoners," he said, "committed a crime of high treason to the fatherland when, at the service of the policy of a foreign government, they bombarded from foreign bases Cuban installations by surprise, and invaded the country with arms in hands . . . and the crime of high treason is universally punished by the death penalty." He referred to the execution of the Rosenbergs as presenting a parallel and said, "By not taking the 1,200 mercenary traitors to the wall to be shot, the Revolutionary Government has had to utilize all its authority with the Cuban people. . . ."

However, Castro still kept the negotiations open. He said he would be willing to meet with representatives of the Kennedy administration, with legislators or with the private Tractors for Freedom Committee. And if the United States continued to insist that this was an exchange, Cuba was willing to swap the invaders for "an equal number of political prisoners from Puerto Rico, Nicaragua, Guatemala, North America . . ." and elsewhere.

A day later, Tuesday, the prisoners left Washington for Miami and then Havana, after having received a document from the committee stating it was willing "to raise private funds from the people of the United States for the purchase of agricultural tractors for Cuba." (The committee already had cabled Castro that it would begin a national campaign to raise the money, estimated at $17 million, and had asked Castro to permit a small group of Americans to go to Havana to complete the details of the agreement.)

The prospects became bleaker, however, as the opponents on Capitol Hill became more vociferous. Goldwater and Capehart now referred to the deal as "blackmail," and there were angry charges that the tractors eventually might be used to kill American citizens, as had scrap iron sent to Japan.

On Tuesday the President, attempting to silence those critics who demanded a statement from him, authorized White House reporters to say he was "profoundly interested in securing the freedom of the anti-Castro prisoners." Typical of dispatches from Washington was a story sent over the wires of the Associated Press citing "authorized sources":

While the various official bureaus maintained a "hands-off" attitude [the story read], Kennedy's approval was seen in a variety of direct or indirect aids from several federal agencies which indicated White House approval.

—A Coast Guard plane brought the prisoners' representatives.

—The State Department indicated it would view sympathetically the application to send tractors to Cuba, something that is now subject to embargo.

—The Treasury said that it is looking into the manner by which it can authorize the deduction from taxes, of the amount contributed for the purchase of the tractors.

—And the White House, it is said, decided that the exchange does not violate the Logan Act—which forbids private citizens to negotiate with foreign governments in matters in dispute with the United States.

The next day, Wednesday, President Kennedy issued a statement personally endorsing the committee. "The Government of the United States is not and cannot be a party to these negotiations," the President said. "But when private citizens seek to alleviate suffering in other lands through voluntary contributions—which is in the great American tradition—this government must not interfere with their humanitarian efforts." He went on to say that "I am confident that all citizens will contribute whatever they can. . . . If they [the prisoners] were our brothers in a totalitarian prison, all Americans would want to help. I firmly believe that all those that fight for liberty—particularly in our hemisphere—are our brothers." The President also said that any contributions would be tax deductible "as though it were for any charitable organization."

This statement only led to more controversy. Barry Goldwater felt that the President had lent "the prestige of the government to this surrender by blackmail." "We shall be lucky," Goldwater said, "if he [Castro] doesn't wind up demanding five hundred hydrogen bombs instead of five hundred tractors." Others on the Hill followed suit. To them the President had gone too far.

But Milton Eisenhower believed he had not gone far enough. "I now realized, in chilling clarity," Dr. Eisenhower wrote, "that the President intended to maintain the fiction that all aspects of the case, from negotiation to critical decision, from raising funds to actually freeing the prisoners, were private."

However understandable Dr. Eisenhower's feeling was, it is difficult to see what more the President could have done. He had stated publicly, and firmly, that he supported the committee without reservation. He had, as Senator Goldwater pointed out, lent the prestige of his office to the venture and he was being strongly attacked because of it.

The coalition of conservative Republicans and Southern Democrats began operating openly against the negotiations. In the Senate, Capehart introduced two resolutions proclaiming it was illegal for a private group to negotiate with Castro, while in the House, Congressman William Jennings Bryan Dorn, a Democrat from South Carolina, introduced a similar resolution. Senator Harry F. Byrd, a Democrat from Virginia and the chairman of the powerful Senate Finance Committee, said the Tractors for Freedom Committee "cannot be considered as a charitable institution" and talked of an investigation of the whole affair.

Thursday the Republican Congressional leaders joined publicly for the first time in attacking the deal, and President Kennedy. "It was," their statement said, "another blow to our world leadership, which constantly diminishes." Senator Everett McKinley Dirksen, speaking on behalf of the group, cited the "disastrous handling of the Cuban invasion" and added, "Now President Kennedy has added to that loss by announcing his official sponsorship of a so-called citizen movement that proposes to make the American people pay blackmail to Fidel Castro."

All the statements failed to mention the prisoners or the responsibility of both a Republican and a Democratic adminstration for them.* Senator Jacob Javits, a Republican from New York, was a lone dissenter in favor of the negotiations. But Javits' voice was drowned out when Richard M. Nixon added to the clamor by issuing a statement asking the President to with-

---

* By then virtually all the mass circulation magazines in the country, as well as the newspapers and television, had trumpeted the extent of the American involvement, beginning with the CIA under the Eisenhower administration and on through to the Kennedy administration. And, on June 13, Dwight D. Eisenhower for the first time acknowledged publicly at a press conference that he had ordered the organizing, training and equipping of the refugees in March of 1960.

draw his approval of the committee. The deal was wrong, the former Vice President said, not only morally wrong, but wrong in that it aided Castro. "Human lives are not something to be bartered," he said.

The President's reply was presented by Hubert Humphrey in the Senate. Nixon, he said, "had acted badly in every sense in attacking the President and the Tractors for Freedom Committee."

Barry Goldwater had the final word. "The only solution open to Kennedy to the serious problems facing the country is to send a man to the moon within the next ten years." And in Goldwater's home state of Arizona, Governor Paul Fannin said he hoped the people of Arizona would "not contribute a dime."

If this were not enough to discredit the effort, a campaign had begun by letter and by phone attacking the use of the bulldozers as aiding Castro's military machine.

"This was the only aspect of the whole fiasco that did not worry me," Milton Eisenhower wrote, "and I telephoned Joe Dodge to tell him so. I had consulted a high military authority on this very point. Cuba had 22,500 wheel tractors and 3,000 caterpillar tractors in use on its farms. If we shipped 500—say 450 wheel tractors and 50 of the caterpillar variety—we would be adding only 2 per cent to Cuba's supply. I was assured that this would have no military significance whatsoever."

However, the critics continued to play upon this fear and in the end it, more than anything else, wrecked the negotiations. For, in an attempt to placate the foes of the transaction, the committee on June 2 cabled Castro that: "Based upon the advice of these agricultural experts [whom the committee had consulted] we are willing to make available 500 agricultural tractors with plowing accessories, disks, and harrows of the types needed the most to increase Cuba's agricultural production and raise the standard of living of the Cuban people."

This proposal was quite different from Castro's original demand for five hundred *bulldozers* of the large type. The committee's letter imposed a deadline for Castro: "We . . . insist on receiving this official confirmation from you no later than 12 o'clock noon (Eastern local time) of Wednesday, June 7 so that we may know that you are prepared to carry out the proposal you made on May 17, 1961."

The prisoners heard the noise of a great crowd outside the Naval Hospital. When they went to the windows and peered through the blinds they saw thousands of people—men, women and children—pushing, shouting and screaming. It was the first visit of relatives who had waited outside for hours. Women began singing the national anthem, guards tried to push them back and a near-riot occurred. The prisoners opened the windows and waved and the throng roared a greeting. Women cried and waved handkerchiefs. One old lady kept calling for her son, Herman Koch. When a militia captain told her the boy was dead, she fainted and was taken to the hospital.

"It was one of the biggest emotions of my life," Pepe San Román said, "to see that building surrounded by thousands—thousands and thousands of people that wanted to see us." A soldier described it more simply. "It was a very big happiness."

Because of the size of the crowd and the confusion only about a hundred men actually saw their relatives that day. The next week relatives were again permitted to visit, and this time there was better organization. The families of those with names from A to G came on Monday, H to M on Wednesday and N to Z on Friday. The guards had been ordered to put Pepe San Román in a room by himself, but instead took him to a large room with other prisoners to greet his aunts and cousins. There for the first time Pepe saw Oliva briefly; and there for the first time he learned of the ten men in the Brigade who died on the trailer truck ride from Girón to Havana.

"I tell you," Pepe said, "I felt very bad about that. That made me sick at my stomach knowing how those fellows died." From that moment on, Pepe said, "I didn't think any more about hating the U.S. All my hate went back to Castro. I will never forget those ten men and how they died."

The ten members of the commission of prisoners had returned and after they had talked to Castro, they were allowed to rejoin the Brigade and spread the good news that they had been promised the tractors. "Everyone was very happy," Sueiro said. The days in the Naval Hospital passed slowly as the men hopefully awaited the final good word from the United States.

The leaders were still in isolation and Pepe had not yet seen Artime, although from time to time he could hear Artime talking to a guard. Artime passed the time writing poems and composing a "March of the Brigade" about the "Legion that fought in Girón to erase the pain from Cuba." He, too, was in relatively good spirits until one day a guard handed him a copy of a magazine and said, "Take a look, Artime, and find out what the Americans really think about you." It was the April 28th issue of *Time* Magazine with, among other things, a picture of Artime.

"I read this article from *Time*," Artime said, "and the article said I was the 'golden boy of the CIA,' that I was an ambitious man, a man of the extreme right who played politics in the training camps. This article hurt me more than a day or two of torture. I kept thinking about the United States and democracy. It was a very bad way to treat those who went to fight for the principles of democracy." *

The deadline of June 7 drew closer. On the 6th Castro replied to the committee in a long cable. The cable contained fourteen points and began:

"With all due respect I wish to tell you the following:

"1.—That your Committee has not taken really practical steps to carry the negotiation towards positive and immediate results."

It was a typical Castro message: vituperative, blustering, threatening and loaded with propaganda. Yet, upon careful reading, one important point is unmistakable: Fidel's position remained consistent with his original proposal. "The Committee," he said, "knows exactly the type and amount of indemnification being claimed, because it received precise information from the delegation of prisoners, and by which the Government of Cuba intends to strictly abide, without entering into struggles of a mercantile nature. [And] it has become known that in the aggression to Cuba the Central Intelligence Agency invested the sum

---

* The *Time* article said: "Of Miró's Revolutionary Council, only the ambitious Artime agreed with the Pentagon-CIA decision to invade immediately. ('He's my golden boy,' a top-level CIA man said.) Artime agreed that something had to be done or morale among the Cubans, chafing under discipline in the Guatemalan camps, would begin to deteriorate. He also agreed that time would only favor Castro, enable him to root his dictatorship even more firmly in Cuban soil." The article thus placed the burden entirely on Artime, who was in prison and could not reply, and implied that the other Cuban politicians had opposed the invasion. Of course neither Artime nor the politicians were consulted about the invasion. But that fact was not known. The *Time* story also said that "by battle's end, he [Artime] reportedly lay dead in the sunken radio ship."

of forty-five million dollars without having to haggle for a single penny with the United States Treasury in connection with the plan that served to destroy the lives of Cuban men, women and children, and caused considerable material damage to our country.* This allows us to qualify as ridiculous and shameful the attitude of those who oppose the indemnification of the material damages that were caused."

Castro asked the committee to send its delegation to complete the details.

By then Milton Eisenhower, weary and showing the strain of being "bombarded with viciously critical letters and phone calls," wrote President Kennedy what he himself described as "the bitterest letter I have ever written." He said the public should have been told from the first and "should even now be told" that only the fund-raising was private; the rest of the transaction, involving foreign policy decisions, was governmental. He described how Castro insisted they accept the principle of indemnification and said Fidel would only accept what the ten prisoners "with whom you asked us to meet told us he wanted, namely, heavy D-8-type bulldozers which are war material, possibly for trade with the Communist bloc." (Why Dr. Eisenhower then evaluated the bulldozers as "war material" when only days before he had told Joseph Dodge that he had been assured they "would have no military significance whatsoever" is not clear.) The committee, as the Eisenhower letter made apparent, was divided: Reuther wanted to continue the cablegram discussions with Castro; Dr. Eisenhower was opposed on the grounds that "if we did so we would be moving into the area of governmental responsibility."

Dr. Eisenhower plainly wanted to end matters there. Nothing written here is intended to portray Milton Eisenhower as the "villain" of the committee. Any thoughtful person must conclude, after reading Dr. Eisenhower's own account of the episode, that his motives were selfless: he was an intelligent, sensitive, charitable man performing a thankless task in the interests of patriotism and service. His very rationale for what happened, his

---

* The $45 million figure was the CIA's estimate of the cost of the invasion in testimony before the Senate Foreign Relations Subcommittee on Latin American Affairs. The figure was reported in the United States press early in May, 1961.

tortured sense of futility and frustration, make clear how difficult the situation was for him personally. It was a job he took on with great misgivings, and apparently he felt that events as they developed justified his doubts.

After much debate, the committee finally decided to send an agricultural delegation composed of Duane P. Greathouse, Ray Rainer, Clarence M. Hansen and John Bruce Liljedahl to Havana with an interpreter. In Havana, Fidel prepared for them. He replaced the militiamen guarding the Naval Hospital with a company of attractive militia women who marched and sang and chanted day and night in an exuberant display of the solidarity and happiness of the new Cuba. On June 13 the delegation arrived, toured the hospital briefly, saw some of the prisoners and then conferred with Castro.

Fidel said he wanted either the five hundred *big* tractors or the equivalent in cash and credits. If the Americans wanted to send only tractors, Castro said he would accept "three hundred bulldozers with blades to clear up jungle and brush, and two hundred with seventeen-pound harrows." At a press conference Fidel referred to the charge that the tractors were war material and asked, "What danger can this agricultural equipment entail us as against stockpiles of nuclear weapons?" But, he went on, if the potential for war material were the objection, "let them give the indemnification in the form of smaller equipment, provided that the total value of the transaction adds up to a value equal to that of the five hundred bulldozers." If it were to be cash only, he placed a value of $28 million on the deal. But, as he told the prison commission later, he was also prepared to accept the indemnification in several forms—some of it in cash, some in credits, some in big tractors, some in small ones.

The experts returned to the United States and reported what Dr. Eisenhower felt were "Castro's impossible new demands." To Eisenhower, "this meant the end of the whole affair." And it nearly was.

Under pressure from the White House and even from Allen Dulles, who personally called Joseph Dodge, the committee reluctantly sent a "last chance" cable, restating its offer of five hundred *agricultural* tractors for the prisoners. This time Castro was given a deadline of noon June 23 for acceptance.

At 11:26 A.M. June 23, thirty-four minutes before the deadline, Castro cabled the committee his reply.

YOUR COMMITTEE LIES WHEN IT ASSERTS THAT CUBA HAS CHANGED ITS ORIGINAL PROPOSAL. IT IS A RUSE CONCOCTED BY YOU IN AN ATTEMPT TO CONFUSE THE NORTH AMERICAN PUBLIC OPINION AND THE RELATIVES OF THE PRISONERS THEMSELVES. THE CUBAN GOVERNMENT INDICATED FROM THE FIRST MOMENT THE AMOUNT AND TYPE OF EQUIPMENT THAT IT WAS CLAIMING AS INDEMNIFICATION FOR THE MATERIAL DAMAGES CAUSED BY THE IMPERIALIST INVASION. THIS WAS EQUALLY EXPLAINED TO YOU WITH COMPLETE CLARITY BY THE PRISONERS' DELEGATION. AND IT WAS REITERATED TO THE COMMISSION OF TECHNICIANS THAT CAME TO HAVANA, TO WHOM WE SAID THAT WHILE WE WERE WILLING TO ACCEPT SMALLER EQUIPMENT, ITS VALUE HAD TO BE EQUAL TO THE TOTAL VALUE OF 500 SUPER D-8'S WITH THEIR ACCESSORIES AND SPARE PARTS, AS INDICATED BY US AS ADEQUATE INDEMNIFICATION.

The message concluded by saying, "The responsibility is exclusively yours." The last sentence was as follows: "The Revolutionary Government will again authorize the prisoners' delegation to go to the United States in order to explain the facts to the North American people."

Within hours the committee sent its final reply:

"Dr. Castro's latest proposal to the effect that a delegation of prisoners whom he holds captive under threat of death or long terms of imprisonment can be able to negotiate the conditions to their own freedom is ludicrous. It is further evidence of his brutality in cynically toying with the lives of the prisoners and that of their relatives."

Castro summoned the prison commission.

"Well, boys," he said amiably, "the Americans are not going to give you those tractors."

He gestured expansively and asked if they would like something to drink. Whiskey? Brandy? Coca-Cola? Anything they wanted. He told them that while they might not get the tractors, the deal was still on; they would still get the money. He was sending the commission back to the United States to explain the situation. Briefly, he referred to the committee: he was most cutting and abusive toward Eleanor Roosevelt and Walter Reuther. Mrs. Roosevelt, he said, was a *"vieja chocha,"* a silly old lady. Reuther was simply a "labor baron," controlling the lives of the workers. When he finished chatting, Castro handed the prisoners a list of the equipment he would accept, which contained substantially the same demands he had outlined to the committee. The ten prisoners were taken to the Havana docks where they boarded the *Arenal,* a Costa Rican freighter carrying a cargo of tobacco, bound for Tampa.

At Key West they were transferred to a PT boat and taken to the U.S. Coast Guard station. There they encountered a United States immigration official who had met them on their first visit.

"We had a long and hot argument with the man," Sueiro said. "He was different than the first time. We were told that we should go back to Cuba."

The official, whose name the Cubans do not know, harangued them about American principles. Lincoln, he told them, had established the United States policy, which was still in effect; and he quoted, "millions for defense and not one penny for tribute." * Ulises Carbó replied angrily, "We have fought more for the ideals of Lincoln than you ever have in your life."

After the argument the prisoners were taken outside where reporters were waiting to question them. Didn't they know the Roosevelt Committee had been dissolved? Didn't they know about the stories in the papers? Didn't they know that the whole country was against Fidel's blackmail scheme? That the tractors could be used for military equipment?

At first the Cubans could not believe that the Tractors for Freedom Committee had disbanded. Politely, but firmly, they declined to answer questions or make any comment. "Anything we might say at this time could be erroneously interpreted by one side or the other side" and any declarations "could place our companions in Cuba in danger."

They were kept apart from the press at Key West until on Sunday, June 25, a Nashville lawyer named John J. Hooker, Jr., who had helped the Kennedys during the presidential cam-

---

* The phrase, of course, was C. C. Pinckney's when Pinckney was minister to France in 1797.

paign and had been named executive secretary of the Tractors for Freedom Committee, arrived from Washington. Hooker broke the news: the committee *had* been disbanded and nothing could be done about the tractors.

The Cubans and the American discussed the situation. The prisoners wanted the negotiations reopened; at the very least they wanted to take charge of whatever funds the committee had collected. Hooker promised he would see what could be done.

On June 30 Hooker told the prisoners it was his "sad duty" to inform them that the negotiations were broken, irretrievably. He offered the prisoners two alternatives: (1) they could remain in exile in the United States; (2) they could go back to Cuba. He would not be able to give them the money from the committee; seventy thousand envelopes that had accumulated in the committee's Detroit postoffice box were going to be returned, unopened. However, if the prisoners wished, they would be given thirty days in which to raise the funds themselves and explain their mission to the American public. The prisoners accepted that proposal as the best possible one under the circumstances. They would be on their own until July 31 when they had to return to prison.

They tried to contact Richard Goodwin. He was not available. They tried to reach Eleanor Roosevelt but were told by her New York secretary that she felt Castro had insulted the committee's honor. They called and wrote to Joseph Dodge, without success. They telephoned Milton Eisenhower in Bermuda, where he had gone on June 15 for a rest and where, as he wrote later, "I was no further from the strain and turmoil than the telephone—which rang in Bermuda with annoying frequency." The prisoners never reached him. They tried to reach a wealthy Cuban named Julio Lobo who had promised to help them and he, too, was not available. In despair they turned to their own people—the families of the men in the Brigade.

On July 5 the commission met at Key West with a group of Cuban parents. From that meeting came the formation of a "Cuban Families Committee for the Liberation of the Prisoners of War." Then the prisoners left for Miami to lay the groundwork for the long and lonely campaign to raise the money.

President Kennedy placed the blame squarely on Castro. At a press conference the President said, "The committee did everything conceivable for the purpose of showing its good faith, but Mr. Castro has not accepted."

The record is not so clear-cut. The prisoners suffered more from domestic politics than they did at the hands of Castro. In the controversy surrounding the exchange, one thing was consistently overlooked: Castro apparently was sincere in wanting to bargain. However, at the time everyone, even those on the committee, seemed to fall victim to the naïve American belief that the "bad guy" never can be trusted. Castro already had proved, at the Bay of Pigs, that the "bad guys" don't always lose. And as events later would bear out, he *could* be dealt with over the bargaining table, if the right techniques were used.

Had the political climate in the United States been less inflammatory, it is not at all unlikely that Brigade 2506 could have been released in June of 1961 for $28 million in tractors, cash and credits. Instead of freedom through tractors, however, the men were doomed to the degradation of a year and a half longer in prison. And in the end the price on their heads more than doubled.

CHAPTER 4

OWLS AND OPTIMISTS

During the days in the Sports Palace and the Naval Hospital, the prisoners had divided into two principal groups: the optimists and the pessimists. The pessimists, known as "owls," spoke constantly of *bolas* (rumors). When a new *bola* would make its way through the Brigade, men would ask if it were a white *bola* or a black one: white meant good news and gave comfort to the optimists; black reinforced the owls. The atmosphere was black when, at three o'clock on the morning of July 17, the prisoners were suddenly awakened and told to gather their belongings together.

As always, they were not told where they were going. As always, they began to fear that the hour of execution had arrived—or perhaps they were being taken to the dreaded Isle of Pines.

They were herded into waiting buses and rode through the quiet moonlit streets of Havana until they approached the harbor. On the first bus a prisoner said to his companion, "If he turns the wheel to the left it means liberty." The driver turned to the right and the buses labored up a long, winding hill.

"All of a sudden we saw ourselves in front of the doors of an old castle and all our happy days of the Naval Hospital were past," said Felipe Rivero.

An owl turned to an optimist and asked bitterly, "What do you think now?" His friend said, "I don't think any more."

Guards shouted for them to get off in groups of twelve, and they were ordered to run across a drawbridge over a deep moat into the enormous stone building. One of the prisoners saw a small chapel with a cross inside a rotunda and he remembered thinking, "I don't know what sin I have committed, but I don't deserve this."

Off to the side in a small room, the three leaders, Artime, San Román and Oliva, were reunited for the first time since the invasion. The director of the prison, a man named Morejón, told them to stand against the wall and ordered the guards to shoot if they spoke to each other. Throughout the night they could hear the sound of their men running through the castle, taunted by the guards.

As the men of the Brigade ran into the fortress, they saw the prisoners known in Cuba as "common prisoners" looking down on them from five floors of galleries. Above these prisoners was a large sign: MENTAL PRISONERS. They shouted and screamed and the guards, too, were yelling, "This is going to be different, you yellow worms." The men were forced to run down a ramp circling lower and lower, past guards stationed every ten or fifteen yards who cursed and pushed and struck them with bayonets, past barking stray dogs, past prisoners who insulted them, down and down into the depths of the prison, filling the empty cells until the last groups were forced into four large dungeons holding one hundred men each. The doors clanked shut. The floors and walls were black stone and water dripped from the ceiling. The dungeons were dark and musty. High up on the walls were small windows with bars. Their spirits broken, the men lay on the floor and tried to sleep.

Two or three hours later they heard men approaching; then the guards appeared, pushing handcarts containing large sacks in which each prisoner had put his personal belongings. While the men crowded forward to the bars and shouted, "That's mine! That's mine!" the guards emptied the bags in a pile out of reach of the prisoners. They could hear the sound of broken glass. The guards held up individual items, waved them mockingly and asked who owned them. Then they threw the belongings into the cells, letting the prisoners fight like animals for a toothbrush, a washcloth, a towel or a piece of soap.

"That was the moment of the owls," one man said later.

That was also their introduction to the *Castillo del Príncipe.*

The Príncipe Castle stands on the western edge of the Príncipe plateau on the highest point overlooking the city of Havana and its harbor. Work on the fort was begun in 1774 and completed in 1794. The castle has changed little since it was constructed. It remains a Spanish fortification of the eighteenth century and for generations prisoners have been housed there. Nine hundred men of the Brigade were confined there for eighteen months.

As the last of the Brigade entered the prison, Artime, San Román and Oliva were escorted into its depths and placed in separate cells called *bartolinas*—the worst cells in the prison. "I thought that only a pig could live there," Pepe said. The cells were dark and filled with rats and cockroaches. The toilet was an uncovered hole in the middle of the floor. Later Morejón, accompanied by a man in civilian clothes, came to their cells and said it was a mistake for the leaders to be isolated. He ordered the guards to take them to the *leoneras*, the "lion's den." This hardly sounded reassuring, but to their surprise the *leoneras* turned out to be the name for the four large cells housing four hundred men from the Brigade. Once more the leaders were united with their men. It was exactly three months since the invasion had begun.

"That first day I lost my voice talking with all the boys," Artime said. "It was the biggest and happiest day that I had in all the time I was in prison."

The reunion, however, was not without its problems. Many men in the Brigade, and particularly Oliva, felt a great resentment toward Pepe: they believed that Pepe had left them to fight on alone. Pepe was aware of this and has said, "I condemned myself very often for not having gone to tell Oliva to retreat instead of sending the messenger. I did not go myself, and I should have."

In the *leoneras* Pepe and Oliva were able to talk about the battle. "Pepe explained to me why I didn't receive the order to retreat," Oliva said. "He explained that he sent Félix Alemán, a member of the transport section, as a messenger because we didn't have radio communications. Then he retreated himself, certain that I had received the message. After that I talked personally to Alemán in prison because Pepe insisted on it and I found out it was true, because Alemán told me that he could not go because the place was under heavy artillery attack and he thought we were dead. Also he told me that a bomb had exploded near him and he was unconscious. After this I talked to Pepe again and I told him that I was satisfied, and Pepe said that he wanted me to know the real truth."

Although Oliva heard the truth, and gradually others learned it, for a long time a cloud hung over Pepe's head. As one soldier expressed it later, "At that time people spoke badly about Pepe. Oliva was the great hero. Later, it was learned that San Román had given the order to withdraw when resistance was useless, and little by little it became apparent that San Román was a brave officer and a good soldier, but in the first moments of defeat and the belief of many that he had abandoned them, he was attacked within the Brigade. But the ones who saw him in war and in prison have to say he always had a lot of dignity."

The men began to exchange stories of combat and in the telling there was a natural tendency to exaggerate: the brave became heroic and the weak cowardly. There were cases, too, of men who had not performed with distinction under fire, but in prison described their exploits on the battlefield in epic terms. One prisoner wryly referred to those early days in Príncipe Castle as the "hour of the false heroes."

While the men waited for the commission of prisoners to return from the United States for the second time, their days began to fall into a pattern. There were occasional fights and cases of personal hatred among themselves, but toward the enemy the men began to unite. Every day a guard with a drooping mustache came to count them, poking each man with his bayonet. The men called him *Pica Culo* ("Pinching Ass") and one said, "We hated his guts the first moment we saw him."

The guards kept the lights on at night, as they had in the Sports Palace. The food was poor and monotonous but edible—rice, hash, sweet potatoes and bananas. There was one toilet (the hole in the floor) for each hundred men and two big laundry tubs, one for washing their tin plates and cups and spoons (they never had knives or forks) and one for clothes. As a diversion, the men resorted to jokes and pranks which might have been childish but helped to ease the maddening thought that they might be doomed to a lifetime in prison—or be shot.

Then a new *bola* swept the Príncipe Castle. The commission of prisoners had returned and the optimists hopefully predicted they were going home.

Using a small office in the Miami Colonial Hotel overlooking Bayfront Park and Biscayne Bay, Alvaro Sánchez, Jr., began organizing the Cuban Families Committee early in July. Alvarito, as he is called by his friends, was perhaps the perfect man for the job. Single-minded, tough, blunt but shrewd in negotiations, he worked tirelessly and at times somewhat fanatically to bring about the release of the prisoners. Like every member of the committee, Sánchez had a relative in prison—his son Eduardo, "my baby," who at the age of seventeen had left his freshman class at Georgia Tech to enlist in the Brigade. Sánchez had been a wealthy cattleman from Camagüey Province and often when talking with Americans he gave the impression that he was a simple man of rural background. Actually, his family had attended school in the United States for three generations, and he held a degree from Harvard.

For Sánchez, the Brigade was a symbol of a free western civilization as opposed to the totalitarianism of the East. It comprised, in fact, the first group of men to fight against communism in the hemisphere. In the months to come he repeated that message over and over to anyone who would listen.

The Cuban Families Committee was organized formally on July 10, and on July 24 it was incorporated in the State of Florida. During that time the commission of ten Brigade prisoners was attempting to raise money. Still hopeful that they could collect enough to purchase a few tractors and show Castro their good faith, they made the rounds of the Cuban colony: women gave jewelry and some their wedding rings for the cause. Toward the end of the month three of the prisoners succeeded in meeting with Richard Goodwin in Washington. Goodwin made no promises, but he did mention the possibility that they might receive tax-exempt status from the government. On July 27, as their thirty-day parole drew to a close, the prisoners called Havana and asked if they could bring the representatives of the Families Committee. They were answered affirmatively.

At the last minute two of the members of the commission, Mirto Collazo and Reinaldo Pico, deserted and refused to go back to prison. On July 31 the remaining eight men, accompanied by Sánchez and Ernesto Freyre, kissed their wives and mothers goodbye and boarded a plane at Miami International Airport. "It was the most difficult thing I ever had to do in my life," said Ulises Carbó.

"They were the bravest men I've ever seen," Sánchez said. "Not even in ancient history is there any record of prisoners going back to jail voluntarily—and these men were going back for the *second* time knowing they had failed in their mission and there wasn't much hope. I remember on the plane how one of the boys kept asking me how many minutes before we got to Havana. But they never complained."

In Havana there was a tense moment when they landed. "There are only eight prisoners," a Castro officer said sharply. "Two are missing."

"No, you are mistaken," Sánchez replied.

"But there are only eight here. I counted them. I know."

"No," Sánchez said. "Ten left and ten have returned."

He counted the prisoners and then pointed to Freyre and himself and said, "Nine and ten. Ten left and ten came back. Freyre and I will make up the difference." *

While Sánchez and Freyre watched, the prisoners were taken to the Príncipe Castle and marched through the gates in single file. Then Sánchez began his attempts to open negotiations for their release.

"When we went there we had nothing," he said. "We started with the idea of raising $300,000 and with that we hoped to bring out the badly wounded—they were virtually stretcher cases—and I was completely sure that if we arrived in Miami at that time with those men we could have got our campaign going and the rest of the men would have come out soon. We never did get to talk to Castro that month [of August] but we did get to talk to his representatives."

Sánchez was optimistic but his son in prison was not, as a letter Eduardo Sánchez wrote indicated. Better than anything, his words expressed the feeling of the men in prison at that time; and they help to explain why everyone who met them became so impressed with their attitude and spirit. The letter is quoted as written:

---

* Sánchez later explained that he was not acting out of bravado. He was certain his proposal would be damaging propaganda to Fidel. Sánchez was right: there were arguments but he and Freyre were not harmed.

My Dear Family:

Today, Wednesday the 16th of August, I spoke with father. Up until now they have not been able to get to talk with Fidel Castro. I do not have much faith in the negotiations. I believe that I face prison, possibly on the Isle of Pines. But I also have something that is worth more than money, even more than liberty. I have the satisfaction of having done something against Communism—for Cuba. Also, I have the honor of having served with the 2506th Brigade.

The only way to bear prison is with honor, with the honor of realizing that I am imprisoned for fighting for a just cause. All of my suffering and privation I offer as a service to God. Needless to say, prison will leave its imprint on my character, but this imprint will be constructive and in no way will it deform me.

At night when I go to bed and remember the sufferings of that day, I feel proud, and even if I had known of them beforehand I would do it again. Many people in Miami, who being able to come did not do so cannot go to bed with such peace. They have not fulfilled their duty. I have.

We are separated now by the sea, by a few yards of concrete, and [undecipherable word]. But spiritually we are more united now than ever. The situation that we are in has united us and, more, we have done our duty. My brother, you were not the only one who suffered because he was not accepted for the camps, when so many were able to go and did not.

Yes, you have a relative in prison. But don't envy those who do not, because you have the happiness of giving something for a just cause and they have not.

As always united with you.

E.

The day after Eduardo wrote that letter his father's hopes were jolted. On that August 17, a young Brigade prisoner named Osvaldo Hernández Campos escaped while en route from the Príncipe Castle to a hospital to be treated for a serious diabetic condition. Campos took asylum in the Argentine Embassy.

Castro was furious. It was the second time in two weeks that prisoners had escaped: first the two men on the commission of ten and now this one. Through his representatives he let Sánchez know that he could not trust the Brigade or its negotiators. Sánchez went to the Embassy and talked to Campos. He explained what it might mean to the cause of his comrades if he did not return; but Campos said he had been advised not to go back.

"In my opinion," Sánchez said, "that's what broke the negotiations."

Sánchez remained in Havana until his one-month permit expired on August 31. In those last days he was unable to see anyone. Then he flew back to Miami.

"I never felt worse in my life," he said, "because when we arrived in Miami there were thousands of families at the airport cheering us and shouting and we were completely defeated. They thought we had accomplished something."

Again Sánchez went to work. He and the members of the committee began drafting a long letter to President Kennedy, asking for the President's aid and support in liberating the prisoners. Sánchez never heard directly from the President, but the letter brought a response from Robert A. Hurwitch, a special assistant to the Assistant Secretary of State for Inter-American Affairs. Encouraged, Sánchez went to Washington. At first Hurwitch kept putting him off and telling him to come back later. But Sánchez was not easily dissuaded. For two long weeks, he kept prodding Hurwitch, "asking for the United States to come in and meet what we felt were its obligations." Finally, Hurwitch told him it was impossible to pay the ransom to Castro: Congress and the public would not accept the terms. Sánchez was certain the United States public would support the Brigade if they only knew the facts. He asked for permission to start a fund-raising drive in the United States, backed by a vigorous public relations campaign. "Put it in writing," Hurwitch said, and Sánchez did.

In Sánchez' memorandum, the Cuban Families Committee asked for the moral support of the White House and the State Department and stressed these points for its proposed campaign:

(1) *Don't be too hard on Castro because it will jeopardize the hopes for freeing the men;* (2) *Don't attack the President or the United States because they were the allies of the Cubans;* (3) *Don't impair the dignity of the Brigade.*

The memo was presented at the end of September and immediately accepted. The government informally approved the campaign.

On October 1 Sánchez left the contentious atmosphere of Miami, where many Cubans were wallowing in despair, playing politics or making bitter accusations, and opened a small, rather dingy office in New York. There were two advantages to this office. The rent was cheap, and a Madison Avenue address lent prestige to the national campaign. There, surrounded by volunteers, most of them Cuban women, Sánchez began the formal campaign to raise a ransom. Immediately, it became discouragingly clear that "everybody was against us. Nobody wanted to touch us with a ten-foot pole."

One August night the men in the *leoneras* were awakened and told to pick up their mattresses. They groped in single file through the darkened castle, back up the winding ramp, and then up many flights of stairs. When they reached the top of the castle, they were ordered to put down their mattresses. They were in the *sanatorio*, the coldest and airiest part of the castle, where the prisoners with tuberculosis were kept.

In the morning it was apparent that their situation had improved vastly. They were enclosed by a concrete wall and for the first time were able to enjoy the sunshine. The *sanatorio* was like a small village with two buildings and a patio in the center. It seemed less like a prison, for below the men could see the streets of Havana. In the middle of the patio were concrete airshafts that resembled little houses. The sounds of prisoners carried up the shafts from below. One house served as an infirmary, another contained a barber's chair. There was also a fountain on the patio where the men could wash their clothes.

"Pinching Ass" came and announced that the revolution was generous; the prisoners were free to move about the roof, within the confines of the wall. Morale soared. For a time everyone was an optimist.

In the *sanatorio* the men met Enrique Ruiz-Williams and other badly wounded prisoners, who had been brought there from the hospital days before. Many of the men had thought Harry was dead. To his surprise and embarrassment, Williams discovered that he had become a hero. First Oliva, and then

Pepe, and then Artime greeted him warmly and congratulated him for the way he had fought. "You really did good," Artime said, "you fought like hell." When Williams asked Artime how he knew this, Artime said, "I know, we all know."

From Castro's standpoint, it proved to be a great mistake to permit the Brigade leaders to remain with the men. The freedom of the *sanatorio* gave the leaders an opportunity to rebuild shattered morale. Slowly, the men began to respond to military discipline. Before long they were united in a way they never had been during the training camp period or in the invasion itself. The cruel treatment they had received in prison was in a sense responsible for this increased solidarity. Many switched their hatred from the United States to Castro when they saw their comrades beaten or when their honor was impugned and they were called cowards and mercenaries.

"We started to get organized right away," Pepe said, "thinking that anything could happen in Havana, that an uprising could occur. Everybody told us who had seen their families that the eyes of all the Cuban people were toward us. If anything happened, they would come to us for leadership. So we wanted to be prepared.

"Also we had information from some guards that Castro wanted to kill us by staging some kind of fighting inside the castle. When that happened they were going to give us weapons and tell us that we were free; that Castro had been overthrown. And when we walked outside they would kill us. Well, we talked about that very much and we decided that if that chance came, we would fight. We would take the weapons and fight. And we decided that those who brought us the weapons would be the first to go outside. So we started organizing different groups for that time."

Rumor or reality, the plan gave the men something to do and further helped to unite them. To guard against the probability that the leaders would be separated from the others or shot, the younger were chosen to carry on. They filled the time by conducting classes among themselves. Men of education and skills passed on their knowledge in formal classes. A few men learned to read and write in prison. Others studied such subjects as philosophy, German, French, English, trigonometry, physics, military science and tactics, civics and democratic principles, constitutional law, animal husbandry and mining techniques. Every day the classes were held at a specific time. Soon the practice spread to other galleries in the prison until the entire Brigade was occupied. The days were carefully organized: cleaning details were appointed and military order was enforced. In their spare moments the men played chess with sets fashioned from cigar boxes and they played poker with homemade cards and chips of paper. At night, before going to sleep, they knelt and said the rosary together.

Strangely, the news of the collapse of the Tractors for Freedom Committee did not break their spirit. And when the men learned that two of their comrades had stayed behind in the United States, this news also brought them together. "We condemned those two," a soldier said, "because they had betrayed us. They had broken their word. This fell on the Brigade's honor. It hurt our position and it hurt our prestige."

Then an incident occurred which placed San Román back in command of the Brigade. Although Pepe had discussed prison strategy with Artime and Oliva, he had continued to withdraw from the men. He still blamed himself for leading them to defeat; he felt he was a failure as a military man and he knew that many men still hated him. (Once, when a soldier accused him directly of abandoning them, Pepe merely turned quietly and walked away.) He spent most of his early days in the Príncipe by himself, learning to paint. One day, however, at lunchtime some men began to quarrel about their position in line. The argument spread up and down the line. Pepe shouted a command, calling the entire group to attention. Everyone responded. Pepe then firmly ordered the men to take their proper places and they obeyed. From that time on Pepe gave the orders and the men followed.

The guards seemed bewildered by the sudden show of unity and spirit. On the night of September 4 Morejón and his assistants came to the *sanatorio* and ordered San Román, Artime and Oliva to follow them. They took the leaders away and separated them but again the jailers made a mistake. Instead of isolating them, each leader was put in a cell with a large group of men. Before long those groups also were organized.

Pepe and Oliva found they were in adjoining compounds separated by a wall. Some of the men drilled a hole so the two leaders could communicate. They called the hole their telephone. In time the men found various means of communication throughout the prison—by sign language and mirrors, by word of mouth and through an occasional trusted guard. However, the most effective and imaginative method of communication was by "Telly-Orange." A small hole would be made in an orange and a message inserted inside. Then the men with the best throwing arms (a few had been professional baseball players in Cuba) would hurl the orange from one compound to another where it would drop with a loud "Plop!" When a new rumor arose, men asked, "Did that *bola* come by Telly-Orange?"

The Brigade soon learned that the approach of unpleasant news was reflected in the behavior of their jailers. On the morning of September 8 when the jailers brought a relatively sumptuous breakfast including chocolate, the prisoners became wary. Later it was announced that five of the Brigade had been shot as war criminals, and nine others condemned to thirty years' imprisonment on the Isle of Pines.

"This hit us very emotionally," Oliva said, "because we had lost our first men, and also we thought that the rest of us would be put on trial."

Pepe ordered the Brigade to wear black armbands and in each gallery an honor guard was formed.

After that the days began to lengthen into months and their lives settled into a routine. On the fifteenth of each month women relatives were permitted to visit them, bringing gifts and food parcels. The women were stripped naked and searched before and after each visit and so were the prisoners. As the months passed and liberation seemed as far away as ever, the visits became harder to endure. Some of the men begged their relatives not to come any more, but most of them kept coming anyway.

On the 17th of each month the entire Brigade stood at attention for a minute of silence in memory of the invasion and those who had died. While the show of unity was impressive, in reality each man felt the effects of prison. As one said, "We weren't the same any more. But we didn't speak about it." Even their letters only hinted at what they were undergoing. The following, written in English on October 24, 1961, from a Brigade member to an American friend in Tulsa, Oklahoma, is typical:

As you probably know, the fight was terribly hard with great odds against us, and without food or ammunition; but to withstand imprisonment, probably requires even greater presence of mind and greater mental and physical strength. Yet, after all we've gone through and are going through, our spirits are high and our minds are at ease because we feel we've done our duty as Cubans, Christians and members of the great democratic world. We've sacrificed not only ourselfs [sic], *but also our families and our fortunes, and though these sacrifices are great, we believe they are all well worth it if they have contributed, even in a small way, to free our country from communist tirany* [sic]. *We've lost the first battle, but not the war itself, and God willing, we shall win at the end. Even our defeat is a moral victory.*

I have not yet given up hope, I never shall, of someday rejoining my family and seeing all my good friends at P. T. & T. [*Petroleum Trading & Transport Co., Tulsa, where he had worked*] *again. When that day arrives, I will be more explicit with regards to my various experiences.*

For the present, I'm as well and as healthy as can be expected due to the circumstances. . . . I try to keep myself busy teaching English and studying Accounting, so the days, though monotonous as hell, go by a little faster. . . .

It was signed, "Carlos, 2506 Assault Brigade."

Telegram: November 22, 1961

THE HONORABLE JOHN F. KENNEDY
PRESIDENT OF THE UNITED STATES
THE WHITE HOUSE
WASHINGTON, D.C.

DEAR MR. PRESIDENT: SINCE THE BEGINNING OF AUGUST THE CUBAN FAMILIES COMMITTEE FOR THE LIBERATION OF THE PRISONERS OF WAR, INC. HAS BEEN SEEKING A RULING FROM THE INTERNAL REVENUE SERVICE OF THE DEPARTMENT OF THE TREASURY THAT WOULD

MAKE THE COMMITTEE TAX-EXEMPT AND CONTRIBUTIONS TO IT
TAX DEDUCTIBLE. WE HAVE BEEN WAITING FOR THIS RULING TO
BEGIN A NATION-WIDE FUND RAISING CAMPAIGN TO FREE THESE
PRISONERS OF WAR OF THE APRIL 17TH INVASION UNDER THE SLO-
GAN—"GIVE THEM FREEDOM FOR CHRISTMAS." ON THE EVE OF THE
THANKSGIVING HOLIDAY, WHEN AMERICANS OF ALL FAITHS WILL BE
GIVING THANKS TO GOD FOR THE BLESSING OF LIBERTY AND THE
ADVANTAGES OF THEIR DEMOCRATIC SYSTEM, WE RESPECTFULLY AP-
PEAL TO YOU FOR YOUR ASSISTANCE. DESPITE THE KINDNESS AND
COURTESY OF THE TREASURY DEPARTMENT OFFICIALS WITH WHOM
WE HAVE BEEN IN CONTACT, WE ARE TOLD THAT OUR APPLICATION
IS STILL UNDER STUDY. ALTHOUGH WE HAVE PLEADED THAT EACH
DAY'S DELAY BRINGS OUR CAUSE CLOSER TO DEFEAT . . . WE HAVE
PATIENTLY EXPLORED ALL OTHER AVENUES OF APPROACH WITHOUT
SUCCESS AND NOW APPEAL DIRECTLY TO YOU. WE PLACE IN YOUR
HANDS ALL OF OUR HOPES FOR FREEDOM OF THE YOUNG MEN WHO
SURVIVED THE LANDING AT PLAYA GIRON.

RESPECTFULLY

ALVARO SANCHEZ, JR., CHAIRMAN
ERNESTO FREYRE, SECRETARY
CUBAN FAMILIES COMMITTEE
FOR LIBERATION OF THE
PRISONERS OF WAR, INC.

While Sánchez waited hopefully for a reply, Castro pre-
empted the stage again. On December 1, during a television
speech that began shortly before midnight and lasted until five
o'clock in the morning, Castro was faced with what Theodore
Draper called "the delicate task of explaining how and when
he became a Communist." The line that attracted the most
attention throughout the world was: "I am a Marxist-Leninist,
I will be one until the last day of my life."

On December 6, the Cuban Families Committee was granted
tax-exempt status by the Internal Revenue Service, officially
establishing it as a nonprofit organization and making all contributions to the committee tax deductible. It can only be con-
jectured whether Castro's speech, with all of the attendant publicity, influenced this decision. In any case it was the first great
governmental boost for the campaign to ransom the prisoners.

During this time the main objective—the overthrow of Castro —had not been forgotten. Already the CIA had regrouped and begun to re-establish its broken contacts inside Cuba. Despite everything the Brigade had been through, a number of its members, both those who had participated in the invasion and managed to escape and those who had served on the infiltration teams in the provinces before the landings, started to work again under CIA leadership. Some men had taken asylum in friendly embassies, some had jumped the fence into the Guantánamo Naval Base and had been flown back to Florida by the Americans.

Progress was slow at first. By the summer of 1961, when the Brigade prisoners were taken to Príncipe Castle, a few members of the infiltration teams had started to assemble new intelligence to send back to the United States. On at least two occasions, in September and in November, the agency was sent information from inside Cuba about probable missile launching sites. One was located in Oriente Province in the mountains, where three large bases were being constructed by Cuban laborers and Russian technicians. The other site was reported by an infiltration team member who saw "cranes and cases of a very special kind entering into Santiago de Cuba port."

Meanwhile, new groups were being trained in Florida. Early in the fall, missions began again from the Florida Keys. Once again, Enrique (Kikío) Llansó was sailing for the agency. Throughout the fall near Key West, a large group of Brigade members was being formed into commando units. One of the men was Roberto San Román.

Two ambitious missions were planned. The first, in November, was to enter Cárdenas Bay on the north coast of Cuba at night, slip ashore and blow a bridge and a key railroad yard.

"We actually went into Cárdenas Bay," Roberto said, "but again intelligence was very bad. They said that Castro was expecting an attack on the south coast and that we would have no problems. So two good Americans, Gray from the invasion, and a new man, 'Bob,' who knew a lot about sailing, went with us. So when we went into the Bay one of Castro's ships picked us up and started following us. We went out of the Bay and after half an hour we had five ships following us. And they followed about a mile behind us more than half the way to

Miami. We couldn't fire on them because we had orders to land in Cuba, blow that bridge and attack the railroad yard. We had to attack that and make it appear like an inside raid, from Cubans inside. So if we engaged the navy outside they will know that we came from the United States."

Immediately after that failure a second, far more daring, mission was planned: to blow the Matahambre mines in Pinar del Rio Province, the largest in Cuba. If the mission succeeded, production would be halted for a year. A specially picked commando group began training intensively in the Florida Everglades.

"They gave us very good training," Roberto said, "with scale models of the shafts and the way they took the minerals up from the mines. And we had big targets and special demolition equipment and all that. We were in that training for two weeks, using the rubber rafts, big ships and small ships, and time clocks for the demolition. And then after all that work they put us in a ship that was good for nothing. At sea, the battery went dead, one engine went out, the ship began taking water and the radio failed. Gray was with us again. And Bob. Two Americans and five Cubans. We spent three days lost in the ocean with enough food for only one day. So again I was in the ocean without food or water. Bob and Gray took the catamaran we had brought along for the landing and tried to make it to Key West. They were picked up by a freighter and taken to Texas. They couldn't say that we were from the CIA and trying to get to Cuba or back to Miami. They made contact with the agency, finally, and a Coast Guard cutter was sent to pick us up. They towed us back to Key West. That is a typical mission. The idea is good and then it breaks to pieces."

When he got back, Roberto was incensed. As he said, "I could not stand this, so I wrote about both missions and I went to Washington to see [an officer in the Pentagon]. We had a very short conversation and he agreed that things were very bad . . . and that I should keep working because things were going to improve."

Reassured, Roberto went back to Miami in mid-December and began helping train Cubans with the CIA—or, as he expressed it, "playing the untouchables around Miami."

That fall the prisoners kept their hopes up by dreaming of going home for Christmas. They knew that Sánchez and the Families Committee had begun a "Give Them Freedom For Christmas" campaign and then they learned that the United States government had granted a special tax ruling. They felt that it couldn't be too long now.

The holiday season approached and to pass their time the prisoners began making Christmas ornaments from paper, cigar boxes and red ink. Already some of the more ingenious had fashioned crude tools with which they made small planes and boxes and a sled. On Christmas Eve, while some of the prisoners pulled the sled and others sang "Jingle Bells," Santa Claus, cotton beard and all, made a brief appearance—until the sled collapsed and the beard fell off. Late that night priests celebrated the Christmas mass and on the next day the prisoners put on a show, produced, written and directed by themselves. Guards, reminding the men how generous the revolution was, brought a special meal—small chickens from Bulgaria. (Some of the owls said the chickens really were vultures.) As the day passed, optimists began picking the next date for their release—New Year's Day. Again their hopes went up and down.

Then it was New Year's Eve. From the *sanatorio* they could see the glistening lights of Havana. As the hour approached men ran from their cells and embraced each other. Some drank hair tonic mixed with lemon; some tried to make wine out of crushed pineapple. It was a futile attempt at conviviality. As the clock struck midnight, signaling the end of Castro's "Year of Education," a Brigade prisoner tried to commit suicide by slashing his throat with the jagged edge of a can. In a small hotel near Times Square, Alvaro Sánchez, tremendously depressed, sat alone trying to ignore the sounds of the celebration far below.

The New Year began bleakly in Havana. The prisoners could hear the Castro celebration—the rumble of tanks and the roar of jet fighter planes (Russian MIGs)—demonstrating clearly that Castro's strength had increased. One week later an outbreak of hepatitis occurred. The men lay in their cells without medical treatment until, in one, a prisoner obviously was dying. Shouts of "Médico! Médico!" came from the cells and were repeated in other parts of the prison. After nearly an hour of shouting, doctors came and took the man, José Borrás, out of the cell, dead. Eleven others were taken to the prison infirmary.

Prison life resumed its monotonous routine, but with a difference: the food was getting worse, the treatment more severe. Then on the night of January 30, the leaders of the Brigade, their staff officers, the doctors, priests and some of the men who had performed courageously during the television interrogations were taken aside, stripped and searched.

"Well, what do you think?" Felipe Rivero whispered to Harry Williams.

"Maybe it's the firing squad," Williams said and shrugged.

Guards then ordered them to put on their clothes and took them to the Seventh Gallery, the place where condemned prisoners were kept.

The priests, Artime, San Román and Oliva were put in isolation. Sixteen others were packed into a cell designed for four men. "It was so dark that you couldn't see your fingers," Pepe said. "We had to live with the lights on all the time. I used to paint at night and that's how I damaged my eyes. We had very strong lights, about two hundred kilowatts, and it almost burned us in there. We felt like hamburgers."

After those "most dangerous" twenty-two prisoners had been isolated, a specific attempt was made to indoctrinate and divide the Brigade. The rest of the prisoners were separated into social classes—the rich in one part of the castle, the poor in another. The poor were transferred to the *sanatorio*, the best quarters in the prison, and received better food and treatment than the others. A commissar named Martínez conducted indoctrination classes; he promised they would receive preferential treatment if they cooperated with the revolution. If they reacted properly, they were told, they also would receive special visiting privileges and they would be able to play games and watch television.

How badly the Communists failed in their indoctrination is indicated by a single incident: when Martínez arrived to begin a class in the *sanatorio* one day, the men deliberately turned their backs on him and walked away.

CHAPTER 5

THE TRIAL

A cryptic item from the *Prensa Latina* News Agency in Havana on March 20 foreshadowed the official announcement. Time had run out for an exchange of the prisoners for tractors, the item said. Two days later a Cuban government radio broadcast the news to the world: the mercenaries would be tried as war criminals.

In New York Alvaro Sánchez reacted by sending a cablegram to Castro, offering himself as a hostage in order to keep the negotiations open. Four days later Castro replied by cable: THE LACK OF INTEREST ON THE PART OF THOSE MAINLY RESPONSIBLE FOR THE ACT OF AGGRESSION ON OUR COUNTRY IN THE GENEROUS OFFER OF THE REVOLUTIONARY GOVERNMENT, EVADING INDEFINITELY ITS ACCEPTANCE, JUSTIFIED IN ITSELF THIS DECISION [to "bring to trial the invaders of Playa Girón"] . . . NOW THIS MATTER IS IN THE HANDS OF THE REVOLUTIONARY TRIBUNALS, WHO ARE THE ONLY ONES WHO CAN MAKE ANY DECISION. The cable was signed, CORDIALLY, FIDEL CASTRO.

In the Príncipe Castle Brigade 2506 first received the news on the morning of March 22 when a common prisoner scrawled on a wall in large letters: TRIAL ON 29. The news traveled rapidly throughout the Brigade. From each gallery came evidence of doubt and apprehension. Everyone wanted to know what to do. In the Seventh Gallery the leaders of the Brigade conferred; and out of their deliberations a decision was reached.

"We decided," Artime said, "to take the same position that Christ took in front of the Jews—to ignore them and not to say anything."

The decision was passed on from gallery to gallery. In the

week before the trial, while the Communists called some of the men who had weakened before the television panel in the Sports Palace and threatened them with violence if they didn't co-operate now, the Brigade drew together into almost perfect unity. In one gallery the men continuously sang the national hymn, in another there was dancing and singing. Songs were composed for the occasion. The essence of simplicity, they perfectly conveyed the spirit: *"If you see my wife going by / tell her I am not afraid to die"* . . . *"Here we are with high morale / waiting now for the trial."* Some did not even rhyme: *"Look how beautiful they are going / the 2506 Brigade that will be back"*—and some were a blend of devout and profane expressions. As in the first moments of combat, each man was afraid of showing his fear.

The most remarkable thing about their attitude was their decision not to speak against the United States, no matter how grave the consequences, and in spite of everything that had happened to them. One soldier explained it this way: "The only ally that we have in fighting communism is the United States. And how are we going to go against the only ally we have? And besides, I have a wife and kid, and I want my name kept as it is, straight, vertical."

Two days before the trial, Pepe was taken out of his cell and brought before Martínez, the prison commissar. Martínez was sorry they had put Pepe in such a small cell; now they were going to make it up by setting him free. They had noticed that Pepe seemed to be concerned about the Brigade and that was a mistake—the Brigade no longer existed and the men wouldn't follow him anyway. So they were going to turn him loose. Pepe could forget about the invasion and the Brigade and everything that had happened.

Pepe refused. Nothing, he said, could alter his position. He was the leader of the Brigade and he himself never would deny that before his men. He was taken back to his cell where he waited for the trial to begin.

It was the largest mass trial in Cuba's turbulent history. In size, it recalled Stalin's purge trials of the early 1930s. But there the resemblance ended.

On Thursday morning, March 29, 1962, the men left their cells and walked to the courtyard in the center of the prison as if they were going to a party. There were jokes and laughter and shouts of *vivas* to comrades from other galleries whom they had not seen in months. When they were seated in the bright sunshine on the rows of narrow benches, Morejón brought Artime, Pepe and Oliva into the yard and took them to the first bench. Without any command the men stood at attention and sang the national hymn; then they cheered and began gathering around the leaders. A Negro named Carrillo embraced Artime, and Martínez shouted for Artime to stop acting like a politician with a Negro. But Carrillo said, "You are wrong; this is my brother."

The noise rose and in the confusion a militia guard struck another Negro. Torres Mena, of the tank company, instantly leaped forward and hit the militiaman in the face with his fist. When Martínez tried to halt the fight, a prisoner hit him. The Brigade was almost out of control. Sporadic fights began, two prisoners were bayoneted, some were hit with rifle butts. A bloody riot seemed inevitable.

Captain Pedro Luis Rodríguez rushed to Pepe and Oliva and begged them to control the men. Pepe bellowed out a command and the entire Brigade, even those who had been wounded, as well as the Castro guards, snapped to attention. There was complete silence. As one prisoner recalled, "It was so quiet you could hear a fly going around."

Oliva stepped forward to a microphone and said, "If we are going to die, we are going to die with dignity. When they shoot us we will sing the national hymn. This is not the time."

Pepe ordered the men to be seated and maintain their discipline "before the enemy." The men sat down. Then the trial began.

From the bench where the five-man tribunal sat in the shade facing the prisoners, Augusto Martínez Sánchez, the president of the tribunal, called out: "José Pérez San Román. Do you have something to declare?"

Pepe came to attention, walked briskly from his bench to a position directly in front of Martínez Sánchez, halted with exaggerated clicking of heels and said loudly, "*Me abstengo.*" (I refuse to answer.)

Next, Sánchez called on Artime—and Artime repeated Pepe's action. Oliva's turn came—and he followed suit. Martínez Sánchez then asked if anyone in the Brigade wished to make a statement.

The silence was impressive.

Impatient and angry, Martínez Sánchez said, "Well, we'll see. Is there anyone here who is not a member of the Brigade? If so, stand up, you are free." No one stood, even though there were in fact several men from the merchant marine who had come ashore when their ships were sunk and who were not in the Brigade. Next he asked, "First row. Anyone who has a declaration to make, stand up." No one stood. He repeated the question row by row. The prisoners remained seated. In one of the last rows a tall Negro named Luis González Lalonry raised his hand. Martínez Sánchez pointed to him. "Yes, stand up. What do you have to say?" "I want to go to the bathroom," the prisoner replied. The Brigade burst into laughter; the tension was broken.

Instead of the mass declarations accusing the United States that the Communists had hoped for, the trial was taking an unplanned and unwanted turn. It was not the propaganda show they expected. Around the top of the prison, cables and television cameras had been stationed, ready to show Cuba and the world how the worms reacted. But from the first moment when the fighting developed, the trial was not shown on television or broadcast on radio, and no Western newsmen were ever permitted inside the fortress.

Pedro Luis Rodríguez was called as the first witness. He stood at the microphone in front of the prisoners in his fatigue uniform with a pistol in his belt; then he faced the tribunal and began to berate the Brigade. They were worms who had behaved like cowards in the fighting in April, and now they were trying to pretend they were brave. And now the commanders of that Brigade—the commanders who had been so demoralized—were attempting to act bravely. For example, he went on, San Román, the Brigade commander, was so demoralized and so cowardly when he was captured that he gave them many signed papers and documents. Rodríguez read slowly from a document attacking the United States which, he claimed, Pepe had written to Castro. When he finished, Martínez Sánchez called Pepe to come forward.

Again, Pepe snapped to attention and walked stiffly to the microphone, stood at military attention and then parade rest. His action infuriated Martínez Sánchez and also Manuel Piñeiro (Barbarroja), the "Red Beard" who had interrogated Artime months before. Sharply, they ordered him not to assume military position, but Pepe continued to stand at parade rest.

"All right, San Román, what have you got to say? You don't have to talk. You have a defense counsel." Martínez Sánchez motioned to Antonio Cejas, their court-appointed attorney who sat in a leather-backed chair at one side of the tribunal.

"In the name of all the Brigade," Pepe said, "I refuse to accept the defense counsel who has been imposed on us by the government. We don't want anyone to defend us. We don't need any defense."

Rodríguez took over and waved the letter angrily at Pepe and asked, "What have you got to say about the letter? Look at it, San Román, look at your handwriting."

"I did not write that letter," Pepe said. "I recognize that it is a very good falsification. But it is not mine!" He was ordered to move forward and write his name on a piece of paper. He did so, then resumed his military stance before the microphone. Then he was told to sit down.

Rodríguez started reading from another letter that he said Pepe had written to his family in Miami, stating that the Brigade had received false and inexact intelligence information before landing. Once more Pepe was called forward to examine the letter; and again he denied it was his. Rodríguez, by then "mad as hell," tried one more time. He read a letter from a woman Pepe once knew in Oriente Province. Pepe broke in to say that he did not have to speak about women before them. Pepe's trial was finished.

It was then nearly three o'clock in the afternoon and the men had been sitting without a break and without food or water since eight o'clock that morning, staring into the sun. Photographers knelt along the rows—particularly the first one where the leaders sat—ready to take pictures the minute a man dropped his head or appeared dejected. Throughout the day, and for the rest of the trial, it became something of a game among the men to see if they could keep holding their heads up in the direct rays of the sun. A kind of *camaraderie* developed between the photographers and prisoners: smiles were exchanged when it seemed one or the other was not alert.

When Pepe took his seat, Martínez Sánchez called for Artime to come forward. He said they also had something to read of Artime's.

Before Artime reached the microphone, however, Martínez Sánchez for some reason changed his mind. "That's enough for today," he said, and got up and left, followed by the members of the tribunal. Pepe, Artime and Oliva were taken back to the Seventh Gallery, but minutes later they were called out, one by one, and taken away. Immediately, rumors began that the leaders were being tortured—or maybe they were going to be shot because of their performances that day.

Actually the three men were put into separate cells in the lower part of the prison. Into Artime's cell came Ramiro Valdés, the chief of the G-2, and Pedro Luis Rodríguez. For the last time, they said, Artime would be given a chance to sign a statement. They showed him a typewritten document, written under Artime's name, saying, in effect, that Artime had been a puppet of the United States and now he repented. As they left, they said Artime had less than twenty-four hours to think it over. Two guards were stationed next to Artime, and when he dozed off they poked him with bayonets. In another cell, Pepe's experiences were similar—although he was not questioned nor was he asked to sign anything. He lay on a wooden bench, without blankets, and all night guards ran canteens across the bars of his cell to keep him awake. Similarly, Oliva also was deprived of sleep but not questioned.

Outside the walls of the castle, a group of several hundred Cuban women knelt and prayed for their relatives inside. No one knew what had transpired during the first day of the trial. A brief statement over Havana radio that night merely said that the 1,180 prisoners, having been accused of carrying out a "treacherous attack" against the Cuban people at the "direct instigation of the imperialistic government of the United States," had "confessed their crime and announced they wished to make no further statement."

The Friday morning papers in Havana were no more explicit. They all said the mercenaries had "admitted their crime" but aside from the names of the members of the tribunal and the first witness, Pedro Luis Rodríguez, virtually no other details were reported. The newspaper Hoy was typical. All the prisoners, it said, "having invaded their fatherland, having participated in an invasion prepared, organized, trained and financed by Yankee imperialists," said they did not wish to make any further declarations.

Friday morning all of the prisoners except for the three leaders were seated in the courtyard again by eight o'clock. Again, there was a bright sun. That day began even more tensely than the first, for there was great concern among the men about what had happened to the leaders and how they would act *if* they showed up. Shortly after eight o'clock the sound of boots marching briskly toward the courtyard could be heard. Moments later the command "Attention!" was given. The men immediately recognized Oliva's command voice: he and Pepe and Artime were being escorted to their seats in front. That command and the way the leaders walked reassured the prisoners. The second day of the trial began immediately.

Artime was called and stood silently listening while Pedro Luis Rodríguez read the typewritten document. When Rodríguez finished, he asked Artime to acknowledge it as his own. "This is a complete lie," Artime answered. Rodríguez cursed and from the ranks of the Brigade came catcalls and laughter.

An officer from the INRA testified and accused Artime of having stolen money from the peasants while serving with the INRA in 1959. Artime, the officer said, was a man without dignity who "would sell his own mother."

The Communists next tried to discredit Oliva. They began by accusing him of retreating from Playa Larga without fighting hard. Oliva, however, was not called to the microphone. He and Pepe laughed and talked while the brief derogatory words were delivered.

For the rest of the day the tribunal directed its attention solely to the men of the Brigade. Several who had been questioned on television in April and several who had given long statements accusing the United States during the first days of captivity in the Sports Palace were called, one by one, to stand by the microphone. Their statements were read and they were asked to acknowledge them. Then they were forced to listen as their own tape-recorded words were played back over the loudspeakers, booming down on the Brigade.

All but two men denied their statements and even denied their own recorded words. One man, Pablo Organvides, had testified on television that he was really an agent of the CIA and had come to Playa Girón with suicide pills. At the trial he denied ever having said that. Another man, Areces Gutiérrez of the Second Battalion, after listening to his voice, said, "That is my voice, but that was in a moment when many things had happened. Now I deny what I said then. Now I want you to treat me as your enemy."

Out of the entire Brigade only two men made statements. One was Ulises Carbó, who had been the spokesman for the Brigade commission of prisoners that had attempted to negotiate the release through the tractors. Carbó accused the United States harshly, and referred bitterly to the Tractors for Freedom Committee negotiations. He admitted that the United States helped train them in Guatemala and then landed them at the Bay of Pigs.* But Carbó did say he could never support communism and was an enemy of the regime. The second man to make a declaration was Alonso Pujol, who is regarded within the Brigade as a Judas. He blamed the United States for everything that had happened and he said he wanted to help the Castro government in the future. Shortly after the trial Pujol's freedom was "bought" by his father, who had been a wealthy politician in Cuba and at one time a vice president of the country, and who, interestingly, had talked to Castro before the trial began.

For Castro, though, that second day of the trial had been as great a failure as the first, for the Brigade had been tested at its weakest points and it had not cracked.

A recess was declared until Monday morning and the men were taken back to their cells with the leaders still kept apart. That night Oliva remembered hearing the men singing a new song, a song that said the Brigade was ready to go again and fight.

The news of the trial had set off a wave of emotion in Miami —far more, even, than the invasion itself, for nearly everyone expected the men to be executed. In Bayfront Park more than

---

* In fairness to Carbó, he later explained to the author his testimony this way: "I was pressed a lot the night before and told that if I didn't testify they would shoot San Román, Artime, Oliva and others. And I testified, because they told me that was the only way to save them. And the chief of the Brigade thanked me for saving their lives."

Pepe said that Carbó had explained this to him in prison. And Pepe's reaction is: "I think he is right, and I believe what he told me."

a thousand women knelt at night in a vigil for the prisoners. Other Cubans talked about more worldly plans: some were prepared to touch off riots against the United States.

Roberto San Román reacted differently. He went to "Peter," the chief CIA man in Miami, and asked for money to go to Washington to try to gain government support for the prisoners. Peter said no money would be available; it was not "official business."

"Hell," Roberto replied, "these are our people and we have to do something. You have taken me to Washington three or four times when it wasn't my idea. You just told me I should go and I went. Now I'm asking only for money to help our men."

The answer was still no.

From the Cubans themselves Roberto collected $500; then he and two members of the Brigade, Nildo Acevedo and Manuel Reboso, flew to Washington on Thursday night. The next morning they went to the State Department and asked to see Robert Hurwitch, who, Roberto knew through Alvaro Sánchez, was handling the Cuban prisoner problem. In Hurwitch's office, a secretary asked who they were and if they had an appointment. Roberto said they were from the Brigade that was being tried in Cuba. They didn't have any appointment but they had to see Hurwitch. Hurwitch received them.

According to the Cubans, Hurwitch at first was "very, very cold." He explained there was nothing the State Department could do. On that point, Roberto said, Hurwitch was "very clear." If that was the case, Roberto said, then he was certain many men of the Brigade would go back to Cuba to join the men; the least they could do was to share their fate in their hour of trial. Hurwitch said they would only lose their own lives and accomplish nothing. To the Cubans, as they explained it, the Brigade was a symbol of unity for their country, and they had to maintain that symbol.

The Cubans say Hurwitch told them he didn't think the Brigade "represents any kind of symbol."

Nildo Acevedo spoke up. They had gone to Arlington Cemetery just before coming to his office and on their way out they saw a "big stone, just a piece of stone, and some statues on it with a flag. But that represents your efforts to preserve peace and democracy in the Iwo Jima battle. That is your symbol and the Brigade is ours."

Hurwitch was apologetic and said he was genuinely sorry about the men in prison. He had not meant to imply any disrespect for the Brigade. He promised to see what he could do.

By nature, Cubans are emotional and often inclined to act impulsively, but seldom had Cubans acted more impetuously than did the three men from the Brigade. In anger and without much thought, they left Hurwitch's office, hailed a taxicab and went directly across town to the Justice Department and demanded to see Robert Kennedy.

"We were real hot," Roberto said, "and we told the receptionist who we were and that we wanted to see Mr. Robert Kennedy." Within five minutes Roberto was inside the Attorney General's fifth-floor office, while the other Cubans waited outside.

"This man was completely different," Roberto said. "This was like talking to a Brigade man. He was very worried about the Brigade and he wanted to know everything that I knew—if there was any possibility that they would be shot, and how the people of Miami felt about it. We talked about the families and everything. I told him that for sure some of them would get shot, maybe not all of them, but some of them, probably at least the staff, and that Miami was boiling, waiting for some kind of action from the United States. That everybody was waiting. And if these men got shot the United States was going to have a rough problem in Miami. And, believe me, this was really the situation!"

The Attorney General listened intently, asked several questions and then said, "All right, Roberto, we are going to do everything we can. I give you my word we will do everything possible to keep them from being shot." He asked Roberto to keep in contact with him and to "call me ten times a day if you have to." He wanted to know details of the trial as it developed. From that time Roberto and the others worked directly through Robert Kennedy, whom they regarded as caring about their cause—a sentiment they did not feel existed inside the State Department.

Kennedy sent the Cubans to Richard Goodwin that morning. They told their story again and Goodwin also promised to do everything he could. For the remainder of the trial, Roberto

San Román called Robert Kennedy constantly day and night— at his office, at the White House and at his home in McLean, Virginia. As good as his word, the Attorney General was always available. Each time Roberto gave what information he had: from the Cuban Families Committee's representative in Havana, who continually called and cabled what could be learned of the trial; from Alvaro Sánchez, and from Cubans in Miami. Moreover, the Attorney General acted on that information.

In the midst of the trial President Joao Goulart of Brazil forwarded to Fidel Castro an emergency appeal from Washington urging Fidel to spare the lives of the prisoners. Through his embassy in Havana, Goulart informed Castro that Richard Goodwin personally had asked him to intervene in behalf of the prisoners. Goulart told Castro that Goodwin was relaying President Kennedy's thoughts when he predicted that if the prisoners were executed, it would touch off such a storm of protest in the United States that the President would be forced to take drastic new action against Cuba. Once again, as after the invasion, it was a threat of intervention. The administration also put pressure on other Latin American embassies to send notes of protest to Castro about the trial. Castro did not acknowledge the messages.

The week-end recess brought the first public hints that the trial was not going smoothly. On Saturday, a Havana radio broadcast reported that the prisoners had rejected the services of their court-appointed attorney and, in effect, challenged the legality of the proceedings against them. The newspaper accounts diverted attention from what was happening inside the prison by long attacks on President Kennedy and former President Eisenhower. Thus, *Hoy* reported Sunday: "John F. Kennedy, currently U.S. President, personally gave the order for the so-called preliminary operation to the cunning invasion. . . . Kennedy and his predecessor Eisenhower and their lieutenants Nixon and Johnson must morally feel they are on trial as war criminals." That paper carried a revealing photograph of Pablo Organvides standing before the microphone on Friday. The caption recounted how Organvides in April had confessed he was a CIA agent and denounced the United States on television, and then said: "He now ridiculously tries to repudiate himself."

At nine o'clock Monday morning, April 2, more than an hour after the prisoners had been seated in the courtyard, August Martínez Sánchez took his place on the tribunal bench and the third day of the trial began.

Instead of calling members of the Brigade, the government had summoned a number of "witnesses" against the prisoners. Major José Fernández, an operations officer and principal commander in the fight at Girón, gave a lengthy account of the battle. It was Fernández who stated for the first time publicly that American destroyers had been spotted coming toward the beach Wednesday afternoon toward the end of the fighting. He said the ships approached to within three or four miles of the shore, picked up survivors in small boats and left at high speed after he had ordered artillery and tank units to fire at them and called for jets to attack. Fernández was followed by Captain José Alvarez of the revolutionary air force, who made the charge that United States jets attacked and strafed a column of troops advancing toward Playa Larga on Tuesday, April 18, "causing heavy casualties."

In everything that was said, there was a blend of fact and fiction; but the principal purpose of all the testimony seemed to be to demoralize the Brigade by depicting it as cowardly and to place the blame for the invasion on the United States. The third witness was the chief of staff of Castro's army of the west that had fought at Playa Larga. He began by viciously attacking Oliva as a military commander. Oliva, he said, was a coward who tried to abandon his men when the fighting was becoming difficult. The desertion was proved, he claimed, because it was known that Oliva had attempted to get on a plane on Wednesday morning at Girón.

As he spoke, Pepe jumped to his feet and shouted, "That's a lie! You are a liar!"

While the tribunal shouted for Pepe to sit down, Pepe turned around, faced the Brigade and said, "Don't believe any of that. Oliva did not want to go. I wanted him to go, and I had to give him a strong order to go to the plane." Pepe continued to explain what had happened until Sánchez yelled to the guards, "Take him out of here!" Pepe was removed from the trial and missed an embittering moment for the Brigade.

them; then he would say that God exists, and finally pronounce "*Viva Cristo Rey, Viva Cuba Libre.*")

By Friday afternoon, April 6, Berta Barreto, the mother of a prisoner, was unable to stand the tension any longer. She was the liaison for the Cuban Families Committee in Havana, the principal source of information for the committee in the United States, and a strong personality in her own right. After lunch that day she decided to take matters into her own hands. She telephoned Conchita Fernández, whom her husband had known years before and who had an *entrée* to people high in the Castro government. Although she had no authority to do so, Mrs. Barreto explained who she was and said it was imperative for her to reach Fidel; she said she had a firm pledge from the committee of the ransom money. Conchita Fernández listened to her plea and asked Mrs. Barreto to remain at home. Some time later the phone rang. It was Celia Sánchez.

Celia Sánchez, the daughter of a physician, had joined Fidel from his first day in the mountains and has remained at his side ever since. Officially, she is Castro's secretary. Actually, she has been and, as this is written, continues to be the most important person in Castro's life, perhaps the only person he trusts completely. Berta Barreto had never spoken to Celia but she knew instantly how important the conversation could become. Celia was kind and understanding and asked Mrs. Barreto to repeat what she had said earlier. She cautioned Mrs. Barreto to make certain that she was correct about any offer, and suggested that she telephone the United States for confirmation and then call her back.

Immediately and impulsively, Mrs. Barreto put in a call to Washington to Ernesto Freyre of the Cuban Families Committee, whom Roberto San Román had introduced to Robert Kennedy that week. She told him what she had done and said she had promised the $28 million. Freyre told her to call him back in an hour; he wanted "someone" else to hear what she said. She called back and once more repeated her story, certain that someone was listening on another line. There was a pause while Freyre left the phone. When he came back, he said she was authorized to say the committee had pledges totaling from $26 million to $28 million and was prepared to resume negotiations with Castro. It was then about five o'clock in the afternoon.

Elated, Mrs. Barreto called Celia Sánchez and told her the good news. Celia made no commitments or promises, but her tone was reassuring.

At 6 P.M. Saturday, April 7, Alvaro Sánchez sent a cablegram to Castro requesting an "urgent personal interview" with four members of the committee, and informing him officially that the committee was in a position "to carry on negotiations to liberate all the prisoners . . . on the basis of the amount fixed by you in your speech of May 17, 1961." The cable specifically said "the concrete offer we are ready to offer you does not refer to tractors."

Sánchez was *not* acting on his own: he had been told by Robert Hurwitch that "we had the assurance of $28 million in foodstuffs." When he asked Hurwitch how he could prove that to Castro, Hurwitch said, "You'll know when the ships arrive."

Sometime between midnight and three o'clock of Sunday morning, April 8, Pepe San Román was awakened by the sound of voices outside his cell. The door opened and several men entered.

"When I woke up and realized what was happening, there was Fidel Castro," he recalled. "So Fidel came and I started to stretch and he was mad as hell. He stood in front of me and said, 'Get dressed!' I was in my underwear. So I put on my pants and I stood in front and looked him straight in the eyes and he said, 'Why did you deny your letter at the trial?' "

Pepe answered, "All that I'm going to say I've already said at the trial."

Typically, Castro at first reacted violently and profanely. He threw a piece of paper against the wall and began to curse. At one point he tugged at his beard and said, "San Román, what kind of guy are you? I don't understand you. I don't understand what kind of people you are." Then he became conciliatory and said he had always tried to be friendly and had given Pepe everything he wanted. He even said he recognized that many men in the Brigade were valiant. When Pepe asked why he hadn't said that at the trial they began to argue again.

"We are not brave," Pepe said, "the only one that is brave is you. You and your men. For example one of your first majors, Cienfuegos, he was so brave that he put my men on that trailer truck and killed ten of them. That was a crime! That was assassination!"

Castro broke in: "They were not ten, they were nine, and I tell you it was an accident that could happen to anybody. He did not mean to do that. It was an accident."

They argued on until Castro finally shouted, "San Román, you don't deserve to live."

"Major," Pepe said, "that is the only thing that we agree about. I don't want to live any more. I have been played with by the United States and now you are playing with me here. I am tired of being played with. Kill me, but don't play with me any more."

Castro turned and walked away without saying another word —and without telling Pepe why he had come.

Artime was the first to learn Castro's real purpose.

Fidel went directly to Artime's cell. It was the first time Artime had seen Castro since the meeting in the INRA in 1959 when Castro outlined his plan to communize Cuba.

"I thought he was coming to see me before they killed me," Artime said, "just to make a fool of me, because I knew he had done that before to other people. He came with about twenty people around him and looked at me very deeply. Then he said, 'How are you, Artime?'

"I told him, 'Very well, though not as well as you are. You're heavier than you were in *La Sierra*.'"

Castro smiled and said, "Chico, I didn't come to see you before because I knew you were very weak when you came from the swamps. And I didn't want you to think I would come to make fun of you."

He asked Artime what he was expecting and Artime told him, "Death." Castro drew out the conversation by praising the revolution and saying Artime should know better—the revolution did not do things that way. With a shake of his head, he said, "It's a pity you're not a Communist."

"It's a pity you're not a democrat," Artime replied.

Still in good humor, Castro said, "Artime, you are wrong as always. To prove to you that we are truly generous, we are not going to kill you."

Castro had come to announce the tribunal's verdict. They were guilty but the revolution, he said, had spared their lives and sentenced them to thirty years in jail. But because they were so valuable to the Yankees, he was asking for a ransom of $500,000 each for Artime, Pepe and Oliva. The rest of the Brigade would be divided into three groups: in the first group, each man's freedom could be purchased for $25,000; in the second, $50,000; and in the third, $100,000. The total ransom price was $62 million.

Castro left, and gave the news to Oliva. He seemed to delight in asking all three leaders what they expected. Oliva, too, told him death and then, after more conversation, Fidel explained the terms of the ransom. Cuba's "Maximum Leader," as Castro is called, next went to a prison gallery, ordered the lights turned on and announced the news of the ransom. He did it this way: "The Spanish made this castle uncomfortable—so uncomfortable that we're going to take you out of here." A pause. "In four months you'll all be gone." Another pause. "I'm putting a price on your heads." A prisoner called out, "How much?" And Fidel said, "$62 million."

At first they were overjoyed, but then the shock at the size of the ransom set in. If they had not been able to raise first $17 million and then $28 million, how would they ever get $62 million?

"Naturally," a prisoner said, "the owls had their day."

When Castro announced the verdict to the world later in the day that Sunday, he sent a cable to Alvaro Sánchez authorizing Sánchez to come to Havana and begin negotiations for the prisoners' release.

On April 10 Sánchez, Ernesto Freyre, Enrique Llaca and Mrs. Virginia Betancourt de Rodríguez landed in Havana and went directly to Mrs. Berta Barreto's home in the Miramar section of the capital.

One hour later Castro arrived. He was dressed, as always, in his fatigue uniform and brown beret, with a .45-caliber pistol slung at his hip. He was cordial and in high spirits. As he lighted a cigar and sat down at the dining room table, he asked, "Well, what are they saying over there?" Without waiting for an answer, he said, "Do you know what the Yankee papers are saying today?" He quoted from several papers and added, "All of them, with one exception, are favorable."

For the next hour they discussed the negotiations and the "enormous difficulties" the committee had encountered in trying to raise money. Castro retraced the negotiations from the time of his original proposal on May 17, 1961, when he had asked for heavy tractors and then had agreed to any tractors worth the same, and "the Americans offered me five hundred ridiculous little toy tractors worth a little over three million dollars. They chose to have no faith in my offer. As a result, eleven months have gone by."

To the astonishment of the committee, Castro made a sudden offer to prove his good faith: he would hand over to them the most seriously wounded prisoners and let them go back to the United States; when the committee had collected the ransom for those wounded men, it should deposit the money in The Royal Bank of Canada.

After saying he was permitting the representatives of the prisoners to come see them that night, he left.

Castro kept his pledge. Early in the evening Oliva was taken to his office. Castro told him that because the revolution thought highly of him, they were going to keep him separated from Pepe and Artime. And that night, Castro said, Oliva would go to Berta Barreto's house with the eight members of the Brigade prison commission and the sons and husbands of the members of the Families Committee.

"I was shocked when I heard this," Oliva said, "and then at eight o'clock we traveled to Berta Barreto's house where they gave us a nice dinner, with meat that was given by Castro, and for the first time in two years, counting the training camps, I sat at a table with a tablecloth and silverware."

At ten o'clock they were taken back to prison—this time with "lots of hopes because Alvarito Sánchez told us that the negotiations could become true."

Castro, usually so well informed, was only partly correct about the reaction in the American press to his ransom proposal. Virtually all of the press denounced it as barbaric and by no means did they all favor meeting his demands. *The Washington Post* was representative of many: "Plainly every effort must be made to see that the Cubans are returned alive and safe to their families in exile."

From the small middle-western town of Aurora, Illinois, the *Beacon News* offered another typical comment: "Considering that the United States is the only source of such money, the fine really is against this country. We oppose such blackmail. It is wrong morally to barter for human lives. It would be economically wrong to turn this money over to a Communist country toward which we already have set up an economic embargo. The proposed tractor swap for prisoners, which started as a joke last summer, was wrong. This proposal is worse."

The greatest obstacle toward the liberation of the prisoners, however, was neither a critical press nor any opposition in Congress; it was the apathy of the American public. For nearly a year the men had been in prison, forgotten by all but a few. Indeed, the problem really was that the American public knew nothing of them—they were a phantom force, a faceless, nameless band of Cubans, and perhaps, as Fidel said, only mercenaries at that. They were not known as a unit or as a Brigade. From the time of the trial, however, and the ransom demand, the balance began to shift. Slowly, stories began to seep out of Havana and into the American press that the Cuban prisoners had behaved, as Ben F. Meyer of the Associated Press wrote from Washington on April 14, "with great courage and no apparent effects of any brainwashing during their recent trial." As Meyer wrote, "Experts here considered the reported conduct of the prisoners remarkable."

To those who knew something about the men—how courageously they had performed in combat, how they had suffered afterward, and how they might well have been expected loudly to condemn the United States for letting them down—their action in refusing to testify or to discredit America in any way left a deep and lasting impression.

BOOK FIVE

Liberation

CHAPTER 1

HARRY'S STORY

Sixty of the most seriously wounded prisoners were taken into the courtyard of the Principe Castle. "Artime and I saw them through the window in our block cell," Pepe San Román said, "and they saw us and started saluting and shouting. Then Harry Ruiz-Williams came walking toward us with great difficulty and stood at attention and saluted me and said, 'Sir, I am at your orders. What do you want me to do?' And then a guard came running up and took him away. I think Harry was crying."

The prisoners walked through the castle gates toward the buses outside and turned and looked back for the last time. Lining the windows of the prison were the men of the Brigade, distinguishable from the common prisoners by their bright yellow T-shirts. "It was like a cloud of yellow at the windows," said Carlos Allen, who had lost an arm. "It was very emotional because we were leaving our brothers. It was happiness and sadness all mixed together."

The buses left for the Rancho Boyeros airport where Alvaro Sánchez, Jr., and the representatives of his Cuban Families Committee were waiting on the plane that would take the prisoners back to the United States. It was Saturday morning, April 14, 1962, exactly one year after the Brigade had sailed from Puerto Cabezas, Nicaragua, to begin the Bay of Pigs invasion.

In the beginning Harry Williams had not been one of the key men in the Brigade. He had enlisted as a private and gradually had risen to become the second-in-command of the Heavy Gun Battalion; but even in that position he was not involved in the decisions that vitally affected the Brigade. Yet he had qualities of leadership that eventually made him one of the most important men in the Brigade, and later in the Cuban exile colony. Among the men of the Brigade, Williams was admired for his courage, for his judgment and for his boundless optimism. In addition, he had another great asset: he was completely independent, nonpartisan and thus free from attack by the Right or by the Left. He had not been a military man or a *Batistiano;* he had not been a *Fidelista;* he had not been a politician. By profession, Williams was a mining engineer, a 1945 graduate of the Colorado School of Mines. He came from a respected Cuban family and his father, a civil engineer, had been Minister of Public Works. As a geologist, he had worked throughout South America, in the jungles and in the mountains; and by the time of Castro's revolution Williams was the general manager of the Matahambre copper mines in Pinar del Río Province, the largest in Cuba.

Politically, Williams was typical of many middle-class Cubans with college educations. He had been disgusted with Batista and had felt "that the regime was very dishonest." But, again typically, "I never went into politics deeply and I never registered to vote or voted." Even so, Williams had become involved in sabotage work against Batista, had helped to store dynamite in the hills and on several occasions had gone personally into the Sierra Maestra Mountains to supply Castro's rebels. By December of 1958, "it was getting kind of hot" and Williams was forced to leave the country. He was in Chicago with his wife and son on New Year's Day, 1959, when he heard the news of Batista's fall and Castro's triumph. Hopeful that a new era of justice had begun, he returned to his country.

Williams remained in Cuba until the summer of 1960. After the government seized and nationalized the Matahambre mines, he took his family to the United States again and that fall enlisted in the Brigade.

When the wounded prisoners left the Príncipe Castle, Williams was the man who acted as spokesman both for them and for the Brigade in prison. Before he left, Williams had pledged to return to prison if the negotiations failed. On the plane he and Sánchez, meeting for the first time, discussed the wording of a statement that would be issued to the press after they arrived in Miami. It said: "We shall consider ourselves prisoners of war until the last member of our Brigade is free. If we fail to gain the freedom of those who remain behind we shall return to *Castillo del Príncipe* prison to share with honor the fate of our Brigade." The statement concluded: "We have placed our confidence in the people of the Americas. We believe that in understanding our ideals and the purpose of our sacrifice they will give us the support we must have to liberate those who can offer only trust and faith in return."

At Miami International Airport the crowd had begun to assemble early in the morning. By afternoon more than twenty thousand Cubans were anxiously waiting. A roar went up as the big plane taxied into view and a sea of white handkerchiefs fluttered over the heads of the crowd. As the door opened and the first prisoner appeared, a stillness fell over the airport. Twice the crowd attempted to sing the Cuban national anthem. Voices faltered and broke. From the windows of the plane the prisoners saw a color guard composed of men of the Brigade who had escaped and been rescued. They were carrying the Brigade flag, the Cuban flag and the United States flag. One by one the prisoners stepped through the door of the plane—bandaged, on crutches, legs, eyes and arms missing—and saluted the Cuban flag. A band played "The Colonel Bogey March," the theme song of another Brigade that had recovered from disaster, and the men hobbled down the ramp. One of the prisoners knelt and kissed the ground. The crowd broke and rushed forward. Their tears and screams were seen and heard by millions of Americans watching on television.

Harry Williams was the last prisoner to leave the plane. "A lot of women were crying," he said, "and when I came out of the door the first person I saw was Roberto San Román [who had been his battalion commander]. So I gave him a big *abrazo* and told him, 'How are you, boss?' and he cried on my shoulder. Then I kept walking and I saw my boy who was crying and my wife, and I tried to get with them, but I had to go in an ambulance and they took me to Mercy Hospital."

Later Roberto called the Attorney General in Washington.

"I saw you on TV," Robert Kennedy said. "I watched everything."

"That's why I'm calling you," Roberto explained, "because a very good friend of mine came out with the prisoners and I want you to meet him. He will be able to tell you what's happening in prison. His name is Enrique Ruiz-Williams."

"Bring him to me," Kennedy said.

Tony Varona, the most important man in the Cuban Revolutionary Council after Miró Cardona, had visited Harry in the hospital and made a "very, very bad impression. He [Varona] came to me and told me that he didn't know how in the hell we came out, and there wasn't a chance to liberate the rest. And he said we had to go there and shoot it out. Right there I knew he was out of touch. I told him that we had said we were going back if the rest didn't come out and he said, 'Well, that is up to you.' He seemed very disgusted that we had come out."

That night Harry left the hospital to rejoin his family. When he got to the small duplex his wife had rented, he found it filled with Cubans anxious for news, and he began to realize the extent of the responsibilities he had accepted. He and Alvaro Sánchez decided to send seven of the wounded prisoners to New York to begin a campaign of public appearances to raise the ransom for the rest of the Brigade. Sánchez was even more optimistic than he had been the year before that the American people would respond to the appeal if they had an opportunity to see the sort of men who were in the Brigade.

On Monday Harry was interviewed on television for the first time. The next night, April 17, three days after he came out of prison, Harry flew to Washington with Roberto San Román. Their appointment with the Attorney General was scheduled for five o'clock the following afternoon.

"I remember I was thinking that I was going to see the number two man in this country," Harry recalled. "You know, when you come out of prison your brains don't work as quick as before, and I was a little worried about that. I was expecting to see a very impressive guy, very well dressed, and a big office and all that. And when I got into his office there was this young man with no coat on, his sleeves rolled up, his collar open and his tie down. He looks at you very straight in the eyes and his office is filled with things done by little children—paintings and things like that. I liked him right away."

After Roberto introduced them, Harry and Robert Kennedy sat down for the first of many long conversations. Harry, as Roberto remembered later, started by drawing an analogy to his own profession: his mission was to build public opinion for the Cubans step by step, in the same way he faced a new mining job, step by step until the final structure was built. He proceeded frankly, and often bluntly, to tell the Attorney General everything he could about the Brigade: how the men felt, how they had acted during the trial, how united they were, how they knew that the United States was responsible but they "didn't want to play the Communist game," and how "we have to do something for the boys."

The Attorney General said it was going to be very difficult to raise the ransom because the government could not give any money to Castro. He advised the Cubans to organize an aggressive fund-raising campaign and obtain the services of a professional organization. They should realize, however, that such a campaign would be extremely frustrating. He also said it would be easier to collect the ransom money if they could get Castro to accept food and medicine instead of cash for the prisoners. And last, but most important, they should try to form a committee of prominent citizens who had no connection with politics to sponsor their campaign. When Kennedy suggested that they approach wealthy Cubans in exile in the United States, Harry interrupted to say he knew what they were like and "they won't give us a penny."

"I left that meeting," Harry said, "thinking that it was going to be very difficult, but I was not completely disappointed."

That night he flew to New York, checked into an inexpensive hotel and the next morning walked across town to the Cuban Families Committee office at 527 Madison Avenue. "I was looking at New York for the first time in years. It made a big impression on me—the people running back and forth and all that —because after being in prison so long I was nervous. My nerves were not even yet. I could not be in a place where a lot of people were, like a subway. You know how it gets in the rush hour. I could not stand it."

Harry told Alvaro Sánchez of his conversation with the Attorney General and they discussed the formation of a sponsors' committee. That afternoon Sánchez, Harry and the delegation of seven wounded prisoners, all wearing their yellow T-shirts as a symbol of the imprisonment of their comrades, formally opened their campaign to raise the ransom. By a cruel coincidence their press conference at the Overseas Press Club on April 19 was also the first anniversary of Castro's triumph over the Brigade. As the wounded prisoners stepped before the microphones in New York, Fidel was celebrating his victory in Havana with a huge military parade, accompanied by low-flying jets. The New York press conference was more than an opening for the ransom campaign; it was also the first opportunity for the press to question the men about the controversial Bay of Pigs invasion, because the men had been told by Williams not to talk to the press on their arrival in Miami. The experience, as Harry found out, "was very difficult. We could not be too rough or too easy."

As the *Herald Tribune's* reporter described the prisoners, they "talked guardedly of the invasion and its aftermath."

The reporter quoted Harry as saying, "We cannot discuss the general battle plan or the lack of air support." Asked when he realized the invasion was going badly, Harry replied, "When we were running out of ammunition."

The initial publicity was encouraging, and on April 21 Ed Sullivan interviewed several of the prisoners on his television show. (Sullivan already had spoken on behalf of the Brigade during their trial earlier in the month. He was to assist them a third time on May 20, Cuban Independence Day, by televising an appeal for the prisoners.) Publicity alone, however, obviously was not enough. Harry, Sánchez and the volunteers on the committee, particularly two talented and dedicated women, Mrs. Luz María Silverio de Kean and Mrs. Ana María Sánchez, increased their efforts to enlist sponsors. The response was discouragingly slow and, as Harry learned, the rejection by old acquaintances particularly bitter.

Harry and the prisoners and the members of the committee continued to make personal appearances, write letters and make endless phone calls. On May 2 Harry entered a New York hospital for examination of wounds suffered during the invasion. The doctors, however, decided it was too late for surgery; the bones in his feet were too badly damaged. They were surprised he could walk at all. He was discharged from the hospital the same day, still carrying countless pieces of shrapnel in his body. The committee began working on a plan to travel throughout the country, meeting the governors of various states and asking them for assistance. On one point the prisoners were insistent: they were proud men and they had no intention of begging for help. When *Time* Magazine printed a cover story on Cuba and Castro, the prisoners were outraged by the following sentence: "Last week the strongest of the 60 sick and wounded prisoners Castro has sold on credit were in the U.S. to beg funds to buy themselves and the other 1,119 still in jail."

Sánchez spoke for the men in a telegram to Henry Luce:

THESE MEN WHO ONLY DAYS EARLIER FACED DEATH BY THE FIRING SQUAD AS THE POSSIBLE VERDICT OF CASTRO'S CLOSED MILITARY TRIAL DID NOT BEG FOR MERCY FROM THE COURT. THEY ARE NOT NOW BEGGING FOR FUNDS IN THIS COUNTRY. THEY ARE PROUD OF THEIR BRIGADE, AND PROUD THAT AFTER A YEAR OF IMPRISONMENT NOT ONE MAN OF 1,179 PRISONERS OF THE BRIGADE * BROKE DOWN AND "CONFESSED" DURING THE TRIAL. THE 60 MEN NOW IN THIS COUNTRY WERE RELEASED WITH THE CONSENT OF THOSE WHO STAYED BEHIND. THEY ARE HERE TO ASK THE HELP OF ALL AMERICANS WHO RESPECT COURAGE AND INTEGRITY IN FREEING THEIR COMRADES STILL IN HAVANA'S CASTILLO DEL PRINCIPE. IF THEY ARE NOT ABLE TO GAIN THIS HELP, THEY HAVE PLEDGED THEMSELVES TO RETURN. I AM CONFIDENT YOU WILL AGREE, SUCH MEN DO NOT BEG.

* Sánchez neatly bypassed the point that one prisoner out of 1,180 did confess. By then Alonso Pujol's freedom had been "bought" and there were 1,179 men in prison.

CHAPTER 2

THE ISLE OF PINES

On the afternoon of May 27, 1962, a militia guard at Príncipe Castle told some prisoners that everyone with a fine of $100,000 on his head was going back to Miami. Their ransom had been paid. Excitement mounted as the afternoon dragged by with no official word. From time to time guards came and looked strangely at the prisoners—and sometimes they broke into raucous laughter.

Finally at one o'clock in the morning the loudspeakers blared the names of the 211 men with the $100,000 fines. One by one the men ran from their cells into the courtyard, clutching their spoons, toothbrushes and cigarettes. Outside the gates twenty buses were waiting for them. At six o'clock Artime, San Román and Oliva were brought out under separate guard, the last prisoners to be put onto the last bus. The feeling of tension increased. The optimists were still convinced their freedom was at hand; the gloomier of the owls said they were all going to be shot.

As they drove through the streets, Havana looked like a dead city, with weeds growing along the roads and the beautiful Avenida de los Presidentes littered with trash. The buses headed south toward an airfield near the Camp Columbia military base and there the prisoners, heavily guarded by soldiers, were herded into four large planes. Inside, more guards were stationed behind machine guns which pointed directly toward the seats, Artime, San Román and Oliva were put on a smaller plane, and the planes took off. They banked and flew south and soon were over water. A last dim hope flickered: perhaps they would swing around Cuba and head for Miami. Before long the men could see mountains in the distance. A prisoner who knew his geography called out, "It's the Isle of Pines."

The Isle of Pines lies fifty miles from the Cuban mainland, directly in the path of the hurricanes that boil up in the Lesser Antilles to the southwest and whirl their way northeast. The island itself measures about 1,200 square miles. Its soil is sandy, and a large swamp covers a third of the island. By location and by terrain, the Isle of Pines is uninviting, but for Castro's purpose it serves well: overlooking the water, next to a marble quarry, stands the Modelo prison. There, all political prisoners and other enemies of the people are imprisoned, and there the men from the Brigade were taken on May 28. In the United States their transfer went unnoticed, for on that day the stock market took its worst plunge since 1929, with losses exceeding $20 billion.

The planes landed on a provincial air strip, where a horde of surly-looking militiamen waited in the drizzling rain. A bald man in his fifties, with a large stomach, stepped forward carrying a carbine. "So these are the dangerous ones, eh? Well, we'll see who's dangerous here. On the trucks, and watch out! Hold on; if one of you falls we'll shoot you right there."

This was Pomponio, the chief of the Modelo prison guards. When Artime, San Román and Oliva were brought forward and introduced as the chiefs of the counter-revolution, Pomponio sneered and warned that they were about to see a *real* prison. Pepe smiled slightly and Pomponio shouted at him: "Oh, you think you are brave! We'll see how brave you are in a few days."

After an hour's drive they saw the gray cement walls of the prison, with its high towers at the four corners. As the trucks drew closer, they heard shouts and screams and saw shirts and blankets waving from the windows. From some windows, sheets were lowered with large printed letters that spelled out: WELCOME THE MEN OF 2506 BRIGADE. Pomponio aimed his carbine and fired several shots below the windows. The sheets were withdrawn.

"What a welcome!" Felipe Rivero said. "It was worse than when we get to the Príncipe Castle. Our morale was shattered. Then above everything else we heard a scream, 'Fresh meat!

Fresh meat!' "

The militiamen pushed the men inside the prison on the double. In a large room they were forced to strip naked and stand facing the wall, their feet apart and their hands over their heads, touching the wall. If they turned or moved they were struck with bayonets. All the while the guards shouted obscenities. Father Tomás Macho, one of the three Catholic priests in the Brigade, and a man named Arozarena, one of the strongest and darkest Negroes, were pulled from the line and made to jump and run up and down on the wooden floor while guards threw bayonets at their feet.

"I had never known such beasts," Artime said.

Finally all the men but the three leaders, the priest and the Negro were taken to a long, narrow pavilion that would be their home for the next eight months. They were given some clothes and left alone. As they waited in silence, another shrill scream broke out, one that would be repeated again and again during their imprisonment at the Isle of Pines: "*Ahora, sí! Ahora, sí! Ahora, sí!*" ("Now, yes.") It came, they soon learned, from an insane prisoner in another part of the building. Some hours later the guards brought the first meal. To their surprise, it was good —bread and goulash—certainly better than the fare in the last days at the Príncipe Castle. As one man said, "A few optimists began to crawl out."

Artime, Pepe and Oliva were allowed to put on only their T-shirts and were ordered to follow Pomponio to a large dim block cell which was divided into a number of smaller cells. Each cell measured two by four meters, had brick walls on the sides and back, bars in front, and a steel net over the top. A hole in each cell, filled with water, was the source of drinking and bathing water and served also as a toilet. Separated by the brick walls, the leaders were unable to see each other.

Within minutes, fifteen to twenty guards came down to the narrow walkway pushing Father Macho and Arozarena toward other cells, poking them with bayonets, hitting them with rifle butts and fists and shouting abusive language. They called Arozarena a traitor and a dirty Negro and said "the only thing you are good for is to be a cook—or to be cooked." Father Macho received even more humiliating treatment. The guards told him to ask his Saviour for help and said they would test his priestly vows of celibacy by putting a naked fifteen-year-old girl in his cell.

They had to eat with their hands, but the food was good and even included meat. On the third day Major William Gálvez, the director of the prison, paid the leaders a visit. He stood in front of Pepe's cell and said: "Well, you're going to be here until your friends, the Americans, pay your ransom. If they pay, you'll go out; but if they invade—well, you'd better pray for them not to invade."

The major said he was forced to treat them roughly because of their behavior during the trial. Still, he wanted to be generous and he would reunite them with their men. The next morning the three leaders, the priest and the Negro were taken to the pavilion where an unforgettable sight greeted them.

The pavilion was long and narrow, and virtually every inch of it was occupied by the prisoners—row upon row of men, packed together side by side, head to foot. When they lay down on the stone floor they could not turn over without touching those next to them or in the rows above and below them. (One of the prisoners later figured out that each man had exactly three square feet for himself.) Toward the far corner, high up on the wall, was one window, but it did not face the outside so there was no sunlight.

Food was severely limited and their diet remained the same, without variation, for eight months. At eight o'clock in the morning each man received about an inch and a half of lukewarm coffee and bread. At twelve noon they were given small beans that tasted like earth and green potatoes of a kind normally fed only to pigs. In the middle of the afternoon the guards brought bad-smelling soup and noodles. That was all, until the next morning's breakfast of lukewarm coffee.

One toilet was provided, but no toilet paper. The men had no soap or wash cloths or razors or toothbrushes. There was hardly room to move, much less to exercise. They never saw the sun or the sky. From time to time guards shouted for them to stand up and prepare to move; they waited but nothing ever happened.

Pepe said, "The first thing, Oliva and I got together with the officers and the staff and we decided to organize the Brigade battalion by battalion. The complete Brigade wasn't there but at least the men that were there could be organized. We decided to do everything in formation—when we ate and when they came to count us at night. I ordered them to make formations and to give military commands. We also decided if we got out of there our first mission was to free the seven thousand political prisoners already there."

The abbreviated battalions were formed and military discipline was resumed. This display of unity apparently angered the guards, for a week later the three leaders were ordered to leave the pavilion. Pepe called a hasty formation and, when the guards approached to take him away, ordered the men to maintain their unity and discipline in front of the enemy. Then the three leaders were led to the same cell block they had occupied before. They were put into separate cells, each with an empty cell between, and from that moment Artime, Pepe and Oliva never saw their men again.

Isolated, the leaders of the Brigade organized their lives. As soon as they were put back in their small cells, each man made a calendar on the wall. While they were unable to see each other, they could communicate and they carefully arranged their days into a uniform pattern.

Each morning they waited until a guard brought their breakfast of coffee and bread before speaking to each other. Next, they did calisthenics, keeping count in unison. The rest of the morning was spent in individual pursuits. Their guards provided notebooks and pencils and Pepe drew pictures from memory—of his wife, children and friends. Artime composed poems—sixty-seven in all—patriotic poems, love poems, humorous poems and poems to Pepe's and Oliva's families. At noon the guard came with their lunch, a piece of yucca floating in boiled water.

"Then," Oliva said, "we had a nap for about an hour to have good digestion after this good meal."

About 1:30 each afternoon their class periods began. Pepe taught English, Oliva military tactics and Artime communism, democracy, religion, the geography of Latin America and physical anatomy. While one man instructed, the others took notes, asked questions and discussed the subject. The remainder of the afternoon was devoted, as Oliva expressed it, "to thinking about the meaning of the lesson" and to reading books brought from Príncipe, painting and composing poems. Oliva read one book on the philosophy of communism at least ten times and Pepe read and reread a book about Haiti. Supper (of macaroni and potatoes) was brought at about six o'clock. For the next hour they conducted what Artime called the "evening radio show," with Artime as the "announcer." Pretending to use a microphone, he would introduce Pepe who sang romantic songs and Oliva who sang Mexican songs; then Artime himself would sing congas and *guarachas*. "Sometimes the guards got mad because I would give commercials about Socialist products, making fun of them, but sometimes they would laugh. One day I made up this commercial: 'Eat the best product you can eat, eat the meat of the Russian bear,' and they laughed."

After the radio show the three men continued an imaginary trip they had begun around the island of Cuba. Pepe would start from Havana and describe the roads east until he came to a town; then he would describe everything he remembered about the town: the buildings, the population, the churches and so on. Artime began the trip from Oriente Province, Oliva from the center of Cuba, and all three argued spiritedly about the accuracy of the details. That trip around the island took two months to complete. Then Artime initiated a tour through Latin America, describing the countries, the physical terrain, the people and their political problems. That took another two months. Pepe conducted a trip in the United States—or in the part of the United States he knew—and Oliva talked about Mexico and Central America. When those trips were finished, the men related their personal lives—from birth to the present. The period reserved for the trips was from about 7:15 to 9:45 each evening. Then they had what they called a "bread party," when they ate bits of bread saved from breakfast. Before eating the bread they proposed elaborate toasts—to the future of Cuba, to their freedom, to the Americans who were coming, to a wedding anniversary or to a birthday. After that they prayed together and said good night.

"Then you were with your own thoughts," Oliva said.

During all the months of isolation their guards tried to break the leaders' spirits. Sometimes insane prisoners would be put into the adjoining empty cells. One continually called for his horse and his bicycle. Another heard voices that told him to kill himself. A third went berserk and hurled plates and beat on the bars. However, the one who affected them most was a young, blond American who sat in his cell for an entire month without uttering a sound. Then he was led away, passing in front of their cells, his face blank and completely expressionless. At times they became aware that someone had entered a cell farther down the corridor—someone they never saw and who never spoke. The jailers themselves added a bizarre touch: the guard who brought the meals always signaled his approach by singing the "Internationale."

The life in the pavilion was an endless hell of starvation and degradation. Friction among the men became almost unbearable and there were brief but violent fights. Old antagonisms became more intense; new problems such as homosexuality developed. During their eight months on the Isle of Pines the men received no visits or mail. They developed an ingenious system of communicating with the political prisoners in other parts of the building by using sign language and pieces of paper flashed in code through the window, but otherwise they had no way of knowing what was happening. Some had brought books and magazines from the Príncipe, but these were soon ripped up to use as toilet paper. The men knew they were slowly dying: they could see it in each other's emaciated faces and feel it as their strength ebbed away. They knew that if they survived they would never be the same again.

"The strain on the mind was awful," one man said.

"I began to see people in a different way," another said.

As they grew weaker, they began fainting from hunger. Medical attendants gave them intravenous glucose injections as they lay on the floor and kept them just at the point of death. There were constant outbreaks of diarrhea, and once more than ninety were violently sick at the same time with dysentery. As one prisoner put it, "Everywhere was high fevers, the violent cramps, men falling down unconscious. We were all lined up for nights for the toilet, doubled over in pain. I figured out that each man had the toilet for 4½ minutes each day, and when we were sick we couldn't make it to the toilet."

Every twenty days each man had to serve on the cleaning teams appointed by the commanders. "The night before it was your turn to serve was like the night before going to the *paredón*," a man remembered. "We used coffee sacks for mops and with the diarrhea and the vomit and the condition of the toilet, the things we had to do were indescribable."

Yet, despite the horror of their existence, the men maintained their discipline. Roberto Pertierra, a gambler in civilian life, summed up the situation best. "I know the human race," he said. "I know it by heart. But there we all worked together. When one man was sick another cared for him, he washed him. If he [defecated] a friend carried him away and cleaned him. It was something to see."

Brotherhood and charity were not their only motives: the men realized they had to remain organized or they might perish. The worse their situation became, the more they were harassed and tortured physically and emotionally, the closer together they drew. Their suffering united them even more.

At the Isle of Pines most of the prisoners became owls; pessimists never had their hopes shattered. It was easier to think only of each day, and not to dream of liberation. Their only hope rested with their comrades in the United States who were trying to raise their ransom. As for escape, they realized that was impossible, especially after four political prisoners in an adjoining compound tried to escape and were immediately captured. The men were stripped, beaten with rifle butts and thrown into an open cell, where the beatings continued and the captives were doused with buckets of ice water to keep them awake. Through an entire night the Brigade heard their screams.

On one occasion the political prisoners went on a hunger strike, and the Brigade joined them and refused to eat. After forty-eight hours the strike was crushed. The men, forced to capitulate, said they would resume eating. In the morning they desperately waited for coffee and bread but none came. Instead, half of them were taken, stripped and forced to stand with their hands high over their heads touching the wall while the guards insulted them. They had come full circle and were back where they started at the Isle of Pines.

After the transfer of the Brigade members to the Isle of Pines, the treatment of the nine hundred men who remained at Príncipe Castle became more harsh. Three hundred men were thrown back into the *leoneras*. Their daily food consisted of coffee (sometimes with sugar) and bread in the morning, macaroni and soup for lunch, and noodle soup at dinner. As a special treat, twice a month they were given the legs and stomach of ox, which had a revolting smell. Visits and mail deliveries were canceled, no cigars or cigarettes were allowed and later even their periods of outdoor exercise ended. Periodically, the prisoners were subjected to "shakedown" inspections—always conducted in the middle of the night. The prisoners would be called out and forced to strip while guards searched their clothes and cells.

However, at Príncipe, too, the Brigade's discipline remained firm. Daily classes continued and the men still sang to the accompaniment of improvised instruments made from broken bottles, trash cans, a thermos canister and cigar boxes.

One rainy night in July José Dearing González and Juan Manuel López de la Cruz lowered a rope they had fashioned with their clothes and, while the prison spotlight shone away from them, jumped the remaining thirty feet to the ground. They managed to get as far as the town of Marianao several miles west of Havana. Two days after their escape they were captured, returned to the Príncipe and placed in isolation in a small room without lights. After that the guards became even more sadistic.

"I have their faces in my head," a prisoner said. "I only want to put them in jail—only, only—and give them the same—the same—that they gave to us."

CHAPTER 3

THE DONOVAN MISSION

Harry Williams, the incurable optimist, was discouraged. He and the prisoners had appeared at more than one hundred luncheons; had held conferences in a number of cities with executives from companies, corporations, associations, veterans' and religious organizations; had met with governors, politicians, and well-known public figures; had appeared on radio and television and been the subject of articles in the daily press and national magazines. Still, the principal goal—raising a ransom of $62 million—remained as distant as ever. The publicity had brought a response, but the Cubans had not been able to collect enough money to ransom even one of the sixty wounded prisoners, to say nothing of the men at the Príncipe Castle and on the Isle of Pines. Their public relations experts predicted that their problems would be solved if a prominent American citizen agreed to serve as chairman of the sponsors' committee. But no one wanted the job.

When the problem seemed insuperable, Harry turned to the man he called his friend, Attorney General Robert F. Kennedy. On June 19, he saw Kennedy in Washington and told the Attorney General of the difficulties.

"Enrique," Kennedy said, "you don't need a chairman. You can get a chairman under any rock in the trail. What you need is a man who knows how to deal with Castro. You need someone who can represent you. I think I know of a lawyer who might help."

"Who is he?" Harry asked.

"Donovan."

Harry flew back to New York and reported the interview to

Alvaro Sánchez, Manuel Gamba and Robert W. Kean, Jr., an American businessman who was helping the committee. They decided to try for an appointment with James B. Donovan, and delegated Kean to make the call.

"We thought Donovan was a very important guy and since we were Cubans maybe we wouldn't be able to get in touch with him," Harry remembers.

At nine o'clock on June 20, Kean telephoned Donovan's office and to his surprise received an appointment for that afternoon. At three o'clock Kean and the Cubans were ushered into a large paneled office, lined with bookcases and prints and commanding a magnificent view of the Brooklyn Bridge and the East River. Behind the large desk was Donovan, a stocky man of medium height, with white hair, pale blue eyes, a ruddy complexion and an extraordinarily prominent forehead.

When Bob Kean began to speak, Donovan interrupted: "I know who you are. You are Robert W. Kean, Jr., president of the Elizabethtown Water Company. You are married to Luz María Silverio, a Cuban whose brother is a prisoner and your father was . . . Now, you are interested in what?"

Kean said they were interested in liberating Brigade 2506. He introduced the Cubans and for nearly two hours they explained the work of the Cuban Families Committee. At the end Donovan agreed to represent the committee *pro bono publico*—without fee, donating his time and talent for the public good—with one stipulation: he would have to determine from Washington whether his mission would conflict with government policy toward Cuba, or whether it would violate the Logan Act, which prohibits private citizens from negotiating with foreign governments over matters in dispute with the United States. In the meantime, Donovan said, the Committee could list him publicly as a sponsor. He asked them to prepare a memorandum outlining present and past activities—and he particularly wanted all available material about the Brigade and about Fidel Castro. He said he would have to study Castro's personality intensively.

"We were very happy," Harry Williams said. "You could see that Donovan was very smart and a very tough Irishman."

Later, Harry called Robert Kennedy to say that Donovan had agreed to be their lawyer. "That's a good job," Kennedy replied.

James Britt Donovan had been involved in mysterious affairs ever since his early twenties when, fresh out of Harvard Law School, he had worked under Vannevar Bush with the U.S. Office of Scientific Research and Development, the agency that developed the atom bomb and radar. After being commissioned in the navy, he served throughout World War II as general counsel of the Office of Strategic Services, the predecessor to the CIA, on the personal staff of Major General William J. (Wild Bill) Donovan, who was no relation. At the end of the war he assisted the late Supreme Court Justice Robert H. Jackson in the prosecution of the major Nazi war criminals at Nuremberg, Germany; and it was Donovan who was primarily responsible for introducing the films of Belsen and Buchenwald as evidence. Five years later Donovan was a partner in Watters & Donovan, with offices in New York and Washington, and an eminently successful insurance lawyer representing a string of important and profitable clients.

Donovan became a public figure in 1957 when, at the request of the United States District Court in Brooklyn, a committee of lawyers appointed by the Brooklyn Bar Association recommended him to defend Rudolph Abel, indicted as chief of Soviet espionage in the United States. Later, in 1962, he was the man chosen by the U.S. government to negotiate the exchange in West Berlin of Abel and U-2 pilot Francis Gary Powers.

Obviously Jim Donovan's credentials suited him for the mission the Cuban Committee had asked him to undertake, but in the end his success or failure would be determined more by force of personality than by past experience. Donovan's most important asset was his versatility. He could be gregarious, relaxed and disarming in his conversation. He could also be tough and blunt and discuss realities of politics, domestic and international, with the coldest clarity. Donovan, in short, was a complex, shrewd, ambitious and fascinating person—and so was the man he had to deal with, Fidel Castro.

While Donovan turned his full attention to studying his adversary, the Families Committee continued to solicit sponsors and on June 26 formally announced the list. The original fifty-two sponsors were prominent men and women representing the arts, industry, education, labor and religion. Among them were Princess Lee Radziwill, Jacqueline Kennedy's sister; Richard

Cardinal Cushing, Roman Catholic Archbishop of Boston; the Right Rev. James A. Pike, Protestant Episcopal Bishop of California; James A. Farley, General Lucius D. Clay, General Elwood Quesada, Dame Margot Fonteyn, the ballerina; former Senator Herbert H. Lehman, William D. Pawley and David J. McDonald, president of the United Steel Workers of America. The committee, as *The New York Times* commented editorially, was "impressive." The *Times* added:

So far as United States citizens are concerned, the overriding consideration was well put by the three American religious leaders who gave out statements on behalf of the Cuban Families Committee for Liberation of Prisoners of War, at 527 Madison Ave., New York City. Cardinal Cushing, Bishop Pike and Rabbi [Louis] Finkelstein [chancellor of the Jewish Theological Seminary of America], all said essentially the same thing, which was that we North Americans have a responsibility for the plight of these prisoners. We do, for it was the United States that recruited, trained, equipped and dispatched the tragic invasion of April, 1961.

At President Kennedy's press conference a day later a reporter asked if the President approved "of public subscriptions to ransom these prisoners and don't you think this money would contribute a great deal toward easing Castro's economic difficulties?"

Kennedy replied: ". . . I certainly sympathize with the basic desire, which is to get a good many hundreds of young men out of prison, whose only interest was in freeing their country. So, I'm certainly not critical of any efforts that are being made in this field."

That day other efforts were being made that would lead to the opening of Donovan's formal negotiations. Mrs. Berta Barreto, the Families Committee's liaison in Havana, who had been in the United States for a month, was given a bulky package to take back to Cuba. It contained nine separate documents, including a lengthy memorandum to Castro detailing the committee's activities since April 14 when the wounded prisoners were released. Also included were a complete list of sponsors, clippings from various newspapers reporting activities of the

wounded prisoners, and—the key item—a five-page letter to
Mrs. Barreto from Jim Donovan.

"He [Donovan] never asked me to show it to Castro," Mrs.
Barreto said, "but I knew from the way he acted and spoke that
that was what I was supposed to do."

Donovan's letter to Mrs. Barreto recounted what he described
as "much that is encouraging in this preliminary phase." He had
been approached by the Committee only seven days before he
wrote the letter, but meanwhile had been studying Castro's history and speeches. In the last paragraph Donovan, in effect, spoke
directly to Castro for the first time, in order to set the stage for
possible personal negotiations.

"It is my personal opinion," Donovan wrote, "that in his heart
Fidel Castro is proud of his fellow-Cubans now imprisoned for
their participation in the invasion of April 17, 1961. Fidel is a
Cuban before he is a Marxist and he must have pride that fellow
Cubans—however misguided or misled he may believe them to
be—would risk their lives for what they thought to be in the best
interests of Cuba. If reasonable conditions can be brought about,
in the interests of the Cuban people, I believe he will carry out
his Pledge with respect to these fellow-Cubans and demonstrate not only to Latin America but to the world that he wishes
to be regarded as the compassionate leader of all the Cuban
people. It is in this belief that I have agreed to assist your cause
toward a prompt accomplishment of its objectives."

While Mrs. Barreto prepared to return to Havana, Donovan
planned his next step: the visit to Washington. Again, Harry
Williams was the indispensable man. Harry was en route from
Miami to New York with his family when Sánchez called him at
a motel. Donovan wanted to see the Attorney General, Sánchez
said. Would Harry arrange it? Harry telephoned Kennedy that
day, July 2, and set up an appointment for 9:30 the next morning; then he drove straight through to Washington and met
Donovan's train at Union Station. At the Justice Department,
Harry introduced Donovan and Kennedy. They never had met
or talked to each other until that moment.

The Attorney General and Donovan conferred alone. Donovan
received the assurances he wanted: the mission was in the
national interest and any negotiations with Castro would not be

a violation of the Logan Act. Later that day he held further discussions at the State Department with, among others, Robert Hurwitch.

The next move was up to Castro. There was still the question of whether or not Donovan had judged Fidel's personality correctly.

Berta Barreto, who already had acted so courageously during the trial of the Brigade, now assumed an even more important role. In a letter written from Havana at 8 A.M., July 5, she reported her activities to Sánchez and Harry Williams.

"Just a few lines," she began, "after being two days in bed, because frankly I feel desperate. Officially the people of the government could not have been nicer to me. They gave me all the facilities at the airport; they let me pass the drugs I was given in Miami and Celia S. [Sánchez] called me. . . . I arrived Friday at 2 p.m. and went straight to bed as, because of my heart trouble, I felt weak, and Saturday Celia called me to tell me she and Fidel would come to see me that day anyway; I told her if they wished it, I could go over there, but she answered, 'Don't bother, I know you are sick and we will go with pleasure.' At 10 o'clock that night she called me and asked if it was all right for them to come at 11 because Fidel was expecting some gentlemen and could not leave until they arrived. At 11:15 she called again and said, 'Berta, Raúl has just arrived with the gentlemen and Fidel has to go with them; he says, if it is just the same to you, I will come there (in the end I am the one who reads and studies the documents) and then he will let you know his answer by the middle of the week personally.' I said yes, to come, and she arrived at . . . 11:30 and left at 2:15; locked up with me in the room, she studied all you sent; I believe of *everything*, the only thing that was of any interest to her was Donovan's letter and the list of sponsors. . . . Here, the government is informed of everything you do there, step by step, what comes out in the papers, of my letter to Kennedy,* of my visit to

---

* On June 5, a week after the transfer to the Isle of Pines, Mrs. Barreto had written the President, "as a mother of one of the prisoners," requesting a personal interview to inform him "of the real and actual situation of our prisoners of the Bay of Pigs." She did not receive a reply.

Washington, of the time I went with you and the time I went alone; *everything*. How? I do not know, but he even knows the cts [contacts] we have. 'I assure you (I said) that we are in the *home stretch* if you will only give us time, and in this I hope you will be our sponsor.' 'All right, Berta, I will let you know. So that you can see Fidel the middle of the week, and he will give you his answer. With reference to visits, passing of food and medicines, etc., you must try by all means to see that the rich immediately deposit their money, so that in that way I may be able to help you better and give those benefits to your prisoners.' Then she left. Today is Tuesday and she has not answered, I suppose waiting for the deposits of the rich. My mission is accomplished in principle; now if it is successful or not depends on the speed with which you act. . . ."

Mrs. Barreto gave them discouraging news of the prisoners. At Príncipe Castle, she said, the guards had been changed and all of the new ones were related to those in Castro's forces who died at the hands of the Brigade at the Bay of Pigs "and others, that the men already saw at the trials, whom they consider foreigners." Their rations had been cut and they had posted signs in the prison windows reading: WE ARE HUNGRY. SOS FOOD. More than six cases of nervous breakdown were reported. Conditions were even worse at the Isle of Pines. "Besides not having soap, or toothbrush, or clothes, *or anything!* they sleep on the bare floor.

"In my absence a group of ladies, desperate because of my delay coming back, went to the ministry. . . . They were told that when I arrived, and depending on what I would bring, the prisoners would be given facilities, and not to forget, that those were very special prisoners and that if there were any expeditions, invasions or disembarking here, they would be immediately *shot*.

"I know, Alvarito [Sánchez], that all this news will annoy you because of the helplessness in which you find yourself, the reality makes you mad. I understand perfectly. . . . I live here, living the reality, and it is necessary that you *act* and that you *act in haste*. Raúl's trip to Russia worries me extraordinarily. Tell Ruiz-Williams as one of the Brigade to go immediately to see whoever he has to see and to move heaven and earth to get the men *out of here* as *soon as possible!!* . . . Yesterday was my birthday, and among the flowers I received were some very beautiful ones from the men, which made me cry when I read the card. And I feel desperate with my impotency and full of fear for those men, prisoners of their worst enemies and under great peril always. . . ."

Ten days later Mrs. Barreto was permitted to visit some of the prisoners at the Príncipe Castle and to distribute a memorandum on the status of the negotiations. She wrote, "Alvarito Sánchez, together with Ruiz-Williams, works daily and tirelessly from eight o'clock in the morning to six and seven o'clock in the evening, Saturday and Sundays included. . . . [They] have asked me to tell you of how deeply they have felt your plight, and that they know how restless you must have been throughout this long wait, but that they are doing all that is humanly possible to hurry matters; that they are optimistic, because if they weren't they would be among you, sharing your fate."

Her son gave her a handwritten note from another prisoner:

Inform Berta that we are starving to death . . . that they should hurry up because we cannot stand it any more and we either will go on a hunger strike or provoke a mutiny or whatever is necessary. Those in the sanatorio *cannot stand it any more. And in the* vivac *either. This will work out if they get out some [time] soon. Forgive me but we are out of our minds.*

Within two weeks of that note, three hundred prisoners clashed with their guards at Príncipe and four men were wounded.

On July 29 four prisoners arrived in Miami after their families and friends had paid a ransom of $175,000 to the Cuban government. Opinion within the Families Committee and the Cuban exile colony concerning their liberation was divided. The strategy of the Families Committee was to bring out the entire Brigade; it was felt that to ransom only the wealthy would create friction and bitterness in the Brigade itself and among the relatives in the United States. If the negotiations degenerated to the point where the men were bargained for individually, many were destined to remain in prison. Furthermore, most families financially able to ransom their sons, husbands and brothers had refrained from doing so for the good of the entire group. Now they were uncertain about what action to take.

Despite this problem, the ransoming of the four men did not upset the plans for negotiations with Castro; in fact, the newly released prisoners probably helped the situation. They had all lost from forty-five to sixty-five pounds: with their skin drawn tight over their faces and their sunken eyes, they were reminiscent of victims of World War II concentration camps. One man who had been on the Isle of Pines, Fabio Freyre (no relation to Ernesto) looked like a skeleton. Without rancor and in perfect English, he described to reporters what life was like there.

Early in August Harry Williams took him to see Attorney General Kennedy, who later sent the two men to the State Department. There Freyre and Harry spoke to Edwin M. Martin, the Undersecretary of State for Latin American Affairs; Godfrey H. Summ, officer in charge of Cuban affairs; and Richard Goodwin, about the condition of the prisoners and the treatment they were receiving.

Several days after those meetings, Celia Sánchez called Berta Barreto in Havana. Donovan had asked for permission to come to Havana, the Cuban representative to the United Nations had told Fidel. Celia was calling at Fidel's request and she asked Mrs. Barreto to transmit the following message to Donovan:

"Although Fidel answered [Donovan] already through [Raúl] Roa [Minister of State], he, Fidel, prefers that Donovan interview him personally and prefers that this gentleman, in coming to Cuba, stay at your house, so that everything will develop just as when negotiations were newly opened. . . ."

Mrs. Barreto said she would be delighted to have Donovan stay at her home. Celia asked her to write a letter to Donovan and to take it to the airport early the next morning. The copilot of the plane would carry it by hand.

James B. Donovan held a press conference on August 30 at his New York law office, explained the purpose of his negotiations and appealed for prayers for a successful mission. Then he, Alvaro Sánchez and Ernesto Freyre boarded a plane for Havana. At 3:30 that same day, he met with the Attorney General of the Cuban government, Dr. Santiago Cubas, in Berta Barreto's villa. The meeting was brief. Donovan explained that he had come to Havana to reach an agreement for the liberation of the prisoners that would enable Fidel Castro to announce that an indemnification had been paid. Thus, at the outset, Donovan conceded that the transaction would be an indemnification—something that previous American negotiators had refused to admit.

The next afternoon, August 31, Donovan, Sánchez, Freyre and Mrs. Barreto were ushered into the ministers' hall of the Presidential Palace. Castro was seated at the long table, alone.

Donovan, who does not speak fluent Spanish, had Alvaro Sánchez as his translator. He had instructed Sánchez to translate literally every word that was said, neither adding nor deleting nor interpreting. From the beginning Donovan was the sole negotiator with Castro. The members of the Families Committee, all of whom had relatives in prison, had asked him to make the decisions for them, fearing that their emotions might influence their judgment. In addition to this responsibility, Donovan began the negotiations under a singular handicap: he was *not* in a position to offer cash. The Cuban tribunal had imposed a ransom sentence of $62 million in *cash,* and Castro had made it clear to the Families Committee earlier that he intended to get just that: he wanted Yankee dollars. For practical and political reasons, however, the Kennedy administration would have no part of a deal in which cash was paid to Castro. (There is even some indication that the CIA had pledged to certain Senators that no American dollars would be sent to Castro.) Even if the administration *had* approved the ransom in cash, it is most unlikely that such a sum could have been raised—either through public or private subscription. Donovan had to get Castro to agree to accept the ransom in some other form.

At great length Donovan stressed that his was a humanitarian mission, free from political involvement by either government, and both sides could reach an agreement with honor and dignity. For his part, Castro would be able to inform his people that a substantial indemnification had been paid; and the American people, as well as the rest of the world, would be satisfied that more than a thousand prisoners of war had been liberated. Donovan emphasized that he was a private lawyer acting only on behalf of the families of the prisoners; he was *not* authorized to speak for the United States government.

Castro asked questions and Donovan answered them—or seemed to. Sánchez translated, calmly, methodically, almost ploddingly. After four hours had elapsed, Castro had agreed to give "some thought" to three main proposals: *first,* that the Donovan mission would be considered independently of the earlier negotiations in April with the Cuban Families Committee, when a cash indemnification of $2,925,000 had been pledged in return for the freedom of the sixty wounded prisoners; *second,* that the payment of the indemnification for the remaining prisoners would be accepted in food products and medicines; and *third,* that the value of these products in the world market would be equal to the indemnification imposed when the prisoners were sentenced.

It was not victory, but it was a great step forward.

The next day there was another meeting—this time at Celia Sánchez' apartment on Eleventh Street, with Celia present. Castro was cordial, ordering coffee and lemonade, and talking expansively of education and real estate; he and Donovan exchanged pleasantries and seemed to enjoy each other's company. Then Castro got down to business. His government, he said, had approved the basic proposals of the day before, including acceptance of food products and medicines as ransom. Using the world market as a basis for prices, the Minister of Health and Welfare and the Minister of Commerce would prepare a list of products most necessary to the Cuban people and submit it to Donovan. However, nothing should be regarded as a final commitment. Donovan, in turn, pledged to do his best to fulfill the requirements of the list as soon as he received it.

The next morning, September 2, Donovan returned to the United States to await the list. At nine o'clock that night, Alberto Mora, the Cuban Minister of Commerce, gave Sánchez, Freyre and Mrs. Barreto a list of products in seven different categories, with desired quantities indicated and the average dollar value of the products in the United States. A list of medical products would follow. Mora estimated that at least thirty ships would be required to transport the goods to Cuba. The list was sent to Donovan "by hand" via the captain of the first Pan-American flight leaving Havana on the morning of September 3.

Only four days had passed since the negotiations began. Alvaro Sánchez was convinced that Jim Donovan was a miracle worker. "He's the greatest poker player in the world," Sánchez said later. "He began negotiating with nothing and kept it up face to face with Castro for hours. As a businessman I told him he had to put up something, but he kept it up with nothing. Nothing! He just said, 'You say in Spanish exactly what I say, word for word, and tell me in English exactly what he says.' And that's what I did."

During September, while Donovan remained in the United States, the hopeful beginning of negotiations seemed only a false start as problems increased. For a number of reasons the shipment of food to Cuba was not feasible, physically or politically. Anywhere from thirty to sixty-eight ships would be required to transport the food, too many for the American government or public to accept in view of the rapidly deteriorating Cuban-American situation. Furthermore, a new United States embargo on shipping to Cuba had been instituted that month and, finally, a longshoreman strike was threatening to tie up the ports from Maine to Florida. Donovan would have to start all over again.

Donovan himself was coming under attack because he had reluctantly accepted the Democratic nomination to oppose incumbent Jacob Javits for a U.S. Senate seat from New York. Republicans now charged that Donovan was using the prisoner exchange to further his political career. A number of highly placed Democrats were equally critical, maintaining that Donovan was hurting the party because he was not free to wage an aggressive full-time campaign. Others felt that Donovan was jeopardizing the cause of the prisoners by becoming actively involved in politics and therefore exposing the negotiations to partisan controversy—the kind of controversy that had wrecked the Tractors for Freedom Committee efforts.

In the midst of such criticism and at a time when the Cuban issue was daily becoming more explosive, Donovan flew to Havana on the afternoon of October 3. The next morning he and the Families Committee members met at Mrs. Barreto's house with Dr. Santiago Cubas and Captain Abrahantes, the sub-Secretary of the Minister of the Interior. Donovan reported that because of the "difficult situation that grew worse each day," it was impossible to transport the food products by sea: however, two major private pharmaceutical corporations in the United States, the Charles Pfizer & Co., Inc., and Merck, Sharp & Dohme, Inc., had agreed to fly large quantities of medical products to Cuba. Also, he had established two letters of credit with the Royal Bank of Canada, one covering the debt of the sixty wounded prisoners, and another guaranteeing delivery of drugs and medicines in sufficient quantity to cover the ransom. That was his new offer to Castro.

Twenty-four hours later Captain Abrahantes returned and briefly discussed Donovan's new proposal. He asked if food for children and surgical equipment could be included along with drugs and medicine. Donovan said he believed so. The captain then invited Donovan to a private conference with Castro and indicated that his car was outside. They drove through Havana and onto the open highway straight east along the sea, and for forty-five minutes they roared around curves at speeds up to a hundred miles an hour. For Donovan, who was suffering from a painful attack of bursitis with one arm in a sling, it was a particularly memorable experience.

When the car pulled up to a deserted villa at Varadero Beach in Matanzas Province, Fidel Castro and his personal physician Commandante René Vallejo were waiting. By then Donovan and Castro had established both a working and social rapport. Fidel seemed to respond when Donovan would tell wry jokes or say, with a smile, "You know, Fidel, when I get out of here and you talk about me, please say nothing good about me in public: with a few friends like you, I don't need any enemies."

As the afternoon passed, Sánchez, Mrs. Barreto and Freyre became alarmed when they had no word of Donovan. By nightfall, as Mrs. Barreto said, "We were certain something had happened to him." Finally, after eight hours, Donovan returned. He was optimistic and impressed with Commandante Vallejo who, with Celia Sánchez, had encouraged Castro in the negotiations. Castro had indicated that drugs and medicine would be acceptable in place of food but he wanted the products at wholesale prices, thereby increasing the quantity for the same amount of money.

At noon the next day Captain Abrahantes again came to the Barreto villa. This time he brought a tough new proposal: as an additional guarantee, all Brigade officers, including Artime, San Roman and Oliva, would remain in Cuba until the entire operation had been completed and all of the ransom paid. Donovan immediately rejected this; the negotiations were for *all* members of the Brigade.

That night Donovan talked for almost four hours on the phone with Celia Sánchez. She explained that the government was concerned about the validity of the banking guarantees and wanted to make certain that the ransom would be paid when the men were out of Cuba. Donovan assured her that they would receive the best international guarantees and he pledged to study the matter further. In the morning (of October 7), sick with fever and in severe pain, Donovan flew to Miami and checked in at the Dupont Plaza Hotel, using Harry Williams' name. He was examined and treated at the hotel and advised to enter a hospital. Instead, he returned to Havana the next day.

Despite his physical discomfort, Donovan was in good spirits when he and the other Cubans arrived at the Presidential Palace to meet with Castro at four o'clock on the afternoon of October 10. He carried news which he was sure would close the deal.

But instead of the cordial and accommodating Castro they had come to know, they were greeted by an unmistakably hostile atmosphere. Besides Castro a number of hard-line ministers and technicians were present: Alberto Mora, Minister of Commerce, and Dr. Machado Ventura, Minister of Public Works, led the team.

Donovan spoke first and reported that he had obtained an increase in the credit and now had the backing of the highest official banking organization in Canada. This could be verified by checking with a Señor Berry, the Havana representative of the Royal Bank of Canada, or with the Canadian Ambassador to Cuba. Donovan then handed Castro copies of a "memorandum of agreement" that contained nine major points. In substance, the memorandum said that, through the cooperation of the two large American pharmaceutical companies and because of the humanitarian nature of the mission, the Cuban government could receive drugs, medicines and surgical equipment at a 60 per cent discount, or at the wholesale prices; that the insurance, packing and transportation charges would be borne by the Families Committee; that baby food would be included in the shipment, and that the banking arrangements would guarantee completion of payment from six to nine months after the operation began. As an indication of good faith, Donovan said that the first shipment, containing 20 per cent of the total, would be made immediately by air and before any prisoners were liberated.

Castro replied that, while he had agreed in principle at their last meeting, his government technicians felt that the wholesale prices in the "catalogues" of the pharmaceutical companies were too high—they should be reduced by 35 per cent. He was against releasing all the prisoners for only 20 per cent of the goods; the committee "would not have the same interest" after the men were free. In addition, all of the shipping costs should not total more than 12 per cent of the ransom, instead of the 20 per cent the committee had estimated. Finally, Castro's technicians had agreed that the merchandise planned for the first shipment was "not as necessary in Cuba" as at first believed; they were going to prepare a *new* list of products.

At that point the conversation came to a halt. Berta Barreto, in despair at the sudden turn in the negotiations, impetuously stepped forward and spoke directly to Castro in Spanish.

"As a mother of a son in prison, I beg you to keep negotiating. Don't let it end this way!" She began to cry.

Castro seemed to soften. Ernestó Freyre, speaking in rapid Spanish, impetuously engaged Castro in a long conversation. Castro was obviously dictating to Freyre the conditions necessary to reach an agreement. Freyre was nodding, taking notes, and occasionally saying, "*Sí, Primer Ministro, sí.*"

During this exchange Donovan was cut off from the conversation: it was happening too fast for Sánchez to translate. Furious at being bypassed and excluded, and not knowing what Freyre had promised Fidel, Donovan turned, said, "That's it!" and walked out. The negotiations were broken.

While Donovan was preparing to go back to the United States to announce the failure of the mission, Alvaro Sánchez came to his room at the Barreto villa. Sánchez said he knew how Donovan felt and he agreed with him, "but the boys are not responsible. They will die if we end it now." Donovan agreed to keep trying. Ernesto Freyre never again participated in the face-to-face negotiations.

The next day Donovan wrote a personal message to Castro, asking Fidel to determine what drugs Cuba needed and to indicate when he was ready to bargain once more. Donovan handed the message to Alberto Mora and left for Miami. His second trip to Havana had lasted eight days.

On October 19, Ernesto Freyre delivered a new list of drugs and medicines to Harry Williams at the airport in Miami. Harry immediately flew to New York and gave the bulky sealed envelope to Donovan the next morning. Donovan scanned the list quickly and said, "Impossible! They want to break the negotiations." The new list quoted drug prices from Japan, Poland, and Italy which were lower on the world market than those of United States firms. Harry called Bob Kennedy and Donovan contacted friends in the drug industry. A report on the possibility of meeting the prices would be presented the next week. But on the following Monday, October 22, 1962, national attention was focused on another matter.

The leaders of the Brigade first became aware of the tension when their guards appeared wearing steel helmets and ammunition belts and loaded with weapons. Extra locks were put on the leaders' cells. Major William Gálvez, the commander of the prison on the Isle of Pines, said to them, "Well boys, your suffering is about to end. It looks like the Americans might invade. We're not going to torture you or mistreat you. But you can count on this: if they come, you are going to be the first to go." The lights in their cell block were turned out and they remained in total darkness for the period of the Cuban missile crisis. At the Príncipe Castle the news came when guards whispered to the prisoners that "the gringo is coming."

James B. Donovan heard the news in the town of Oneonta, in upstate New York, where he was about to make a speech before a college audience. "I sat down in the lounge crowded with students and faculty members," he said, "and watched Kennedy make his famous missile speech on TV. Then and there I had to decide what to say—'no comment' or 'wait and see' or what. As soon as the speech was over I made the following statement: 'The President exhibited his characteristic combination of firm courage and statesmanlike restraint. In my opinion if he firmly adheres to the position set forth in his speech the missiles will be removed, the Russians will leave, and not a shot will be fired.' This was the most difficult decision I had to make during the negotiations. I knew whatever I said would be read by Castro, and I ran the risk of irreparably destroying my mission."

That it did not destroy the mission is a matter of history. Perhaps the most astonishing aspect of the Cuban crisis is that the negotiations for the Bay of Pigs prisoners remained open all those searing hours.

Initially, the case of the prisoners was almost put aside for the duration; but after a conversation between Robert Kennedy and Harry Williams the bargaining continued. Harry had gone to see the Attorney General to discuss what part he and other members of the Brigade in the United States might play in a possible military action against Cuba. The subject of the prisoners was mentioned and Kennedy said they would have to forget about the exchange during the crisis. Harry protested. It was absolutely necessary, he said, to keep the negotiations open, even if only to protect the men from worse treatment.

The Attorney General responded immediately, "You're right. Keep it open. Keep it going."

At least twice every day during the crisis Harry called Alvaro Sánchez in Havana, reporting imaginary progress with imaginary firms and expressing confidence that despite the blockade the mission would be successful. Frequently the calls were interrupted—once it took Harry twelve hours to complete a call. Donovan also did everything he could to keep the lines clear. On October 26, for instance, he sent this telegram to Sánchez in Havana:

RECEIVED YOUR TELEPHONE MESSAGE TODAY STOP THE LIST SENT BY THE CUBAN GOVERNMENT RECEIVED LAST SATURDAY OCTOBER 20 STOP IMMEDIATELY WE STARTED DISCUSSING THIS LIST WITH THE VARIOUS COMPANIES THAT PRODUCE THESE TYPES OF MATERIALS AND THEY ARE GIVING IT SERIOUS STUDY AND DEEP CONSIDERATION STOP WE WILL BE CONSTANTLY IN TOUCH WITH YOU REGARDING NEW DEVELOPMENTS AS WE HEAR FROM THE VARIOUS COMPANIES STOP BEST REGARDS STOP

JAMES B. DONOVAN

When the crisis was over, Sánchez was permitted to see a few prisoners at the Príncipe Castle and visited the Isle of Pines on November 16. At both places he was shocked by the physical condition of the men. He, Mrs. Barreto and her husband flew to New York on November 19. All were dejected over what seemed a hopeless situation but tried to maintain a show of optimism. At a press conference reporters asked if the prisoners would be liberated and Sánchez replied, "Yes. Yes."

CHAPTER 4

ALL THEY LACKED WERE THE CHAINS

Alvaro Sánchez spoke quietly but with great emotion. "Mr. Attorney General, the President, your brother, at this moment is in a honeymoon with the American people. After the way he solved the Cuban crisis he can do anything he wants. Now is the time to free these men. Bring them home to their families by Christmas."

Not only was it the proper moment, Sánchez told Robert Kennedy, but if there was any more delay it would be too late. He described his visit to the prisoners at the Príncipe Castle and on the Isle of Pines, and said he had particularly noticed the backs of their necks. As a cattleman, he could say that they looked like animals who were about to die. "If you are going to rescue these men, this is the time, because if you wait you will be liberating corpses."

Harry Williams, who had asked Kennedy to meet Sánchez, was intently watching the Attorney General. "You could see in his face how he felt," Williams said.

Kennedy waited a moment and said, "You are right. I think this is the moment."

Roberto San Román asked what the chances were and Kennedy replied, "Fifty-fifty." From the American side, there would be no problem; the big question was Fidel Castro.

That meeting between Robert Kennedy and the three Cubans on a Saturday morning at the end of November, 1962, at the Waldorf-Astoria Hotel in New York initiated an operation without precedent in American history—an operation in which the government threw its power and its prestige into raising millions of dollars to ransom 1,179 prisoners from a foreign nation.

Robert Kennedy had been deeply involved in the prisoner exchange from the beginning. To him, it was always a clear-cut issue, a simple matter of right and wrong. The United States was morally responsible for the men and the United States had to do everything it could to free them. Aside from the ethical considerations, he believed that the Cuban prisoners were brave men who had fought for their country and in a larger sense for western civilization, and they had responded to adversity in a remarkable manner. This alone was enough to commit the Kennedys—both the Attorney General and the President—for at all times the Attorney General was acting with the knowledge and consent of his brother.

However, in order to liberate the Brigade more was required than the backing of the Kennedys. In the past, partisanship had wrecked the negotiations. By early October of 1962, however, the prisoner exchange had become a bipartisan venture. General Eisenhower had been contacted and had let it be known that he would not oppose the liberation efforts. The same was true of Republicans in Congress. For this reason there were virtually no political protests raised over the final attempts to free the men.

After the conversation with the Cubans in New York, the Attorney General set out to accomplish a goal of freedom by Christmas. He already had devoted time and energy to the negotiations strategy; now he accelerated the pace. Under his personal direction, the Justice Department became the nerve center of the operation.

When Robert Kennedy became committed to a goal of freedom by Christmas, the negotiations with Castro had been dormant since the October missile crisis. Throughout September and October James B. Donovan had explored with industry officials—especially executives of Pfizer and Borden's—the possibility of obtaining contributions to meet Castro's demand of $53 million worth of drugs and chemicals, medical and surgical equipment and baby food. Donovan also had looked into the possibility of income tax deductions for those who made contributions. His discussions remained fairly general in nature, however, and little progress had been made toward assembling contributions and arranging for the collection and transportation of the goods.

A few days before the end of November Secretary of State
Dean Rusk asked Secretary of the Treasury Douglas Dillon
whether the Treasury, through the Internal Revenue Service,
could be of any assistance in the liberation effort. Dillon took
up the problem at a regular Treasury staff meeting attended by,
among others, Mortimer Caplin, the commissioner of Internal
Revenue, and Stanley Surrey, assistant Treasury secretary. As a
result of that meeting a conference of top officials of the Departments of State, Treasury, Justice and the CIA was scheduled
for Friday, November 30, to discuss the liberation of the Brigade.

On that Friday Robert Kennedy had lunch with Louis E.
Oberdorfer, the assistant Attorney General in charge of the
Department of Justice's Tax Division. Kennedy stressed the importance the administration attached to the prisoner exchange
and told Oberdorfer that the goal was to liberate the prisoners
by Christmas.

"Lean on it," Kennedy said.

From that moment Lou Oberdorfer, quiet, tough-minded and
efficient, like Kennedy himself a doer, worked full time to coordinate all of the activities in connection with the exchange.

Later that day Oberdorfer and Deputy Attorney General
Nicholas (Nick) deB. Katzenbach, who had been a prisoner
of war himself for two years during World War II, met with
Stanley Surrey of the Treasury Department, Robert Hurwitch
of the State Department, Mitchell Rogovin of the Internal Revenue Service and two men from the CIA. They determined that
the $53 million would have a cost in the United States of only
about $17 million at wholesale, and discussed Castro's demand
that 20 per cent of the goods had to be delivered before any
prisoners would be released. For the first time it was suggested
that the manufacturers might be willing to make direct contributions in goods, thus eliminating the necessity for cash—
all of this depending, of course, upon whether the corporations
were assured that their contributions could be considered as
tax-deductible gifts. Rogovin, Surrey and Oberdorfer agreed to
work over the weekend to prepare a tax memorandum for the
Attorney General.

Oberdorfer also informally approached Lloyd Cutler, a Washington lawyer and counsel to the Pharmaceutical Manufacturers
Association, about the possibility of contributions by the drug

companies. Cutler, who had been contacted earlier when Dono-van's negotiations were progressing, said he thought there was still a chance. But he made it clear that in order to do the job the companies would have to be able to work together without fear of subsequent antitrust or other action. And, he pointed out, because of the unfavorable public and political image of the drug manufacturers stemming from Senator Estes Kefauver's investigating subcommittee in 1960 and 1961, the companies would need some assurance from the administration that they would not be attacked because of their participation in the prisoner exchange. They also would have to be assured that they would not be required to disclose their cost and markup data in order to secure tax deductions.

On Monday, December 3, Oberdorfer went to the White House, gave Robert Kennedy the tax memorandum, told him the position of the drug companies and reported that the project appeared feasible. The Attorney General then briefed his brother, the President. At noon that day Bob Kennedy called Oberdorfer and told him to proceed—after first advising Assistant Secretary of State Edwin Martin what was to be done.

From then on, the operation moved forward with the full weight of the United States government behind it. Everyone was conscious that speed was vital and there was a genuine feeling of urgency, of men's lives at stake. Through Lloyd Cutler, Oberdorfer learned that the entire board of directors of the Pharmaceutical Manufacturers Association would meet in New York on December 11. That date immediately became a target for the formulation and presentation of the final plan to the manufacturers. While the Internal Revenue and Justice Department officials worked intensively on their tax and antitrust rulings, a meeting was arranged between the chairman and counsel of the pharmaceutical association and the Attorney General for Friday, December 7, in Washington.

In the meantime, Jim Donovan conferred with Oberdorfer and other officials. Don Coppock, the assistant Commissioner of Immigration, and John Jones of Justice joined the project. On December 6 John E. Nolan, Jr., of the law firm of Steptoe and Johnson, was recruited as a private volunteer to assist with legal work, followed by E. Barrett Prettyman, Jr., John Douglas (Senator Paul Douglas' son) and Raymond J. Rasenberger. They worked as assistants to Donovan, establishing and maintaining contacts with the various private companies, soliciting and expediting contributions or pledges and arranging for donated transportation services by air, rail, truck, and ship. Robert Knight, who had recently returned to private practice after serving as general counsel for the Treasury, headed a similar team of volunteer lawyers based in New York. The Internal Revenue Service maintained a staff of twelve persons on continuous call to answer questions and to issue specific rulings.

As the project accelerated, it became apparent that the Cuban Families Committee did not have a sufficient administrative organization to carry through such a large endeavor. Oberdorfer and Katzenbach, with the approval of Jim Donovan, asked John Wilson, the executive vice president of the American Red Cross, if the Red Cross would coordinate the transportation of the goods to Miami and then to Cuba. The Justice Department officials pointed out that contributors would feel more comfortable if the name of the Red Cross were involved in the transaction.

The Red Cross agreed; the operation, therefore, was conducted officially in its name. In actual fact, however, the operation at all times remained centered in the Justice Department, where the major plans and decisions were made. But the participation of the Red Cross helped to overcome public opposition to dealing with Castro.

That decision set the stage for Robert Kennedy's meeting with the top officials of the Pharmaceutical Manufacturers Association, probably the most important meeting of all in the U.S. December 7 was a blustery day, and as the Attorney General stood to speak the wind whipped the American flag outside, forming a backdrop through the windows. Robert Kennedy himself was at his best. While he may lack the special grace and felicitous turn of phrase his brother had, the Attorney General can be extremely effective in his own right, particularly in a private conference. His determination, intelligence and enthusiasm were especially impressive that day.

Kennedy said the prisoners, in their attempt to liberate their native country, had been assisted by United States personnel and supplies; that the plans had been initiated during the Eisenhower administration and continued in the present one; that the

Kennedy administration felt a moral obligation to assist the men, and that he believed the American people also felt this moral obligation. He had been informed that the prisoners were in poor physical condition, that some were starving and that if they were not rescued soon some would die. He told of how impressed he was with the courage and determination of the men of the Brigade he had met, and he described the events on the boat on which Roberto San Román and the others escaped. He said he believed that the Brigade represented the cream of Cuba's youth; the aim of restoring democracy in Cuba would be served best by liberating these men, rather than letting them die in prison. He explained why it was not advisable for the United States to become directly involved; such action might be misunderstood and there was also the risk of disastrous diplomatic reaction in the event the operation was not successful. He pointed out that the list of items requested by Castro had been reviewed by the Defense Department, the State Department and the CIA; it did *not* contain any items of strategic value to Cuba or any items (such as tractors) which could add to Cuba's productive capacity.

One of the drug officials expressed concern that his industry might be criticized if it participated in the exchange. Kennedy replied that the sight of the prisoners arriving in the United States on Christmas Eve would silence any critics. He also made it clear that all contributions would be voluntary—no company could expect, or would receive, special considerations from the government. Neither would there be adverse consequences if contributions were withheld.

Two days later, on Sunday, the Attorney General repeated his presentation before representatives of various baby food manufacturers. On both occasions the businessmen were obviously impressed.

Mortimer Caplin, the Commissioner of Internal Revenue, issued a ruling on December 11 stating that contributions of merchandise would be deductible at a value measured by the lowest wholesale catalogue prices at which the manufacturers customarily sold their products. Armed with that ruling and with a similarly favorable antitrust ruling of December 8, Oberdorfer and James B. Donovan attended the meeting of the board of directors of the Pharmaceutical Manufacturers Association in New York. They also carried with them the list of drugs requested by Castro, now contained in a 237-page document, typed and single-spaced. The list was composed of ten thousand items, specified by brand name and manufacturer; the desired quantity and dollar value of each item was noted. Only a coordinated action by the drug industry could meet these requirements. At that meeting Eli Lily pledged one million dollars in drugs.

Government and industry worked together with as little fanfare as possible. It was essential to avoid publicity which might arouse political opposition, frighten off the drug industry, or perhaps lead Castro to increase his demands. Because of the newspaper strike, then under way in New York, the necessary atmosphere of secrecy could be preserved. Less than nine days after the directors' meeting, the forty pharmaceutical manufacturers represented at that meeting had put together a shipment of drugs worth $12 million, and meeting Castro's specifications.

There was in this industry solidarity a certain mordant satisfaction, for big business, and particularly the drug industry, felt no love for the Kennedy administration. It was good public relations to assist in the prisoner exchange, and at the same time some executives felt they were mitigating former grievances in their role of extricating the Kennedys from the Bay of Pigs debacle. Then, too, because of the high markup for drugs, it was possible for some manufacturers to realize a "windfall"; the tax benefit granted to a corporate contributor (amounting to 52 per cent of the wholesale price) might exceed the actual cost of the product. Although such tax benefits were legally permissible and did not arise solely because of the prisoner exchange, the government suggested that such profits be contributed to charity. The decision, of course, was left to the individual companies.

Despite these advantages to the drug manufacturers, their motives concerning the ransom operation were humanitarian as well as personal, and the reaction of one drug industry spokesman to criticism of the tax writeoffs was understandable. "It's a little like helping a traffic victim into the ambulance," he said, "and then meeting a guy rushing around the corner to accuse you of picking the victim's pockets."

The operation now was moving forward rapidly, with Lou

Oberdorfer's office in the Justice Department as the command post. Additional desks and telephones were installed and office space in adjoining rooms was made available to the private citizens working as volunteers. During the month of December 344 long distance calls were placed; forty-two trips were made between Washington, New York and Florida, and nearly nine hundred hours of overtime were recorded. The key to the operation was to get private industry to contribute goods and services under existing laws and without the expenditure of government funds. (The Cuban Families Committee eventually bore the expenses incurred by the government employees.)

As problems arose, the government and the lawyers solved them. In two hours the Civil Aeronautics Board handed down a ruling permitting airlines to donate their planes to haul prisoners and freight. The railroads and the truckers received a similar ruling from the Interstate Commerce Commission. Immigration and Naturalization officials conferred with the Department of Health, Education and Welfare, the CIA and the air force to coordinate the reception and processing of the prisoners. The Commerce Department issued export licenses for the shipment of merchandise. And President Kennedy himself, at a press conference on December 12, stated he was most sympathetic to attempts to secure the release of the prisoners.

The last hurdle before the negotiations could resume was to meet Castro's demand for an "irrevocable" letter of credit to guarantee all the shipments. James B. Donovan already had established tentative credit lines with The Royal Bank of Canada in Montreal, but Castro demanded an ironclad guarantee. The pledges of 140 food, drug and transport companies were not enough: Fidel wanted a cash backing so that if any part of the deal fell through the remainder of the ransom would be paid in dollars. Donovan contacted Henry Harfield, an authority on letters of credit, and Harfield immediately came to Washington and talked to Oberdorfer, Katzenbach and Henry Rathbun, one of the lawyers of the Pharmaceutical Manufacturers Association.

On Friday, December 14, Harfield, Katzenbach and Rathbun flew to Montreal to negotiate the credit with The Royal Bank. It quickly developed that the bank was not interested in having the letter of credit secured by pledges; it insisted on formal guarantees from American banks. Furthermore, the letter of credit had to be approved by the board of directors of the bank, who were to meet on Monday, December 17. Thus the guarantees from the American banks had to be obtained over the weekend. Three things were needed: a commitment of $53 million from an American bank or banks to the Canadian bank on the application of the Red Cross; a commitment from the Red Cross to be bound by such a letter of credit; and a surety bond from an accepted insurance company which would guarantee to the American banks that the Red Cross would meet its obligations.

On Saturday Katzenbach, preceded by a call from the Attorney General, visited Red Cross Chairman Roland Harriman in New York. Harriman agreed without hesitation, and without consulting his board, to commit the Red Cross to ultimate responsibility for the $53 million letters of credit.

"It was," Lou Oberdorfer said later, "a decision carried out in the best traditions of Elihu Root and bipartisan American diplomacy."

By Monday two $26.5 million letters of credit had been obtained from the Bank of America and the Morgan Guaranty Trust Co. of New York. Those letters were backed by bonds issued on behalf of the Red Cross by the Continental Insurance Group of New York. Jim Donovan said the bonds issued by Continental—in effect an insurance policy underwriting delivery of the ransom—secured the deal. There again Donovan was instrumental for he is one of their attorneys. Continental issued the bonds without charging a premium, and without requiring collateral security, and there were no charges to insure the merchandise in transit.

That weekend marked the point of no return for the operation. Supplies had been accumulating at various locations, but no action had been taken to move them to Florida. Then on Sunday, December 16, Lou Oberdorfer gave the order for the first shipment of drugs to be transported to Florida and loaded on planes at Opa-Locka airport and at Port Everglades on the S.S. *African Pilot*. Once that order was given the operation was fully committed.

Throughout November and December the news began to

filter through the Príncipe prison, but by then even the optimists were skeptical. José Eugenio Sosa, a fifty-three-year-old cattleman, spoke for many in his prison diary:

November 20, 1962:
. . . this prison cannot endure forever and for that reason I am going to recover my liberty and go on living. . . . Now . . . the food is still deficient and always the same: in the morning macaroni and red beans with 80% of it sauce, and in the afternoon noodle soup and rice. Sometimes we have yucca and sweet potatoes, boiled, and once a week Russian meat that we get half an ounce for each of us. I am trying hard to eat the soup, but until now I can't, but I am sure that the appetite is going to win, and at last I am going to eat the soup . . .

November 26:
Today is a month and 5 days that I have been without sun. We have been in a dungeon without a patio since the declaration of the blockade.
A week ago Alvarito Sánchez and Berta Barreto came and saw their sons and some of the boys. They said they are going to the U.S. to complete some changes in the articles ordered by Cuba for the negotiation, and in 8 or 10 days they will be back.
Well, another merciful lie. I am grateful for what they have done . . . trying to resolve our situation. It is a pity that they had such bad luck. . . . Well, until another day that I feel like writing so I don't forget that I know how to write.

December 5:
. . . today is 7 months since the last visit, and of course [we are] isolated. The truth is that this regime is rough the way they treat the prisoners. . . . I am sure that I am going out of here and not in a long time. . . . Last night I dreamt of my little son Ignacio. I saw him very big and he is a little American. How I desire to give him a kiss! Also to my grandson José Angel and María Luisa, the little girl that I haven't seen yet.

December 10:
Last night I had a toothache and with a terrible fear I went to see the dentist. He told me to wait to see if he could fix it . . . *

---

* The prisoners dreaded going to the "dentist" because almost always teeth were pulled out without novocaine and with crude instruments—

December 15:

. . . today we received news that looks to me like a lie, but later I read today's newspaper in which it said that Donovan made some declarations, with the authorization of President Kennedy, and he expects to take us out of jail before the 24 of this month. This made me feel a little happier, but I don't want to have many illusions because after it is going to be worse.

December 17:

We are receiving news they are sure that Berta Barreto is in Cuba with Alvarito Sánchez since the 9 and last night arrived Ernesto Freyre with Donovan. [This was all false.] *. . . Still I don't want to have many hopes, but everyone is nervous and it's easy to understand. Isn't it? . . . I think that if I go out, after having my favorite steak, I am going to have a complete stuffed turkey that is sold at the big groceries. How hungry I am.*

December 18:

Very early in the morning when I was standing at the door of the gallery the director came and, something very rare, he said in a nice way 'Good Morning.' He told us that we have a chance to leave, that our situation was better, and probably we will have Christmas dinner out. After, we received other news that made us feel optimistic, but after checking . . . it looks ambiguous to me, so I lost a little of my hopes even if I never lose my faith, I always have it.

December 19:

We woke up today a little pessimistic. The food is terrible . . . but it is absolutely true that Donovan and Sánchez arrived yesterday, also they were with Fidel since 4 to 8 at night, and today they will go on with the interview. It looks like the thing is good right now. I am really optimistic; I don't think that Donovan and the Commission will come if they don't have something definite! . . . "

On the morning of December 18, Jim Donovan, Alvaro Sánchez, Berta Barreto and Mrs. Virginia Betancourt of the Families Committee left Miami International Airport on a plane for Havana.

sometimes even hammered out. Because of their diet many suffered constantly with infected teeth and gums.

Before the day was out they had met with Castro for four hours and a tentative agreement was reached. One problem arose, however. Castro's technicians were not familiar with some of the items on the list of drugs supplied by the American manufacturers and they questioned the substitutions and the values. Castro himself expressed doubts about the good faith of the Americans and wanted further clarification about what the first shipment actually contained. The next day, Wednesday, Donovan flew back to the United States and Dr. Leonard A. Scheele, former Surgeon General of the United States, was contacted. The two men spent that night going over the list of drugs, and in the morning flew to Havana.

The negotiations continued. When Castro still seemed suspicious about the value and size of the first shipment, containing 20 per cent of the ransom, Donovan suggested that Fidel send his own inspectors to examine what was being loaded on the *African Pilot*. He called Washington and permission was given for the Cuban technicians to enter the United States and inspect the goods. Their trip, however, was not to be made public.

Friday, December 21, was the pivotal day. Just before noon the vital letter of credit from The Royal Bank of Canada was issued formally and delivered to the Cuban purchasing agent in Havana. It was immediately confirmed by Castro's government.

Late in the afternoon Donovan called Washington to report that he and Castro had signed the Memorandum of Agreement, pending a final inspection of the supplies by Fidel's technicians. Throughout the negotiations for the release of the Brigade, Donovan also had discussed the possibility of release for twenty-three Americans held captive in Cuba. He felt he was making progress toward their liberation as well,* and in his phone call said it was vital that the initial shipment, or down payment, contain a high proportion of items especially needed by the Cubans. This, more than anything, would be proof of America's good faith. Donovan's call triggered a last-minute rundown of the pledge documents and various shipping logs. As a result, the down payment was "sweetened" by about $500,000 worth of prime goods.

Early that evening Harry Williams received word in Miami

* The Americans were released in the spring of 1963.

that the Attorney General was trying to reach him. From a phone booth, Harry called Kennedy at his home in McLean. "You got it, Enrique," Robert Kennedy said. "This is it. That guy with the beard has accepted. Now what you've got to do is move fast."

In a daze, Harry stepped from the booth. Within minutes John Nolan arrived and asked if Harry would serve as a translator for three Cuban doctors who were due on a special flight at one that morning to check the supplies. The Cubans landed and were met by Nolan, Dr. Scheele, Barrett Prettyman, Williams and Ben Lovejoy of the Red Cross. Until daybreak they checked the list of products and examined boxes and crates still waiting to be loaded at Port Everglades on the *African Pilot*. Tempers flared several times and there was a general atmosphere of ill will; the Cuban technicians said they would not accept certain goods—Listerine, or Alka Seltzer or Aspirin. Each time there was dissent, Nolan or Scheele firmly but diplomatically said the goods would be useful in Cuba.

Once, a Castro technician demanded that certain material be unloaded from the ship. "That's impossible," Nolan said, "they're already aboard and we can't disrupt everything now. We're not going to unload that ship. Everything that's on there is going to Cuba."

"Everybody was sweating there," Williams said later, "and I was thinking that Fidel had sent them to break the negotiations."

At daybreak the Cubans announced they would stay over— and "maybe go back on Tuesday," Christmas Day. This meant that the Brigade could not be liberated as planned.

"I realized," John Nolan said, "that we had to do something drastic."

The Cubans and Americans, tired and tense, went to Barrett Prettyman's motel room to discuss what would happen next. Nolan spoke up, addressing the Cubans.

"You should ask yourselves," he said, "if you are going to help the negotiations by staying here." He referred to the one hundred fifty thousand Cuban exiles in Miami, and added, "As far as your own protection is concerned, *I think* we can take care of that, but we can't do anything about the criticism from the press when they see you here, and you know as well as I do how many people are opposed to the deal."

The Cubans conferred alone for a few minutes and then said they wanted to call Cuba. Nolan tried first and failed to get through to Havana; then the Red Cross tried, with success. The Cubans were told to come home.

It was Saturday, December 22. That night, after the final papers were signed, Castro unexpectedly came to Mrs. Barreto's house. He brought a bottle of Scotch and he, Donovan, Sánchez, Mrs. Barreto and Commandante Vallejo held an impromptu celebration. It was a moment of goodwill and they talked at length about communism, democracy and religion. In the morning the liberation was scheduled to begin, but before it could one more problem had to be solved.

Lou Oberdorfer had flown to Opa-Locka Airport that morning to supervise the final loading of goods. As far as he knew, everything was ready to go. Instead, he found that the goods had been pouring into Port Everglades and Opa-Locka at such a rate that no inventories had been made of what actually was on the *African Pilot* and the planes. The Cubans certainly would demand that specific information—at least about the down-payment— before they would release the Brigade. Oberdorfer called Washington and an aide, Frank Michelman, began working with what records were available—invoices, pledge documents, Red Cross shipping logs. By the time Michelman had compiled a summary it was night. Although he had never operated a teletype machine, Michelman, using the hunt-and-peck method, transmitted the lists to Opa-Locka, finishing at midnight. Then, with the original documents to back up the lists, he took a plane for Miami.

One other incident that day exemplified the determination of those behind the operation. Oberdorfer wanted some supplies of a better quality loaded on a donated commercial plane for the first shipment. The plane would have to be unloaded and packed again. The air force colonel in charge of the "volunteer" Air Force loading crew objected, saying he had neither the manpower nor the time.

Oberdorfer, quietly but firmly, said, "Colonel, do you want to order these men to re-load that plane, or do you want the Secretary of the Air Force to order it?"

At Príncipe and the Isle of Pines the prisoners were given better meals—including bags of black sugar and water to help them regain weight rapidly. Toward the end they were allowed patio privileges and basked in the sun. "The hope," a prisoner said, "was so big it was just driving us mad."

On December 22, Major Gálvez, the prison director on the Isle of Pines, came to the three leaders and said, feigning surprise, "What are you doing with those beards and that long hair?" Pepe San Román replied, "Your imagination must be playing tricks. We are perfectly shaved and our hair is nice and short." Gálvez said, "Tomorrow you are leaving." Sarcastically, Artime asked, "May I ask which *bartolina* we are going to now?" Gálvez said, "To Miami."

"We couldn't feel the happiness," Oliva said. "We couldn't realize it was true."

They were taken out, shaved and given haircuts, shoes and fresh uniforms. They still feared another cruel hoax. That night guards brought sacks of food to each prisoner, food donated by their families for delivery on Christmas Day. For the first time they dared to believe they were going to leave. The bags contained pork, ham, turkey, chicken, cheeses, fruit. The prisoners feasted and gorged themselves, almost delirious with excitement. Throughout the Isle of Pines and Príncipe Castle men ate until their shrunken stomachs rebelled and they became violently sick. No one slept that night.

Sunday morning, December 23, the guards came at 7:30 A.M. Pepe, Artime and Oliva were taken from their cells. With elaborate solemnity, they said farewell to the large posters of Lenin that had been placed on the wall in front of them during the Cuban crisis. Then they and the other 211 prisoners on the Isle of Pines were flown to the San Antonio de los Baños airfield in Havana Province. They arrived about 10:30 A.M. and were herded into a large hangar. New beds with fine mattresses, sheets, pillows and new blankets made in China were arranged in rows. Each man was given clothing and shoes—either military or civilian issue, whichever he wished. It was the last, carefully staged propaganda show, for such goods were scarce in Cuba. Indeed, matters were so bad that guards at Príncipe Castle begged the prisoners to leave their old boots, saying they would be able to get new ones easily in the United States. Some prisoners say they walked out of Príncipe barefooted.

The airport was alive with activity. Castro militiamen were everywhere, all carrying loaded weapons. Berta Barreto and her committee of ladies, some twenty in all, were seated at tables with their lists of the prisoners. Farther down the line the Castro government officials arranged their final check point, and at the very end were the U.S. Immigration officials. In back of them were the planes. The day was clear, the sun was shining and there was a steady breeze across the field.

At noon lunch was served: meat, chicken, rice with beans, beer. One of the American Immigration officials said, "Things in Cuba aren't so bad. They really have a lot of food."

A woman from Berta Barreto's committee overheard him and said loudly, "You know something? This is the first time I have eaten meat in ten days. Where I live there is no meat."

Then at two o'clock the *African Pilot* docked and a tense waiting period began.

No matter how strained the situation, Donovan's sense of humor never left him. Perhaps that was the quality that Castro admired most—or, at least, Castro certainly appreciated it. Once that afternoon while Castro, Donovan and a large group were standing together on the air strip, four MIG jets unexpectedly roared low over the field, making a deafening sound. Instinctively, everyone ducked. One of the Cubans shouted, "What is it?" and Donovan, still in a crouch, instantly replied, "It's the invasion." Fidel laughed uproariously.

In the middle of the afternoon buses began arriving carrying the men from Príncipe. "When I saw them," Harry Williams said, "I didn't recognize many of them because they had changed so much. After twenty months they were used to being in files and being quiet and not showing their emotions. Two young fellows jumped up and said 'Hello' to me, but I knew it wasn't wise to talk there and they knew it too. So I talked to them little by little as we used to do in prison so the guards wouldn't notice."

Berta Barreto asked Donovan if he would speak to Fidel about permitting a group of relatives, including Oliva's wife and child, to go back on the *African Pilot*.

Donovan told Fidel it seemed senseless to send empty ships back to the U.S. when Fidel could use them to rid himself of liabilities. Fidel thought a moment and asked: "How many of these worms can we get on that empty ship?" A thousand, Donovan answered. "Get a thousand and let them go out. We don't want these worms here. All they do is give us trouble and eat our food. Every mother, father or relative who wants to go out, let them go." Speaking to Mrs. Barreto, Castro said, "Berta, make up a list and get them ready. This will be my Christmas bonus."

Turning to Oliva Fidel said, "I have presented five points to the United States government and they have been accepted and we will go into co-existence." *

"In that," Oliva said, "we agree. We will never commit the same mistakes again."

At 5 P.M. Donovan gave the signal for the *African Pilot* to be unloaded. Donovan and Castro each had been waiting for the other to make the first move. Donovan acted first. Then the prisoners were permitted to begin boarding the first plane. In about a half hour it took off, with 108 men.

"Just watching the first plane take off made it all worth it," Jim Donovan told a reporter. "It was like the slave trade. All they lacked were the chains. It really choked me up."

On the plane the men were excited and jubilant until Harry Williams said, "Look to your right. See those men who haven't been liberated yet. From now on, in everything we do, we have to remember that they are not free. We have to control our actions, until everyone is free." For the next twenty minutes Williams spoke to the men over the microphone. He told them about the negotiations and warned them not to make any bitter statements to the press or say anything that would hurt the precarious relations between Cuba and the United States. They should avoid answering questions about the invasion, about air cover, and talk only about their prison experiences.

On each of the flights back to the United States Harry had placed men from among the sixty wounded prisoners already liberated, so that they could brief the new prisoners. For that reason almost nothing of consequence was reported about the Bay of Pigs invasion, and in fact long afterward the men of the Brigade maintained a discreet silence about their experiences. Indeed, at this writing, most of the men in the Brigade are still extremely wary of talking about the invasion for fear it might jeopardize their chances of returning to Cuba. The Kennedy administration never suggested or hinted that the men should keep silent: the decision not to talk was made solely by the Cubans.

* No such agreement was made.

At exactly 6:06 P.M., as the brilliant winter sun was setting, the first plane landed at Homestead Air Force Base and taxied slowly toward a ramp while fire trucks and ambulances followed. A Cuban woman clutched at her throat, screamed, "My God, they're really here!" and fainted. An air force lieutenant colonel announced that the second plane was already on its way. A cheer went up from the large crowd of newsmen and television technicians and Red Cross and Immigration officials. It was dark by the time the plane stopped and the engines were cut off. Spotlights played about the field. One by one the men came out.

As in April, Harry Williams was the last to leave. He saw the members of the Cuban Revolutionary Council embracing the men and then Tony Varona came to him and said, "We did it! We did it!" It was the first time Harry had seen Varona since April when Varona had said there wasn't a chance to liberate the men. Tired and angry, Williams cursed. Then he turned, walked away and waited to take the plane back to Havana.

The prisoners were fed, examined by doctors, given new clothing if they needed it and then taken to the Dinner Key Auditorium in Miami, where they were reunited with their families. By 8:55 P.M. the fourth flight of the night had landed at Homestead, bringing the number of prisoners liberated to 426. Then it was announced that no more planes would arrive that night.

Castro brought up the old debt. He said he still had not received the $2,925,000 that the Cuban Families Committee had pledged to pay in April when the wounded prisoners came out. It was a cash debt and the committee was clearly obliged to pay it.

Although everyone from Robert Kennedy down knew about the debt, there was a reluctance from the United States side to pay the money—principally because it might affect the terms for liberating the twenty-three Americans. So far, no cash payment had been made to Castro and there were hopes that Donovan might be able to perform another miracle and persuade Castro to accept more goods in place of dollars. Once the cash payment was made, a precedent would have been set, a precedent that could substantially raise the price for freeing the Americans. However, Castro insisted the money had to be raised, and raised immediately. Fidel was specific: no cash, no more prisoners.

Donovan parried for time, reminding Castro that it was Sunday and all the banks were closed. Then it was decided that Nolan should return to the United States to attempt to raise the money. That evening they casually mentioned the projected trip to Regino Boti, Castro's Economic Minister, and Nolan explained that he was going to handle some "last-minute details." Boti, who seemed eager for the success of the deal, understood the true situation immediately and offered to drive Nolan to the airfield. Nolan thanked him but said that kind of service was unnecessary. Boti insisted and asked if there were anything else he could do.

"Yes," Jim Donovan answered and as Boti, still anxious to please, leaned forward Donovan whispered, "When you get Nolan to the airport, don't defect!"

Nolan left on an American plane at 2:30 in the morning with Harry Williams. As someone said later, "The whole ball game was riding on that trip."

Lou Oberdorfer of the Justice Department met Nolan at the airport and they telephoned Nick Katzenbach, the Deputy Attorney General, in Washington and explained the critical developments. At a quarter to five Katzenbach telephoned Harry Williams at his home.

"Hell," Harry said, "we can't get the boys out without the money."

"Why?" Katzenbach asked.

"Because it's been promised a long time. That money is for the sixty of us. Unless we go back it's got to be paid. This is cash money."

When Katzenbach asked if the Cuban Families Committee couldn't raise it through their public relations efforts, Harry said that if they hadn't raised half a million dollars in eight months they could hardly get nearly $3 million overnight.

At 5 A.M. Nolan called the Attorney General. For forty-five minutes Nolan, Kennedy and Katzenbach discussed the problem on a three-way connection conference call. The money had to be raised by 3 P.M. December 24 or the deal was off. Bob Kennedy took over. With one phone call to Cardinal Cushing in Boston, Kennedy raised a million dollars. The Cardinal, one of the sponsors of the Families Committee, long before had promised Alvaro Sánchez that when the time came he would do as much as anyone for the prisoners. Bob Kennedy then called General Lucius Clay, also a sponsor. Clay, Robert Knight and Robert B. Anderson set to work immediately.

John Nolan flew back to Havana and when Donovan asked, "How did it go?" he replied, "All right. I think it is going to work out all right." Both men tried to appear confident; neither mentioned the subject again.

Castro permitted two planes to leave Havana in the morning, the second one arriving at Homestead at 11:45 A.M. That brought the number of men liberated to 643. Then there were no more planes and the agonizing wait began. In the United States there was no explanation for the sudden delay. At the San Antonio de los Baños airfield the prisoners shuffled and talked nervously among themselves. It was the last moment for the Owls.

Hours passed and the 3 P.M. deadline approached. Alvaro Sánchez turned to John Nolan and boiled over in anger. If the money didn't come, Sánchez said, he was going to stay in Cuba. "Before they shoot me I'm going to get on that radio and read that document we signed before we got the wounded prisoners out, promising that we'd pay for them in cash. And I'll say that Castro was right."

The problem of raising such a sum was formidable enough but, to make things even more difficult, the banks closed at noon the day before Christmas. General Clay borrowed money against future pledges, on his signature alone. The note was deposited in The Royal Bank of Canada just before noon, but it took several more hours to obtain the necessary documents from banks in New York, Washington and Montreal. At almost three o'clock The Royal Bank notified Havana that the $2.9 million could be released on written authorization from Donovan. Castro, Donovan and Nolan met in the Canadian Consul's office, where the final document was signed.

At the airport the last three planes received the signal to leave and the leaders of the Brigade were put on board. "Seeing San Román, Oliva and Artime sitting there next to each other was very moving," Sánchez said. "They were the ones everyone thought would never come out."

After the last prisoner had boarded the last plane, Donovan

returned to say farewell to Castro and to sign a required receipt for the prisoners. Fidel was puffing on a long cigar, surrounded by militia. Said Donovan, in a loud voice: "You know, Premier, I have been thinking of all the good I have been doing for the people of Cuba these past weeks. I have relieved you of almost 1,200 liabilities and also I have been helping the children, the sick, the poor and the elderly among the Cuban people. I think that when the next election is held I'm coming back and run against you. I think I can win." Castro, with a long look and a long puff on his cigar, replied: "You know, doctor, I think you may be right. So there will be no elections." The two men shook hands, and Donovan boarded the plane.

The plane landed at Miami at 9:45 P.M. Pepe was asked to leave first so that members of the Brigade could salute him. When Roberto San Román saw his brother he wept. Minutes later a call came from Washington and the Attorney General congratulated each of the three leaders. Robert Kennedy told Pepe, "I'm looking forward to seeing you soon, and I think the President would like to speak to you also."

"We were taken in a bus to a place where our families were waiting for us," Pepe said. "It was the Dinner Key Auditorium. There we found lots of people, members of the Brigade that had escaped, and others that had been left behind in Base Trax and they tried to take us on their shoulders. Then I saw my mother and then I saw my wife, and I ran to them but the crowd wouldn't let me get to them. The same thing happened to Erneido and Manolo. Finally I got to them and I almost killed my mother and my wife and my kids with the embrace I gave them. It was a very great moment because I never thought I would see them again. And then they came and took us, Erneido and Manolo and myself, to the microphones, and Manolo spoke for us and I don't remember what he said because I was just crazy with happiness. And when he finished we were taken on the shoulders of our men and they walked around with us until I had a chance to get down and I went back to my family."

CHAPTER 5

THE ORANGE BOWL

They found that the value of freedom lay in the enjoy-
ment of small things: drinking as much milk as they
wanted . . . seeing the sky and the ocean . . . walking in the
sun . . . wearing clean clothes . . . sleeping in a bed. They
were, as one man said, "starved for life," and they clutched at
each new experience as if it might be their last.

Not all of their experiences were pleasant. The day after
Christmas Harry Williams met Oliva in a hotel lobby before a
television interview. They walked down the street in the bright
morning sunshine, and Harry suggested they stop for breakfast.
Oliva said they would have to be careful because some places
in the United States would not serve Negroes and he didn't
want to create a problem. At the first restaurant the waitress
refused to serve them. "No, sir, I can't," she said to Harry.

"I was looking at this man who had come out of prison and I
felt so sad to see how he looked," Harry said. "He was very quiet
but I knew it hurt him very deeply. So I said, 'Come on, we'd
better go.' And we left."

Two days after Christmas Pepe, Artime, Oliva, Harry, Roberto
San Román and Alvaro Sánchez drove from Miami to Palm
Beach, at the invitation of the President. They sat around a long
dining room table and President Kennedy told them he was
sorry for what had happened at the Bay of Pigs. He referred to
the international problems the United States had faced at that
time and specifically mentioned West Berlin as being a factor.
He also asked if they really had expected jet air support.

Pepe, who did most of the talking while Harry translated,

said they had not been told at the briefing that they would have
jets, but because of the way things were handled and the obvious backing of the United States, "naturally we expected it
because we had been told the sky would be ours and we knew
the B-26s were not enough." The President looked serious. "It
was very easy to see," Oliva said, "he felt responsible for what
had happened to us and for our long time in prison."

The President then introduced the Cubans to his wife Jacqueline, who spoke to them in Spanish, and introduced the
leaders to the Kennedy children as the heroes of the Bay of Pigs.
Mrs. Kennedy addressed many questions to Pepe and particularly wanted to know everything about prison. "Did you ever
think you would come out?" she asked. Pepe spoke candidly
and answered that he had never expected to be freed.

The President and the men posed for photographs, after which
the leaders held a press conference. Pepe announced that the
President would come to Miami that Saturday, December 29,
to inspect the Brigade in the Orange Bowl. At that ceremony,
Oliva told the reporters, the President would be presented with
the Brigade flag which had flown over the command post at
Playa Girón for three days. After the dispersal, a soldier had
taken the flag and kept it with him until he succeeded in reaching asylum in an embassy in Havana.

"We will be giving President Kennedy the greatest treasure
we possess at the present time," Oliva said.

Press Secretary Pierre Salinger left with the men to discuss
plans for the Orange Bowl ceremony, and they were having a
drink in Salinger's motel when the phone rang. It was the President. Salinger relayed the message: "Would you ask the Brigade
officers if they would like my wife to go with me?"

There had never been a ceremony quite like it. A deafening
roar went up from the thousands in the stadium when the white
convertible carrying the President and his wife entered the
Orange Bowl. A thousand flags, many of them homemade,
waved in the warm Miami sunshine. The President walked
toward the platform set up on the fifty-yard line and shook
hands with Pepe, Oliva and Artime. They stood at attention together while the band played the national anthems of the
United States and Cuba. Then he strode across the grass to the

Brigade and moved through the lines of men in khaki uniforms, greeting them and shaking hands. Washington reporters said they had never seen the President act so informally and with such enthusiasm. The Brigade returned his enthusiasm. As the President reached the paratroop battalion, Tomás Cruz, the Negro company commander who had told Castro he hadn't gone to Cuba to go swimming, impulsively stepped forward and embraced the President.

The formal ceremonies opened and Pepe San Román spoke for the Brigade. "We know how precious liberty is and we know that Cuba has no liberty. The 2506 Brigade, we offer ourselves to God and to the free world as warriors in the battle against communism. . . . We don't know how or in what form the opportunity will come for us to fight in the cause of Cuba. Whenever, however, wherever, in whatever honorable form it may come, we will do what we can to be better prepared to meet and complete our mission."

Pepe turned toward the President. "Mr. President, the men of the 2506 Brigade give you their banner—we temporarily deposit it with you for your safekeeping."

One of the wounded soldiers, Rolando Novoa, was standing on crutches, near the platform, holding the folded gold-and-blue banner against his chest. He quietly handed the flag to Oliva and Oliva gave it to the President. "It was the great moment of my life," Oliva said later. The President unfurled the flag and stepped to the microphone with obvious emotion. He asked the Brigade to be seated on the grass, turned toward Pepe and José Miró Cardona and said:

"Commander, Doctor, I want to express my great appreciation to the Brigade for making the United States the custodian of this flag." He paused, and then his voice rose emotionally. "I can assure you that this flag will be returned to this Brigade in a free Havana."

The Brigade rose and cheered wildly. Shouts of "Guerra! Guerra!" and "Libertad! Libertad!" came from forty thousand throats. Some men wept.

"I wonder if Señor Facundo Miranda, who preserved this flag through the last twenty months, would come forward so we can meet him," the President continued. After Miranda approached and shook hands, the President said, "I wanted to know who I should give it back to."

Again the stadium rocked with applause.

Keeping his remarks extemporaneous, the President went on: "I always had the impression (I hope the members of the Brigade will sit down again)—I always had the impression that the Brigade was made up mostly of young men, but standing over there is a Cuban patriot fifty-seven, one fifty-nine, one sixty-one. I wonder if those three could stand up so that the people of the United States could realize that they represent the spirit of the Cuban revolution in its best sense."

Next came the formal address. On behalf of the government and the people, President Kennedy welcomed the Brigade and brought "my nation's respect for your courage and your cause." "Your small Brigade is a tangible reaffirmation that the human desire for freedom and independence is essentially unconquerable. Your conduct and valor are proof that although Castro and his fellow dictators may rule nations, they do not rule people; that they may imprison bodies, but they do not imprison spirits; that they may destroy the exercise of liberty, but they cannot eliminate the determination to be free." He urged the Cubans in exile to submerge their differences in a united front. "Keep alive the spirit of the Brigade so that some day the people of Cuba will have a free chance to make a free choice," for "The Brigade is the point of the spear, the arrow's head."

"Gentlemen of the Brigade," he said in closing, "I need not tell you how happy I am to welcome you here to the United States, and what a profound impression your conduct during some of the most difficult days and months that any free people have experienced—what a profound impression your conduct made upon not only the people of this country, but all the people of this hemisphere. Even in prison you served in the strongest possible way the cause of freedom, as you do today.

"I can assure you that it is the strongest wish of the people of this country, as well as the people of this hemisphere, that Cuba shall one day be free again, and when it is, this Brigade will deserve to march at the head of the free column."

Cheers almost drowned out the President's last words.

Jacqueline Kennedy stepped to the microphone and, in Spanish, said:

"It is an honor for me to be today with a group of the bravest men in the world, and to share in the joy that is felt by their families who, for so long, lived hoping, praying and waiting. I feel proud that my son has met the officers. He is still too young to realize what has happened here, but I will make it my business to tell him the story of your courage as he grows up. It is my wish and my hope that some day he may be a man at least half as brave as the members of Brigade 2506. Good luck."

Epilogue

December, 1963:

There has been no happy ending. A month after John
F. Kennedy's assassination, a year after prison, three
years after the invasion and five years after Castro came down
from the hills, the Cuban problem remains. The first attempt to
solve it—the invasion at the Bay of Pigs—has taken its place
beside monumental failures of the past, and a new solution has
not been found. Already some of what President Kennedy called
the "sober and useful lessons" of the failure at the Bay of Pigs
are becoming clear.

The Bay of Pigs was more than a mock-heroic tragedy, a
footnote to history. It was perhaps the most heavily publicized
of the many bungled, poorly planned operations since the Light
Brigade charged into oblivion at Balaklava. From the United
States standpoint, however, there were values in the experience.
The Bay of Pigs forced a re-examination of policies, practices
and personalities. The efficacy of that examination became clear
during the Cuban missile crisis. It seems clear now that the
disaster in the Zapata Swamps led almost inevitably to the
confrontation with Russia. From a period of seeming indecision,
inexperience, weakness and defeat, the United States, in October
of 1962, drew an essential lesson. It still possessed the resolution
to take the ultimate risk to preserve its freedom. Today, the
determination to profit by the disaster remains strong.

A special committee similar to the one that investigated the
Bay of Pigs continues to function in secrecy, examining special
governmental policies and procedures with a jaundiced eye.
Such results are hopeful; others are not so encouraging.

As recent events in Vietnam have shown, the Central Intelligence Agency still stands at the center of controversy. The CIA

poses one of the serious dilemmas of the Cold War. It helps to maintain America's existence and yet some of its actions contribute to a lessening of faith in the government. Never again after the U-2 flight or after the Bay of Pigs can citizens take official statements at face value. This adds to the prevailing climate of cynicism. It corrupts and poisons the fabric of a democracy.

As with the solution to Cuba, there is no panacea for the problem of a powerful, secret organization that performs an essential function. However, at least one general conclusion can be drawn. No agency should be permitted to operate without some form of independent, critical outside examination. As the Bay of Pigs shows, the agency should not sit in judgment of itself. The administration, no matter how self-critical, also has a natural vested interest and a public record to defend. One solution may lie in the creation of a Joint Congressional Committee on Intelligence. But given the record of congressional investigations and the need to keep sensitive agencies removed from politics, it is highly doubtful that Congress alone is the place for such examination.

A compromise proposal suggests a bipartisan commission composed of members of the House and Senate, together with private citizens of distinction, similar to the Warren Commission appointed by President Johnson to investigate Kennedy's assassination. Another alternative is a private commission, appointed by the President after consultation with congressional leaders. In that, the example of the notable work of the Hoover Commission after World War II provides a precedent.

Understandably, the CIA would like to bury its Cuban past and conceal its shape in the cloak of "national interests" or "national security." This writer will not soon forget traveling through the Sierra Madre Mountains in Guatemala in the summer of 1963 with one of the leaders of Brigade 2506 in search of Base Trax. High above the Helvetia plantation, in sight of the volcano, with the sound of River Nil far below, we reached a place where the road should have been. It had vanished.

Eventually, from fearful Indian peasants in those mountains and later from Cubans who were the last to leave the camp, the story came out. Two weeks after the invasion all of the records at the camp were placed into a freshly dug hole and a bulldozer covered the hole with earth. Soon after that, Guatemalan soldiers and laborers came. They broke up the camp and carried away every last vestige—including the cement foundations for the barracks. Then the road itself was bulldozed and covered. Now the jungle has taken over and all that one might find to link that territory with the Bay of Pigs is a stray shell or perhaps a rusting can.

Despite attempts to cover the facts, the Bay of Pigs remains an ominous page in our history. Time has not stilled the controversy. If anything, it has become more intensive. There too, for several years, the lack of facts has led to confusion and conjecture. The Bay of Pigs invasion was daringly conceived and boldly led, but because of the series of disasters that befell it attention has been focused on the battle rather than the aftermath. In the process, certain practical considerations of potentially greater significance have been overlooked. In retrospect, too much of the planning centered on the military aspects instead of pointing toward the future, and there has been too much concern with a negative anti-communism rather than planning for a genuinely democratic government.

The real question posed by the Bay of Pigs is not whether the Cubans would have won had they had sufficient support, but whether they could have fashioned a political triumph after their military victory. The record of factionalism, opportunism, self-aggrandizement and even of corruption that marked the Cuban exile political structure boded ill for the future of Cuba. Something more than the tired, often cynical leadership of the *Frente* and the Cuban Revolutionary Council was needed to offset the dynamic personal leadership of Fidel Castro. For the populace to rise in support of a liberating army, the masses had to be prepared and stirred as Castro himself had done so successfully.

Since the invasion the dreary history of exile politics has underscored the difficulties that would have confronted Cuba. For example, on June 20, 1963, the Cuban Revolutionary Council, in an apparent desperate bid for public support, announced with great fanfare a new Cuban invasion. Tony Varona, in making the announcement, issued what he called "War Communiqué No. 1," and Miami seethed with another made-in-Miami report that an army of three thousand had landed. Luis

Botifoll, the Council's spokesman, grandly said, "This is the beginning of the war of liberation." The liberation and the invading force turned out to have been an infiltration of fewer than fifty men.

Immediately after that this writer spoke to Botifoll in the Council's Miami office. While sycophants swarmed through the hallways and crowded the foyer, Botifoll shugged off criticism of the announcement. He spoke of the Brigade and, smiling slightly, said he didn't understand why anyone wanted to write about it. It was, he said, of no importance.

In that the politician was wrong. For in the long run of history the Brigade's defeat may lead to victory. Although the Brigade no longer exists, except in spirit, its story is not over. Symbolically, as President Kennedy said in the Orange Bowl, it is still the point of the spear, the arrow's head, the rallying point, the symbol of action. And from its ranks may come the leadership for future liberation efforts. In that sense, the future of Cuba rests largely on the shoulders of the men who fought at the Bay of Pigs. Their experience has taught many painful lessons and forced home many unpleasant truths. But their example shows that Cubans can unite and work together toward a common goal.

They returned to the cheers of the United States and the Western world and for a long time they basked in that glow. Then the inevitable reaction set in and they found that their dreams of returning to Cuba in glory were not to be fulfilled so soon. Now they are scattered about the United States. There have been personal tragedies and increasingly difficult problems of adjustment. Several men have had nervous breakdowns and at least two are in mental hospitals. The mundane concerns of a job, of supporting a family in a foreign land, of adjusting to the complexities of American life, have created individual problems—problems that must be faced in solitude, away from the cheers, away from the comforting unity of a Brigade. Already many of them are looking back on their days in prison with a sense of yearning and an awareness that there they reached an emotional and spiritual peak that gave an intense meaning to their lives.

Even the scholars are beginning to examine their experiences. As this is written, a preliminary study has been completed on the Bay of Pigs prisoners by the Bureau of Social Science Research, Inc., in Washington, D.C., as part of a continuing examination of the behavior of prisoners of war in Communist territory. The Bay of Pigs prisoners, the Bureau finds, represent a unique group, showing a "reverse process" from the norm—"an uphill one from depths of despair, demoralization, and non-resistance to esprit, organization, and active resistance."

Their spirit of resistance remains as strong as ever. Nearly half of the Brigade, including men who had been seriously wounded, enlisted in the United States armed forces two months after their liberation. Today, they are being trained in every branch of service in bases across the country. They hope their training will assist them in their return to Cuba. The leaders, too, are preparing for that day. Oliva is in the U.S. army. After six months of debating his future and toying with the idea of becoming a commercial artist, Pepe San Román also entered the army. (He found, on his physical examination, that he had contracted tuberculosis in prison, a condition now cured.) Artime, although informed by a doctor that he has a heart condition, has been traveling from the United States to Central and South America, attempting to enlist the support of other countries in a common campaign against Castro. For nearly a year Harry Williams has continued to work tirelessly to bring unity out of division and bitterness. He has not been entirely successful but he still displays the same optimism as in the days when he worked for the liberation of the Brigade, and he talks with enthusiasm of the future and of the kind of democratic government that will enable Cuba to resume its place among the nations of the hemisphere.

For all of them, and especially the leaders, the death of President Kennedy came with shattering impact. The leaders had seen the President, as he had promised they would, once during the year; and they knew that he and his brother Robert, whom they saw frequently, were responsible for their opportunity to serve in the United States military forces. They believed in President Kennedy and he gave them reason to hope for the future. They believed, no matter what mistakes he personally made during their invasion, that he had saved their lives with his strong warning to Castro immediately upon their defeat; that he had kept them from being executed in the twenty months that followed; that he had liberated them from prison; and that he meant what he said in the Orange Bowl—that he wanted them to return at the head of the column to a free Havana, and he wanted to be there on that day.

To the leaders, as well as to many Cubans in exile, John Kennedy already is being regarded as a martyr to the cause of Cuban liberty. And, indeed, Cuba *was* a thread that wound through the President's two years ten months and two days in the White House: from the Bay of Pigs to the missile crisis; from the pledge in the Orange Bowl to his next trip to Miami eleven months later, and still another statement on Cuba ("a small group of conspirators has robbed the Cuban people of their independence") and then, after recalling the lines *Westward look, the land is bright,* the final journey to Texas and the final act in Dallas on November 22 at the hands of a self-professed pro-Castro assassin.

The President did want a free Cuba and he was receptive to plans that would achieve that end. Whether it would have been achieved in his administration is a lasting question mark. But at least one man—Fidel Castro—feared that it might. Although Fidel spoke kindly of Kennedy after the assassination, his real feelings are a matter of record and are worth remembering today.

Ten weeks before the President's death, on September 8, 1963, at a reception in the Brazilian embassy in Havana, Fidel said: "The U.S. leaders must realize that if they assist in the terrorist plans to eliminate Cuban leaders, they themselves will be in danger." (Cuba at that time was being infiltrated by sea and attacked by sporadic air raids which Fidel blamed on the CIA.) Then Fidel added: "Kennedy is the Batista of our time, and the most opportunistic President of all time. . . . The United States are fighting a battle against us which they cannot win. . . ."

Because of the emotional feeling about President Kennedy and because Lyndon Johnson was, to most Cubans in exile, an unknown quantity, the assassination was immediately interpreted as bringing an end to the dreams of liberation for the new year and for the term in office of the new administration.

Yet the dream still lives.

Twelve months ago, when the Brigade prisoners were getting off their trucks at the airport before the flight back to the United

States, one of Castro's militia guards winked broadly at them. When he heard of that incident, Max Lerner remembered the classic passage in Trotsky's *History of the Russian Revolution* in which a Czarist soldier—instead of shooting at the mass of demonstrators—winked at them. That wink, Trotsky said, marked a turning point in the overthrow of the regime.

It is seven years since another small band of freedom fighters was crushed and the light went out in Hungary. Today, in their moments of despair and bitterness, the Cuban exiles often refer to Hungary. They do not know what their future holds, but they are determined they are not going to live a lifetime in exile, in the manner of the White Russians and the Hungarians. Each is waiting to return to Cuba.

ACKNOWLEDGMENTS

Unfortunately, it is impossible to thank all of those who have helped to create this book. To these few, out of so many, I wish to express my particular appreciation: to María Amelia Cosculluela de Ruiz-Williams, Theresa Zubizarreta and Maria-Elena Barrientos, women of Cuba and of the Brigade who worked so selflessly and efficiently in transcribing, typing, and retyping; to Alvaro Sánchez, Jr., president of the Cuban Families Committee, who believed that this book would contribute to Western civilization; to Carlos Arteaga, who compiled an invaluable statistical analysis, by age, profession, education, and birth, of each one of the one thousand one hundred eighty Brigade prisoners; to Albert D. Biderman, Marisol Reyes-Gavilán and James L. Monroe of the Bureau of Social Science Research, Inc., in Washington, D.C., who exchanged information and provided insight on the Bay of Pigs prisoners; to Emerson Beauchamp, Jr., and Miss Carol Houck, who gave sharp editorial criticism; to Christie and William Basham, who helped in so many ways; and to Eric P. Swenson, Executive Editor of W. W. Norton & Company, Inc., whose faith, judgment, and unfailing optimism made the book project both possible and pleasant.

The still photographs so identified are by courtesy of NBC News. From *NBC White Paper*, "Cuba, Bay of Pigs." Irving Gitlin, Executive Producer.

H.J.

BIBLIOGRAPHICAL NOTES

At this writing the literature of the Bay of Pigs consists principally of magazine accounts and an increasing number of references in memoirs to various aspects of the invasion and its aftermath. These notes, in the form of a critical essay, are intended to discuss what the author found of value.

One book has been written. Karl E. Meyer and Tad Szulc's *The Cuban Invasion* (Praeger, 1962) is excellent in its political analysis and understanding of the Cuban problem, and it is unusually good in its over-all grasp, considering that few men in the Brigade were available when it was written. It suffers principally from a tendency to rely heavily on Manuel Ray's viewpoint and to exaggerate Ray's importance.

Out of all the works, popular and scholarly, about Castro and Cuba one writer stands out—Theodore Draper. Until Mr. Draper's history of Castro is completed, his *Castro's Revolution: Myths and Realities* (Praeger, 1962) remains unmatched for incisiveness and brilliance. I have found several other volumes of use. Herbert L. Matthews's *The Cuban Story* (Braziller, 1961) is lucid, fascinating, and useful for its tone, its opinion, and for what it reveals about Matthews and his controversial relationship with Castro.

Jules Dubois' *Fidel Castro* (Bobbs-Merrill, 1959) seems hastily written, but worth reading for the impression it gives of a Castro of promise who has not yet alienated his own people or such astute correspondents as Mr. Dubois. Of lesser value, but some interest, is Nicolás Rivero's *Castro's Cuba: An American Dilemma* (Luce, 1962). In many ways a superficial book, it gives an intelligent, reasonably dispassionate account from the exile's side. Earl E. T. Smith's *The Fourth Floor* (Random House, 1962) portrays a sinister, conspiratorial view of Castro's assumption of power which is thin on facts and long on argument. As the expression of the U.S. Ambassador to Cuba at the time Batista fled, however, it is an interesting document.

From the American side, one must await the publication of the second volume of General Eisenhower's memoirs for any light he may shed on the Bay of Pigs episode. The first volume, *Mandate for Change* (Doubleday, 1963) does refer briefly to the CIA involvement in Guatemala, but its value lies chiefly in what it fails to say about the decisions that were made; and, thus, in a negative manner, it says much about the Eisenhower presidency. Far more stimulating and revealing is Emmett John Hughes' *The Ordeal of Power* (Atheneum, 1963), perhaps the frankest, best-written, and most significant critique of Eisenhower that has appeared.

Richard M. Nixon tells his story forcefully in *Six Crises* (Doubleday, 1962) and gives his account of the presidential campaign of 1960 and of the formation of the Brigade force. For an understanding of both Nixon and Kennedy in that campaign, the indispensable work is Theodore H. White's masterly *The Making of the President: 1960* (Atheneum, 1961). Unfortunately, that book is not of much help on the Cuban issue as debated during the campaign.

On John Kennedy's administration two books are illuminating, for different reasons. Victor Lasky's *JFK: The Man and the Myth* (Macmillan, 1963) is grossly unfair, but it does indicate the kind of opposition the President was encountering. On the other side of the political spectrum is Hugh Sidey's *John F. Kennedy, President* (Atheneum, 1963), breathlessly laudatory, basically uncritical, and yet a vital source in that it recounts, factually and sometimes minute-by-minute, the events of the President's abbreviated term. The chapters on the Bay of Pigs and Robert Kennedy are particularly important.

Others who figured in the Bay of Pigs and who have written about their roles include Milton S. Eisenhower, who tells about "The Tractors for Freedom Committee" episode in *The Wine Is Bitter* (Doubleday, 1963), and Allen Dulles, in his *The Craft of Intelligence* (Harper and Row, 1963), a work which, not surprisingly, skirts the specific Bay of Pigs operation.

Two magazine articles are especially significant. Stewart Alsop's "The Lessons of the Cuban Disaster" appeared in the June 24, 1961 issue of *The Saturday Evening Post* and remains today one of the best accounts of the deliberations in Washington which led to the invasion. In the September, 1961 issue of *Fortune* Charles J. V. Murphy's "Cuba: The Record Set Straight" added further material to Alsop's account. Both articles are factually correct, although Murphy's presents more of the professional military view on the disaster as opposed to the White House side. Another article worth citing was also one of the first. Keith Wheeler's "Hell of a Beating in Cuba" appeared in *Life* of April 28, 1961. It was *Life*, too, which later printed the first general account of the fighting in the May 10, 1963 issue containing two articles by John Dille and Tom Flaherty. While basically correct, Dille's on the fighting is sketchy and marred by a number of factual errors stemming from what Cubans told—and did *not* tell—the *Life* team of reporters. Nevertheless, the article marked the first time the public was informed of the Brigade and its valor, and helped to remove some of the misconceptions.

The magazine which published the most about the Bay of Pigs is also the most misleading. *U.S. News & World Report,* in a number of articles, some of them appearing to be deliberately written to stir controversy without regard to facts, virtually laid the entire blame on President Kennedy. If read with care the articles help to explain why the invasion continued to be so controversial an issue in the United States. Some of them are: September 17, 1962, "The Inside Story—Kennedy's Fateful Decision: The Night the Reds Clinched Cuba" (reprinted in the November, 1962 *Reader's Digest*); December 17, 1962, "After Cuba: Who Stood for What?"; January 7, 1963, "After the Ransom Deal—What Next for Castro?" and "The Real Story of the Bay of Pigs"; January 14, 1963, "We Were Betrayed: A Veteran of the Cuban Invasion Speaks Out"; January 28, 1963, "Robert Kennedy Speaks His Mind" (this was the celebrated interview in which the Attorney General denied that U.S. air cover had been withdrawn); February 4, 1963, "For the First Time: The Story of How

President Kennedy Upset the Cuban Invasion of April, 1961" (perhaps the most misleading of all) and in the same issue, "The Air Will Be Ours: Cuban Fighters Tell Why They Expected Air Cover," an article quoting "Tony" Varona.

One more magazine article is worth examining. The June, 1963 *Esquire* carried a "cover story" by Terry Southern entitled, "How I Signed Up at $250 a Month for the Big Parade Through Havana Bla-Bla-Bla," which purported to be a "hipster-mercenary's version of the Cuban affair." It stated, among other erroneous bits of reporting, that the San Román brothers, Pepe and Roberto, "had taken over" following a "Batista coup" at the camp and were "divvying up the spoils." Terry Southern made no attempt to contact the San Románs, nor, so far as can be determined, any other member of the Brigade, to check the accuracy of any allegations or statements.

Of all the published sources for this book the most significant are the documents from Castro's government. In January of 1962 the Cuban government began printing its history of the Bay of Pigs invasion and in February, 1962, the first of four large volumes was issued. The general work is entitled *Playa Girón: Derrota del Imperialismo* (The Rout of Imperialism) and the individual volumes are called: Volume 1, *La Invasión y los Héroes* (The Invasion and the Heroes); Volume 2, *Reacción Internacional* (International Reaction); Volume 3, *La Batalla de la O.N.U.* (The Battle of the U.N.); and Volume 4, *Los Mercenarios* (The Mercenaries). These works contain material absolutely essential to an understanding of the Bay of Pigs. They present Castro's words, as well as verbatim transcripts of interrogations with Brigade prisoners, and a fascinating view of world events as seen through Castro's eyes. The works bear this editorial imprint: "*editada en la Imprenta Burgay y Cía., sita en Amistad 353, en la ciudad de la Habana, Cuba.*" I cite these sources in detail because Fidel Castro now denies that any such books ever were printed in Cuba. Twice at length he denied their existence while this book, *The Bay of Pigs*, was in preparation. I have been fortunate to have access to them. I also have found two other works published by Castro to be extremely valuable. *Playa Girón, A Victory of the People*, is Castro's speech on television about the invasion, delivered April 23, 1961, and printed in booklet form by "Editorial en Marcha, P.O. Box 6386, Havana, Cuba, 1961." The other is *Cuba Demanded Indemnification: Imperialism Said No!* published by the Cuban Ministry of Foreign Relations in Havana, 1961, and giving Fidel's side of the "Tractors for Freedom" history. This book includes many documents from the "Tractors for Freedom Committee" which have not been made public in the United States.

INDEX

CPSIA information can be obtained
at www.ICGtesting.com
Printed in the USA
LVHW091813180420
653956LV00002B/228

9 780393 331202